# Industrial Relations in China

For socialism, the only progress worth striving for and the only freedom worth dying for.

# Industrial Relations in China

Bill Taylor

*Associate Professor, Department of Public and Social Administration, City University of Hong Kong*

Chang Kai

*Professor, Faculty of Labour and Human Resource Management, People's University, China*

Li Qi

*Associate Professor, Faculty of Labour Economics, Capital University of Economics and Business, China*

**Edward Elgar**
Cheltenham, UK • Northampton, MA, USA

Published by
Edward Elgar Publishing Limited
Glensanda House
Montpellier Parade
Cheltenham
Glos GL50 1UA
UK

Edward Elgar Publishing, Inc.
136 West Street
Suite 202
Northampton
Massachusetts 01060
USA

A catalogue record for this book
is available from the British Library

**Library of Congress Cataloguing in Publication Data**
Taylor, Bill, 1962–
    Industrial relations in China / Bill Taylor, Kai Chang, Qi Li.
       p.  cm.
    Includes bibliographical references and index.
    1. Industrial relations—China. 2. Labor policy—China. 3. Labor—China. 4. Labor unions—China. 5. Labor movement—China. I. Chang, Kai, 1952– II. Li, Qi, 1955–  III. Title

    HD8736.5.T39  2003
    331'.0951—dc21                       2003051344

ISBN 1 84064 578 4

Printed and bound in Great Britain by MPG Books Ltd, Bodmin, Cornwall

# Contents

# Figures

# Tables

# Abbreviations

| | |
|---|---|
| ACFTU | All China Federation of Trade Unions |
| CCP | Chinese Communist Party |
| CC-CCP | Central Committee of the Chinese Communist Party |
| CEC | China Enterprise Confederation |
| CEDA | China Enterprise Directors Association |
| CEMA | China Enterprise Management Association |
| CMRS | Contract Management Responsibility System |
| COE | Collective owned enterprise |
| DRS | Director Responsibility System |
| EDS | Employment director and supervisor |
| FIE | Foreign-invested enterprise |
| ILO | International Labour Organization |
| ICESCR | International Covenant on Economic, Social and Cultural Rights |
| MoL | Ministry of Labour |
| MoLSS | Ministry of Labour and Social Security |
| NBS | National Bureau of Statistics |
| NGO | non-governmental organization |
| OCA | opening corporate affairs |
| POE | privately owned enterprise |
| PRC | People's Republic of China |
| SOE | state-owned enterprise |
| SOU | state-owned unit |
| SETC | State Economic and Trade Commission |
| THM | Taiwan, Hong Kong and Macao (peoples' investments) |
| TVE | township and village enterprise |
| WC | Workers' congress |

# System of referencing

Format of Chinese names. We have followed two different principles in presenting Chinese names. Within the text of chapters and footnotes, the Chinese style of writing family names first has been adopted. Among non-sinologists, there are problems with this when it comes to how to interpret references. For this reason, we adopted Western norms in following the Harvard referencing style. Thus, for example, in the text a reference made to the first premier of China would be Mao Tsetung, but in the bibliography his entry would be either Mao, Tsetung (if first author) or Tsetung Mao if he were not the first author.

Unless specifically noted in the text, translations of Chinese characters into English were by either the original authors (such as the various Chinese government ministries in some cases) or the authors (actually Li Qi). In some cases, verbatim translations are given (often for the titles of official documents) but generally, it is more important to translate the meaning of the original Chinese.

There appears to be a declining rigour to referencing accurately. This especially afflicts second-hand citations and references and can be a particular problem in Mainland China. Thus, we have gone to some length to check the original sources of quotes and references, and rejected (reluctantly at times) numerous references that could not be verified. However, it is doubtful we got it completely right and we apologize in advance for any omissions, misrepresentations or misunderstandings, which are unintentional.

# Acknowledgements

This book evolved out of a meeting in Beijing among the three authors in 1999, arranged to discuss comparative experiences of post-planned economic implications for industrial relations with Simon Clarke, the noted expert on such matters in Russia. Simon encouraged this project, maintaining his critical and informative support throughout the intervening period, and we have deep-felt thanks for this. Thanks also go to Fu Lin for continued friendship and support in the various research projects of the authors. Thank you to the staff of Edward Elgar for a great degree of trust and flexibility, and in particular to Suzanne Mursell in this regard. Whilst the book draws on the research and experience of the three of us in general, we drew on a number of specific research projects, and we would like to thank the Research Grants Council of Hong Kong for funding research on management – labour issues in Japanese multinationals in China (CityU896/96H) and City University of Hong Kong for funding research on trade union reform (7001003).

# 1. Introduction

Since 1978, China has been engaged in a large-scale overhaul of the economy, in which marketization has become an important element in deciding the allocation of goods and resources. The process of change has had fundamental impacts on the political-economic regulation of China. The leadership of the Chinese Communist Party (CCP), in an attempt to maintain its grip on power, embarked on a carefully laid out gradualist path of what is euphemistically called reform, or economic reform.[1] This label implies an improvement over the past, and this is deliberate. Party leaders of China over the past 20 or 50 years see market socialism explicitly as an improvement on the previous Mao period of a communist planned economy.

If we examine the politics of reform, a somewhat more complex picture emerges, in which factions fought over both the meaning and course of reform. We can point to the unevenness of the reform process, the apparent stop-go, or two steps forward and one or two steps back, in policy initiatives of the central state. However, taking the long view, all must admit that China has transformed from a planned economy to one largely regulated through market mechanisms (Howell 1993). This raises two interrelated questions: has the change led to, or can it lead to improvements, for all? What is the meaning of socialism within this context of change?

In this book, we will attempt to answer both questions through an examination of the emerging industrial relations systems in China. Answering the second question is largely a question of ideology, which we would take as a necessary part of intellectual thinking, and not something to be derided. The first question is apparently empirical, but there is an enormous amount of controversy in practice. The conflicts fall into two main aspects: whether or not the Chinese population is better off materially (and perhaps spiritually) under market regulation than it was under communist plans, and whether the role of the state as economic manager is helping

---

[1] Whilst the word 'reform' carries a significant ideological baggage, we will simply use the term to mean change. We continue to use the word reform because (1) change can apply at micro level whereas reform implies a broader sweep of change, and (2) 'reform' is the common parlance and so it could be confusing or stilted to use 'change' in its place.

or hindering the process of change. These conflicts sometimes create interesting bedfellows, such that many management writers from the neo-liberalist school see the Chinese government as interfering with the market, inhibiting market growth potential, whilst many leftist scholars see government intervention as exacerbating inequalities. At the same time, many scholars see increased economic inequality, yet cannot agree how to interpret this, especially in its relation to Party political influence. Whilst some see inequality as a necessary part of market stimulus, which leads to absolute improvement for all, others see rising inequality as leading to differential life changes for rich and poor.

These arguments are the mirror of arguments over welfare states versus free market regimes in capitalist countries. It is important to understand that these arguments exist within China as well as among foreign intellectuals and activists, although the liberalists tend to hold sway at present in much of the academic debate within and outside China.

We will address these questions explicitly in the conclusion, but aspects of these enquiries guide the argument and contents of all the chapters of the book. However, we must narrow down the analysis in a way that is both manageable and systematic. Much (but by no means all) study of China's economic changes has either been atheoretical (which really means the ideological basis is assumed to be non-contentious) or China-studies focused. It is important, however, to understand the changing processes in China in ways that can be understood and reworked comparatively, and overtly informed and defended theoretically. In this book, this will be done using the methodological approach and framework of industrial relations.

## INDUSTRIAL RELATIONS METHOD

Industrial relations starts from the premise that in industrial society, where there is a separation of the owners of production (whether legally or realistically) and workers who engage in some form of productive activity in exchange for wages (in money and or kind), there is an industrial relationship. This relationship has two essential features: it is fundamentally a conflict relation, between owners of the means of production and those who sell their labour, and it is a relation based on power. To Marxists and radicals, this relation exists within a structurally unequal distribution of power that disadvantages workers.

The primary focus of industrial relations is the setting of the price of labour between worker and employer, and the institutional and environmental forces that determine price setting. Whilst this would seem at first sight a reductionist pursuit, in practice it allows us to weave a rich tapestry of links between various institutions and organizations within industrial society and the processes that bind them together and tear them apart. Moreover, the wage exchange is fundamentally both a product of, and at the same time shapes, the political-economic landscape of industrial society. Industrial relations, therefore, is not concerned with the 'market price for labour' in its pure economic sense, but the relations (economics, social, political and psychological) which determine the actual price of labour in both quantitative and quality forms.

Heavily influenced by its economic-rational roots, industrial relations is sometimes divided into macro and micro aspects. Microanalysis examines work-based employment relations, examining a range or workplace-based employment issues, and the operation of the labour process. There is a considerable amount of research and analysis of workplace industrial relations in China covering the full range of enterprises and many employment issues. The main focus of attention has been the way the *danwei* (work unit) has adapted to, or changed because of, reform measures. *Danwei* were not only economic production units, but bases for political mobilization and control of urban workers and managers by the Party-state, and administrative units for the social reproduction of labour (providing housing, medical care, education and so on) within the employment unit. Reform introduced three specific forms of changes which have been studied by various authors: changes in the functions and operation of *danwei* within the state sector (for example Lu and Perry 2000; Warner 2000), the introduction of non-*danwei* labour into public sector enterprises (for example Sargeson 1999), and the nature of workplace employment relations in new private sector enterprises and joint ventures involving foreign investors (for example Chan 2001).

Macro analysis focuses on societal-level institutions, such as the state, trade union organs and employers' organizations, and maps the overall industrial relations framework within society, and it will provide the focus of this book. The rationale is that individual workers and individual managers negotiate either directly or indirectly through labour market mechanisms, to set the price of labour exchange. In order to regularize these negotiations, and reduce uncertainty, employers and workers accept institutional arrangements to settle the price. Moreover, to increase their power in the bargaining process, each forms associations – employers' associations and trade unions. The state, which is either seen as a third party wishing to stabilize employment relations, or to Marxists, acts in the long-run interests of the dominant force (usually the employers) acts to institute regulations and procedures to settle labour prices in predictable fashion, as well as to avoid social disruption from destabilizing levels of poverty or dangerous work environments.

There have been very few studies of the macro-level industrial relations framework focusing on China (Chang 1995a; White 1996; Ng and Warner 1998 being among notable exceptions), although industrial relations participants (employers, the state, workers and trade unions) have been studied in isolation or in relation to particular practices, such as labour markets (for example Solinger 1999, 2002). Because China has been undergoing continued and complex changes for the past 100 years, many writers have found it necessary to place the particular facets of industrial relations they are examining within a historical framework (for example Leung 1998 – trade unions; Sheehan 1988 – labour movement; Walder 1986, 1989 – managerial control).

## INDUSTRIAL RELATIONS DEBATES IN CHINA

Walder (1986: 12–13) summarized the pre-reform industrial relations system with the notion of *neo-traditionalism*, which draws on the 'iron rice-bowl' (*tie fan wan*) perspective of stable wages, employment and welfare provisions. In this system, employment did not fluctuate according to the demands of production and workers were not taken as a factor of production readily separable from the factory. Moreover, wages and welfare were determined in large part by government agencies, and the employing units were the *danwei* which worked to the economic, social and political plans decided by the central state and implemented through government agencies. Like many mainland scholars, Walder perceived this as developing workplaces in which a high degree of worker dependence was created. The workplace was a cell or unit of political control in which the discretion of supervisors was quite broad; workers and management were not recognized as separate parties. Thus, workers were highly dependent economically and socially on the enterprise, politically dependent on the Party and management, and personally dependent on supervisors.

With the onset of reform, some have argued that the 'iron rice-bowl' has been chipped if not completely smashed (for example Leung 1988). Thus, a debate has arisen over the nature and significance of the impact of reform on industrial relations. Whilst it was not quite as simple as to say the wage effort (labour) relationship was decided by an implicit negotiation between state decree and degree of worker compliance, there were certainly no institutional arrangements to bargain over the price of labour in the planned period in China. Now that the plan has gone, and market-based transactions have taken their place in many areas, how has price fixing adapted? Chang (1995a: 42) argues that the government is changing its role from 'administrator' of labour relations to a 'market'-based pattern. This change can be traced to two changes. First, the government transferred primary authority in the allocation of labour (both recruitment and termination) to management and itself retained the supervisory power over these issues (Han and Morishima 1992; Ip 1995; Lu 1996; Wang 1993; Warner 1996a). Second, the government no longer exercises direct control over the income distribution system, leaving management to determine the wage rate, wage form and the ways of payment according to their level of profit and production requirements. The government now only controls the total sum of wages using various macro-administrative measures (Walder 1991; Wang 1993), and this to a declining degree.

Along with the government's partial withdrawal from labour relations within enterprises, it has taken up a more regulatory role designed to manage the labour market, and has tried to adjust labour relations by means of labour legislation (Chang 1995b; Ip 1995; Qi and Xu 1995; Song 1995a). In the labour market, the government takes charge of creating and maintaining new institutions, such as employment agencies, vocational training, occupational guidance, social insurance and labour inspection, which were designed in line with the development of this market (Ip 1995; Wang 1993; Zhu and Campbell 1996). It has gradually isolated itself from direct confrontations, preferring to act as an arbitrator to resolve occurrences of overt conflict between the management and workers (Ng and Warner 1998; Qi and Xu 1995). Generally, the roles of the Chinese government in labour relations are moving towards that which may be described variously as 'regulator', 'administrator' and 'arbitrator', according to some scholars (Chan 1995a; Deery and Mitchell 1993; Zhu 1995). Employment became progressively regulated through the use of labour contracts since 1986 (Han and Morishima 1992; Karmel 1996; Qi and Xu 1995; Song 1995b). Ng and Warner (1998) see labour contracts as leading towards contractual interaction, clarifying the relationship between those working in enterprises into the categories of 'workers' and 'employers'. Warner (1996b), and Zhu and Campbell (1996), also see that the insertion of provisions in contracts dealing with production tasks, duration of probation, working conditions, remuneration, labour discipline and penalties all help to develop a clearer perception of the rights and responsibilities of both managers and employees.

Most scholars in the field generally agree upon the change processes in these areas, but there are two areas of contention. Debate ranges over how to describe the nature of the employment relationship and the role of the different actors, especially managers and the trade unions, and the development path of industrial relations for the future. These may be described as debates around 'corporatism' and speculations on models or theories as to whether Chinese industrial relations is becoming more like, or converging with, practices in other industrialized countries.

## *Corporatism*

Walder (1989) analysed the management–labour relationship in Chinese SOEs (state-owned enterprises) in the 1980s and found that an unspoken agreement existed between management and workers. In this implicit agreement, management tried to garner workers' cooperation by maximizing the bonuses and other benefits distributed to workers, while minimizing contention and conflict by not making working quotas too tight, distributing rewards relatively equally, and keeping a weak link between output and pay. Walder (1989, 1991: 473) argued there were three interrelated causes of this agreement. First, there is very little possibility for the workers to move between SOEs or be dismissed; consequently, the management must be especially sensitive to avoid dissatisfaction among the workforce, preventing them from abusing machines, wasting materials and disrupting the coordination of production. Second, the enterprise is a socio-political community where managers are responsible not only for production, but also for enhancing workers' income and other benefits, and they will be judged by both their superiors and their subordinates on these criteria. Their ability to obtain higher pay and benefits for workers is the primary basis for workers' evaluation (1989: 249). Third, some new kinds of 'soft budget constraint' meant the managers could increase bonuses using retained profits by concealing slack capacity, evading accounting regulations, and bargaining for preferential treatment in taxation, credit and pricing (1986: 32) from their supervising agencies. Walder also argues that in the early 1990s 'paternalism' remained an effective means to extract obedience and tacit consent from the working class in return for an improved material life. In this case workers in SOEs have even increased their advantage to bargain for managerial concessions regarding wage and bonus distribution (1986: 307).

Unger and Chan (1995) argue that corporation developed as a move towards increased economic decentralization from the Maoist era of complete authoritarian domination. The essential argument is that intellectuals and economic planners were brought into the state power structure to broker economic reform whilst incorporating their values so as not to allow economic reform to threaten the political dominance of the Party-state. However, as local-level cadres gain greater economic autonomy, Unger and Chan (1995: 46–7) argue the central Party loses control over their actions. Corporatism in this sense means little more than warlord-like fiefdoms, run by local party bosses and business interests, which firmly excludes any role for the workers and peasants except as waged labour (1995: 51–2; also Chan and Senser 1997).

Lee Ching Kwan (1999) argues strongly against the corporatist argument, developing the concept of 'disorganized despotism', declaring that neo-traditionalism has been eroded by drastic reform, even in SOEs. Lee argues that reforms have resulted in three impacts on labour relations in SOEs. First, after removing enterprise paternalism, social insurance and welfare reforms have not remained effective in enforcing a new safety net for workers. The workers confront the stark reality of finding themselves trapped in a 'transition gap' between two systems (enterprise insurance and state insurance) (1999: 48). Second, the reform has enhanced managerial autonomy within the triple alliance (Party, management and trade unions). While labour contracts make it easy for the directors of SOEs to dismiss workers through 'no-fault causes' in employment contracts, the Party and trade unions are unable to provide legal protection to workers' rights (1999: 57). Third, the external labour market also provides an important condition for managerial domination inside the enterprise as well as conflict between migrant workers and veteran (urban) workers (1999: 60). Under these impacts, workers in SOEs are subjected to a new managerial despotism, which produces a new kind of labour subordination different from the past pattern of organized dependence of Walder's theory (1999: 47).

## *Convergence*

A burning issue for both local and overseas academics in the study of industrial relations in China, as with all reform studies, is the degree to which China is converging with variously defined Western models of industrial relations. Convergence relates to discussing whether China is changing to some form of employment practices and industrial relations structures that resemble those in capitalist economies. The 'is China going capitalist?' (Prybyla 1996) question is rather more obliquely addressed in the Mainland because of the political dynamics of industrial relations, but studies making pains to delineate differences between Chinese reform and Western industrial relations systems (Chen 2001; Hu and Yang 1999) reveal that conscious comparisons are still being made. Many business school writers (for example Ahlstrom et al. 2001; Li et al. 2000) have rather assumed convergence. Chan and Norlund (1995) indicate China is diverging from Vietnam with a faster pace of reform towards a market economy, whilst Chan (1995b, 1997) makes considerable play of arguments of China's industrial relations converging with those of Japan.[2]

Apart from a brief interlude after Tiananmen, most authors, such as O'Leary (1998), Brown and Porter (1996) and Warner (1995), have argued that the trajectory was towards convergence. Warner, in various writings (Ng

---

[2] However, Chan's understanding of the nature of industrial relations in Japan was insufficient to undertake such analysis (Taylor 1999a).

and Warner 1998; Warner 1993, 2000), has argued that there is a tendency to convergence that is checked by the state, leading to a hybrid form management-labour relations, 'with Chinese characteristics' blending with Western or East Asian practices. In this pattern Warner argues:

> Old and new managerial characteristics may combine in the key sectors of the economy, whether involving State Owned Enterprises, town and village enterprises, joint ventures or private firms. Residual elements of the plan may blend with the market; hence, reforms will frequently be incomplete. As in previous phases of economic and organizational development, the position is far from neat and systematic. (1995: 162)

To support this claim, Warner (1996a) analyses Chinese labour system reforms in terms of labour contracts, wages and social insurance. He found that labour contracts represent a move away from an institution where the industrial workers enjoyed tenured employment. However, dismissals are generally as low as before, even though the management has the formal power to make them (Goodall and Warner 1997; Warner 1996b). The wage system is moving towards a more performance-based system and the old eight-level grade system is being replaced by the new 'post plus skill' system. However, the elements of the reward system common in pre-reform SOEs are still in evidence, such as the traditional age-related, equality-based elements and a larger proportion of subsidies (Goodall and Warner 1997; Warner 1996a). Moreover, although a social insurance system has been established, redundant personnel could not be pushed to the labour market (Goodall and Warner 1997). Warner (1995; also Ng and Warner 2000) develops a 'middle ground' between reform and restraint in industrial relations, which he identifies as a form of 'hybridization', which is attributed to the state's need to maintain 'social peace' (that is maintain political stability). He takes the view that the fear of disorder has always been a prime preoccupation of the Chinese top leaders, echoing the dominant academic reasoning in China.[3] Warner (1996b) concludes that the management–labour relationship will develop into a 'marketized' hybrid form, although the exact form of the new species is unclear. Whilst the push–pull nature of the hybrid model allows a

---

[3] This is also the dominant view among China politics specialists, such as Han and Morishima (1992), Walder (1989 and 1991) and Zhu and Campbell (1996), who have all emphasized the delay of political reform in China in general. This point is emphasized in discussions of the relationship between the CCP and the All China Federation of Trade Unions (ACFTU). Hannan (1991) also argues that when social conflicts, such as during reform, cause widespread grievances and potential threats to CCP power, the maintenance of stability is given explicit priority. This can be well illustrated by examining how the post-Tiananmen leadership of the CCP, headed by Jiang Zemin, took over power in 1989, and placed primary emphasis on dealing with the challenges presented by different interest groups, which effectively stalled economic reform until 1992.

more dynamic analysis than simply linear convergence (or lack of change as a whole) allows, because analysis depends on examining each element of the employment relationship in isolation, it is difficult to understand the nature of the system itself.

White et al. (1996) provide a complex argument of the development of industrial relations, one in which the gradual pace of change means convergence is not occurring and that economic change alone is insufficient to claim convergence without political change as well. However, there is a point at which economic change without political adaptation reaches a breaking point. At this point rapid if not sudden change in the political economy occurs, but it is uncertain what the post-ruptured system would look like. Each spring for the past five years there have been waves of labour protests, and one often wonders if this will mark the beginning of the break. However, the split may be less cataclysmic but just as powerful, and indeed this seems a more likely scenario, especially if the Party disintegrates into factionalism or entrepreneurs take control of key coastal city governments.


## CONTENT OF CHAPTERS

The book is arranged into two parts 'Institutional Arrangements' and 'Industrial Relations Processes' and seven substantive chapters, plus a Conclusion.

Part I will detail the industrial relations framework, examining each of the main actors in industrial relations in turn: state, employers, workers and trade unions. Each of the four chapters in this section has a similar format, which is briefly to discuss the historical changes in the role of the actor in the period 1949 to 1978 and in the post-Mao era, leading to a more detailed explanation of the present situation. Analysis will compare and contrast different forms of enterprise and, where appropriate, contractual relations and geographic variations, to discuss the causes of the similarities and differences in the system of industrial relations currently emerging within China, especially between different forms of enterprise.

Chapter 2 'The role of government' outlines the changing role of the government from that of state planner and administrator of all aspects of China's political economy, to a more complex role today. The chapter will examine the objectives of the government and outline the specific ways in which it becomes involved in industrial relations in the public and private sectors of the economy. A large part of the chapter will be taken up with outlining collective and individual legislation and the regulatory framework relating to industrial relations and their implementation down through the organizational structural to the level of enterprises. Relations between the other actors and the state will be outlined to support the argument of the continued central role of the government both indirectly but also, in many respects, directly in industrial relations.

Chapter 3 'Enterprise and managers' outlines the historical importance of the state enterprise sector for the present political economy and then outlines the development and changes in both the public sector and the growing number and forms of private enterprises. The chapter will examine patterns of governance and control in these different types of enterprises, and argue that, despite the primacy of the market, political considerations still have a significant influence over decision-making in all but few enterprises. Whilst less certain than before the reforms began, the CCP maintains a number of formal and informal mechanisms to both push reform, and yet at the same time retain some level of political control over enterprises and their senior local managers. Finally, the chapter examines the emergence of new forms of manager, quite different from the communist era cadre manager. The argument is not so much the development of a 'managerial class' as a divergence of forms of manager, which can be understood through analysing the changes facing different types of managers in terms of income, social status, economic and personal power, and personal freedoms and autonomy in different types of enterprises.

Chapter 4 'Workers' discusses the meaning and symbolic role of the industrial or urban worker in China before the reforms started, and their changing role at present. The chapter goes on to detail a few aspects of the physical work environment and status of workers in different types of enterprise. There have always been differences between rural and urban workers, but economic reforms, in terms of changing ownership, allocation of goods, employment guarantees and so on, have initiated more divisions, and a much more complex picture has arisen. The chapter will explore some of these complexities through illustrations of the fragmentation of urban worker consciousness, with increasing differences based on gender, age, location and so on.

Chapter 5 'Trade unions' outlines the pressures imposed on the Chinese trade unions after reform started, leading to changes in the roles and functions, and their responses to the changing context in which they operate. Moreover, the chapter discusses the relationship between trade unions and the other actors in industrial relations (the Central Committee of the Chinese Communist Party, the government and entrepreneurs). These issues will be explored through two dichotomous ways of characterizing trade unions in China, depending on whether one takes an industrial relations or a China studies perspective. In the former, unions are either seen as instruments of the state or as moribund labour representatives, and in China studies, they are seen as corporatist organs acting as transmission belts between state and worker, or as a communist anachronism. The chapter will argue that there is considerable gap between the official role claimed by members of the ACFTU and the reality of their role. However, it will also be shown that the ACFTU is acutely conscious of its own lack of role under reform, and the debates as to what should be its appropriate role are analysed.

The overall arguments that come from the chapters are that each of the industrial relations actors is to some degree heterogeneous and that the tensions between planned control and market chaos act upon them differently. Nevertheless, at an objective level there are divergent interests being formed between progressively more class-based actors. These are increasingly being shaped by the well-established market mechanisms for allocating resources and, as such, provide some markers to indicate convergence with capitalistic industrial relations systems, although the chapters in Part II will to some degree counter this view.

In Part II, three chapters will apply the structural framework detailed in the previous chapters, to illustrate how industrial relations take place in practice. Each chapter is organized in the following way. First, each chapter will outline the theories of structures and meanings related to the process being analysed (collective bargaining, conflict and participation), in the capitalist context as a framework of analysis for the chapter. Second, each chapter will discuss the present arrangements in different forms of enterprise. Third, each chapter will identify their origin and causation, and then conclude with a comparison to the Western models of industrial relations processes.

Chapter 6 'Participation' examines the formal structures, such as workers' congress (WCs), 'opening corporation affairs' (*changwu gongkai*) (OCA) and employee directors and supervisors (EDS) which have been developed under socialist China for the purpose of promoting what is called 'democratic management'. The chapter then outlines what workers appear to demand from participation and what is the role of trade unions. It will be shown that participation is not a management ploy to subvert unions but is a genuine part of the administrative apparatus in enterprises to promote the interests of the CCP. However, the transition period has placed a question over who really owns the enterprises and who are the 'masters'. This is addressed through examining Chinese academic and political literature that discusses these issues, to explore the power of different actors in the participation process. The argument presented is that current initiatives in democratic management are as much to do with maintaining Party discipline over managers as to do with worker involvement.

Chapter 7 'Labour conflict and settlement' addresses both the nature and the occurrence of conflict in China, as well as the formal and informal mechanisms by which conflicts of interest are handled so that the occurrence of overt conflict is minimized. The chapter examines both individual and collective dispute handling, and particular attention is paid to the sensitive issue of collective labour disputes, as to their causes, the types of issues, the forms disputes take (including complaints, work stoppages, strikes, petitions and demonstrations), and how disputes develop. The chapter will also examine the institutional arrangements, both formal and informal, to deal with these disputes (including mediation, arbitration, concession and suppression), and the role taken by different actors in seeking to settle labour disputes. It will be argued that the ACFTU mostly plays a minimal role in dispute resolution, with workers relying much more on direct appeals to management or the government.

Chapter 8 'Collective contracts' explores how the 'collective bargaining' system has been implemented by the ACFTU, which aimed to protect the interests of workers as well as its own status in a changing society. This chapter outlines the nature and implementation of collective bargaining in China and draws a distinction between implementation in private and public-owned enterprises. The chapter places particular emphasis on aspects not widely covered in the literature thus far, especially the implementation procedures, the process of bargaining or consultation and the nature of the clauses in collective agreements. Through this analysis, it will be shown that collective bargaining in China should not be equated with bargaining in most capitalist situations, but is a blend of administrative guidance and a reflection of the complex roles of three actors: state, union and management. In conclusion, it will be argued that collective contracts may be seen as an attempt to gain a role for the official unions but, in fact, the government hopes to ensure little other than that the legal provisions are known about and implemented as the enterprise level.

The second part follows a 'Chinese' view of industrial relations. The selection of topics attempts to cover all the main areas of institutional arrangements designed to coordinate different aspects of industrial relations processes and to explore areas to which the government has explicitly paid attention in the past decade. The general way in which issues develop to become government concerns is that either the union or a government department raises a policy initiative, and this may eventually become a guideline or a legal provision, on which the ACFTU, the Ministry of Labour and Social Security (MoLSS) and other government agencies or quasi-government organizations can then organize implementation strategies. Each of the three chapters covers explicit policy initiatives on 'Participation' (Chapter 6), 'Labour conflict and settlement' (Chapter 7), and 'Collective contracts' (Chapter 8). However, each chapter also sets these initiatives within a broader context, both historically and in terms of an examination of the broader issues which the policy is supposed to address. The argument comes through in all three chapters, that whatever the needs, interests or context, little happens institutionally until the government steps in and officially sanctions a policy solution. This has a number of implications. First, the primary interests being protected in any initiative are those of the Party-state. In capitalist contexts, we tend to think of the state as primarily protecting the interests of capital, but in China it is the Party. It is often popular to equate the Party with the ruling elite, but it is more complex that this. Just as capitalists need to be disaggregated into often competing and contradictory interests, the CCP contains similar factions and heterogeneity. Nevertheless, both capitalists and the CCP share a common concern in industrial relations: self-preservation. The disagreement is only on how that is to be achieved. Second, there is no significant space for 'civil society' relevant to industrial relations. Chapter 7 discusses the development of autonomous, often spontaneous and transient labour organizations, which may present 'opportunities' for civil society to form. However, at present their leaders generally call for the government to address issues the aggrieved feel are being neglected. Rather then call for independent trade unions, they call for their unions to be more responsive. Rather than call for more autonomy, they call for government to crack down on corruption. Whilst contentious, we think the evidence shows that industrial relations actors, perhaps reluctantly at times, rely on the government to both set the industrial relations scene and to regulate the content and processes of industrial relations in China. Third, the market, whilst a politically instituted and regulated mechanism to bring about change in China, is, as liberals like to emphasize, something the government cannot control. Part II thus demonstrates the central role the government plays in industrial relations, not as a third party but as a direct participant. Moreover, the section shows how the system has gradually been changed over the course of the last 20 years, but that a number of fundamental problems have now been exposed.

The final chapter (Chapter 9) will draw out specific conclusions as to both the nature of industrial relations in China, and the impact such relations have had on the development of reform in the country. Moreover, the Conclusion will return to the broader questions of how to locate industrial relations in China within a broader theoretical framework. A conflict between marketization and the meaning of socialism of labour will be discussed, to conclude that whilst the rhetoric is of a marriage between the two (marketization plus socialism), reality indicates Chinese labour lost much in the period of transition. Moreover, whilst the pace of reform has slowed, there are structural and political impediments to prevent workers recovering their position in the near future. The chapter will argue also that behind the fragmentation and declining power of labour, there is an objective class formation based on objective economic interests, which was previously not possible given the divide between urban worker and rural peasant.

# PART I

Institutional arrangements

# 2. The role of government

The national flag of the PRC consists of one large yellow star and four smaller stars around it, set on a red background. The red represents the ideology of communism, the largest star the Party, and the four smaller stars represent the workers, peasants, petty bourgeoisie (mainly entrepreneurs) and national bourgeoisie (mainly intellectuals). Thus, the early leadership of the Chinese state from 1949 maintained a strongly pluralist view of civil society, in which the state was to be led by the Party but also recognized and legitimated different political economic groups.

However, partly through the influence of Russian advisors and partly because of factional conflicts within the CCP, a more unitarist model was adopted. The evolutionary model of communism gave way to a state-orchestrated movement to state authoritarianism, in which Mao argued a near constant state of revolution was required to build such appropriate forms of socialist consciences among the masses. The peasants were organized into communes, as were many of the urban workers, whilst other workplaces were nationalized and new state-run units were established. Economic reform eradicated private ownership, and political reform led to a fall from grace for the bourgeoisie. The Party became integral to the whole government process, and although they were and continue to be structurally separate organizations, integration has been near total.

At the level of industrial relations, the establishment of public ownership led to both an official removal of 'conflicts of interests', and a standardized pattern for managing labour by the state. As a result, industrial relations in many aspects began to resemble the 'unitary model' defined by Fox (1966: 2; also 1973 for a more sophisticated analysis). Q. Li (2000, 2002) refers to this situation as a 'magnified' unitary model because central planning of the economy sought to remove all forms of civil society and conflicts of interest, in which all factors were combined into a single organization (or actor). Whilst this was never complete, a strong unitarist ideology pervaded urban industrial relations up until the late 1970s.

By nature this was a vertical administrative relationship, or as Chang (1995b) defined it, an 'administrative labour relation', between two actors:

the state and workers. The state was the single 'employer' who was in charge of allocating labour, setting national wage scales, determining social welfare standards, unilaterally formulating work rules and so on. Managers were not independent actors but agents of the state, responsible for transforming the government's policies into practice. The directors of SOEs, like other workers, were the employees of the state (Chang 1995a; Wang 1993). Whilst it is easy to argue that this meant suppression of all other interests except those of the Party-state (totalitarianism), the official line was that interests were aligned vertically, from bottom to top. This means that the interests of workers were contained within (not in opposition to) the interests of managers, which were contained within the interests of the enterprise, and so on up the hierarchy. Going up the hierarchy of course, there are more and more interests to contend with, and there may be an implicit argument that the peasant and workers' interests were more simple and basic than those of people higher up. Moreover, we would expect that interests would start to conflict at a certain point. The official line under the planned period was that all the interests were the same, but this was never considered as more than rhetoric by the leadership. The question was how to align reality with the rhetoric. Thus, the government set in place a series of measures to standardize industrial relations practices and thus 'administer' conflicts of interest to their minimum. This included minimizing pay differentials, providing high job security, establishing the *danwei* style of corporatism and so on. Moreover, it meant that the organizations at higher levels should represent and safeguard the interests of organizations and individuals at lower levels. In this model, the government was the representative of state assets as well as the employer of workers.

This role gradually changed from the late 1970s as the government initiated economic reform, which gathered pace in the early 1990s as the CCP decided to transform the economic system. There were essentially two forms of substantial change the government wished and wishes to pursue. The first was a transition in the economic system, replacing the planned economy with a market economy. The second transition involves a change in the social system from one based mainly on peasant agriculture surrounding pockets of industry, to a 'modern' industrial society. These are creating a new kind of labour relations, in which the role of government is also undergoing great changes. This chapter discusses the government's function and its evolving role in initiating, and in many respects controlling, both the context and content of China's different forms of labour relations, as well as the relationships between the government and two other actors: trade union and employers.

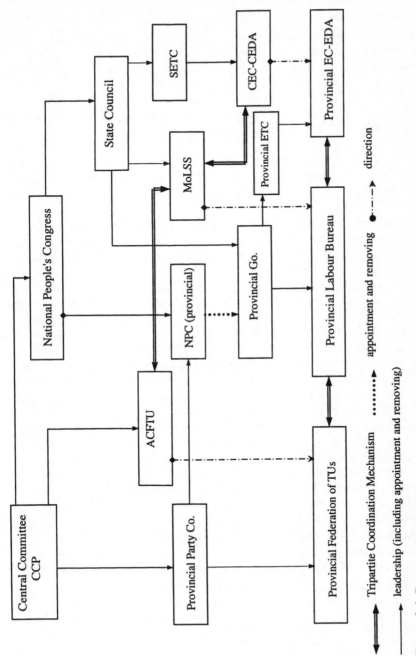

Central Committee CCP

National People's Congress

State Council

SETC

CEC-CEDA

Provincial EC-EDA

MoLSS

Provincial ETC

ACFTU

NPC (provincial)

Provincial Go.

Provincial Party Co.

Provincial Labour Bureau

Provincial Federation of TUs

Tripartite Coordination Mechanism ........

leadership (including appointment and removing) ──────▶

appointment and removing ●········▶ direction

*Figure 2.1 Government structure*

19

## GOVERNMENT INTERESTS

The formal system of the Chinese central government, which is largely replicated at the provincial level, reflects a separation of government from Party. As can be seen in Figure 2.1, the Party has its own organization network, which replicates the government system. However, the figure also indicates the formal power hierarchy, such that the highest authority is the Central Committee of the Chinese Communist Party (CC-CCP), which oversees the National People's Congress, as well as the ACFTU and its own Party structure. Formally, the ACFTU, because of its close linkages to the CCP, is of a higher status than the MoLSS, although in practice that has now changed. The State Council, which organizes the government bureaucracy, controls both the State Economic and Trade Commission (SETC) and the MoLSS.

The very existence of states with national boundaries has some impact on employment patterns and opportunities. It is generally acknowledged that governments play active roles in shaping industrial relations both directly, though laws and regulations, and indirectly, through examples set by the industrial relations practices engaged in with their own employees (public or civil servants). Therefore, the study of government intervention in labour markets is not whether it should intervene but rather what degree of intervention, in what areas and for what objective it should do so (Salamon 1992: 253). As China moves from the planned economy to a market-led system, the role of the state is particularly complex and often contradictory. The features of the Chinese system may be grouped into four characteristics.

First, it is impossible to establish a market mechanism without guidelines from the government. This is because the administrative base of industrial relations in China was a 'stable state continuing' in which change would only occur if either the workers or the state made substantial demands for change. Within the authoritarian structure of the planned economy, this meant in practice change would only occur if initiated by the state, albeit within the context of fears of latent forces for change from below.[4] Moreover, given the Chinese government's wish to initiate marketization as a specific form of economic development, it is inevitable that they should also wish to 'manage' the development of industrial relations within this overall context.

Second, as the economic system changes this necessarily results in the reallocation of economic, political, cultural and information resources (He

---

[4] This is slightly different than Sheehan's (1998) argument that labour has been more active, shaping government policy, or Brown's (forthcoming) argument that state policy is largely determined by its struggle to retain power in the face of contestation with workers. Instead, the state has tried to balance the interests of the army, the peasants and the urban workers all at once, trying to read signals of discontent among such and react accordingly.

2000). This, in turn, creates tensions among various groups in society, as both the perceptions and realities of new power relations between 'winners' and 'losers' begin to occur. Because the government initiated change in China, individuals and groups will naturally hold the government accountable for any 'losses'. Whether they act upon their grievances in some way depends on their power and resources. The state cannot simply abdicate responsibility to some mythical notion of the laws of market regulation. This is a truism in all economic change situations, but given the previous rhetoric of socialism, the Chinese government is held especially to account.

Third, in carrying out reforms in urban areas, the government plays the role not only of policy designer but also of the representative of state assets. In designing and readjusting the layout of the state sector the government has to redefine its functions and its relationship with public sector work units, particular the SOEs. This has two implications. In the first place, as the owner of much of China's productive assets, the state has a vested interest in ensuring economic reform does not erode its asset base substantially. In practice, this has been more a concern of provincial and local governments, who rely more heavily on the revenues generated by these enterprises. On the other side, as the employer of SOE workers, the government is responsible for workers' financial losses and jeopardy to job security brought about by these changes. Those workers who consider they have contributed their life to 'socialist construction' especially hold the government accountable as the (ultimate) employer.

Fourth, whilst the government has initiated economic change, which relies heavily on major structural changes to economic institutions, there has been little or no change to the political structures of China. In maintaining political control, the CCP has effectively prohibited the development of unofficial or autonomous organizations. Whist such organizations do spring up from time to time they rarely have the networks or stamina to represent workers' interests for long, and whilst the government will often respond to their grievances favourably, the leaders are invariably persecuted. Thus, workers have little alternative but to rely on the government to have any hope of realizing their interests.

Taken together, these characteristics mean that the government should not be seen purely as having 'third party' status in the development of industrial relations in China, but a party with direct interests in shaping both the process and outcomes. This argument can be seen more clearly if we examine the ways in which the government has gone about seeking to legislate the development of industrial relations.

After much deliberation, the Third Plenum of the 11th CC-CCP in 1978 adopted a trial and error approach that called for a 'gradual or evolutionary' process of reform.[5] The CCP chose a process of concentrating rapid reform on a few 'key' areas to initiate fundamental change to the market system, but then instituting gradual reform in other areas (Gao 1999). After the success of reform in rural areas during the 1980s,[6] the central government and the CCP, at the 14th National Congress of the CCP held in October 1992, stated clearly the aim of establishing a 'socialist market economy' as well as the blueprint for reform of the economic system. This blueprint was to establish a market economy that allows diverse sectors of the economy to develop side by side. In this system, the public sector, which includes enterprises owned by collectives, was to remain the predominant form of ownership, with the private sector, which includes individually owned and foreign-owned enterprises, providing a supplementary position. Different sectors of the economy could operate jointly in different ways on a voluntary basis (Jiang 1992). At the Third Plenum of the 15th CC-CCP in 1999, it established a principle that reform should proceed within a framework in which public ownership would remain the main form of ownership and other forms of ownership would be developed simultaneously. The Amendment to the Constitution of the People's Republic of China, adopted at the Second Session of the 9th National People's Congress of the PRC on 15 March 1999 states that:

> The non-public sectors of the economy, such as the individual and private sectors of the economy, operating within the limits prescribed by law, constitute an important component of the socialist market economy... The state protects the lawful rights and interests of the individual and private sectors of the economy, and exercises guidance, supervision and control over the individual and the private sectors of the economy.

Thus, it can be seen that the government has created a market system of regulation to allocate products and resources through gradual reform of the public sector and nurturing the development of a private sector. The result

---

[5] The 12th National Peoples' Congress of the CCP declared that, in a socialist economy, planning was primary and market regulation secondary. The Third Plenum of the 12th CC-CCP stated that a commodity economy was a stage that could not be by passed in socio-economic development and that China's socialist economy was a planned commodity economy based on public ownership. The 13th National Congress of the CC-CCP reaffirmed that the socialist planned commodity economy should be a system that integrated planning with market regulation. The Fourth Plenum of the 13th CC-CCP concluded that the goal was to facilitate the development of a socialist planned commodity economy (Jiang 1992).

[6] In terms of introducing the contract responsibility system based on household production, giving peasants the power to make their own decisions about production, almost entirely doing away with the unified purchase of farm products by the state and by removing price controls over these products.

has been a change from government as state planner to market regulator. In promoting the market, the government has stressed reform policies that favour capital owners and management. This tendency is shown by a series of reform policies, such as devolution of autonomy to SOE management, encouraging the development of private enterprises and promoting the privatization of public enterprises. The result of this has had a great impact on the nature of labour relations, effectively undermining the unitarist system and creating considerable tension between workers and employers.

However, it is not in the Party's interest to promote reform to the extent, or in the manner, that will threaten its own interests. This explains the gradual approach to reform, and explains why political considerations sometimes outweigh economic ones. Conflicts of various kinds, including labour unrest, religious activism, community protests and so on, during the reform era have at times undermined the authority and even threatened the stability of CCP power. Sometimes, dealing with these problems becomes more important than intensifying reform.

When the first round of reform (1987–89) eroded workers' interests, some politicians, such as Deng Xiaoping, warned fellow leaders of the potential for political instability in China. He pointed out in 1987 that 'the first precondition of the development of China is to keep political stability ... the second, is to maintain current policies unchanged, unchangeable-ness also means stability' (Deng 1994a: 215–22). Deng (1994b: 62–66) remarked that 'reform in China is neither a social revolution of overthrowing a power, nor a re-selection of the basic social regime. It is a process of self-perfection and self-development, on the basis of adherence to the socialist system and relying on our own capability.'[7] After the 1989 Tiananmen Square protests, the government decided to establish dual goals of deepening economic reform and maintaining social stability. In the second round of reform, begun in 1992, the government has been reluctant to declare its role of representing and protecting the rights of owners and management, especially the interests of private owners, because of this second objective. When its reform policies are confronted with resistance from workers, and social stability is thus threatened, the government has been forced to respond by employing its power and resources to set some restrictions upon employers' behaviour or intervene in their management. Whilst such measures help to maintain social stability and remove threats to Party hegemony, it also means the government takes a direct coordinating role in industrial relations. In the absence of alternative forms of organization to represent workers' interests in

---

[7] The emphasis on self-reliance reflects one of the main driving foci of the economic reform programme, to develop China in order to protect the country from foreign influences. Russian military expansionism in Asia, Japanese economic power and Western capitalism were all seen as threats (in that order) in the 1970s and much of the 1980s.

negotiating the pace and form of reform, workers appeal directly to the state to resolve such issues. For its part, the government also has significant motivation to respond to workers' calls, both to prevent social unrest and to stifle the space available for alternative representative groups to form. As such, the government continues to play a direct role in industrial relations, unable and unwilling to confine itself to that of a 'third-party'.


## GOVERNMENT ROLES IN INDUSTRIAL RELATIONS

The dual interests in reform and stability create a degree of contradiction between stopping and starting reform. Conscious of this, the government has developed three types of strategy, or roles, in seeking to manage the changing terrain of industrial relations. These may be thought of as roles to maintain the status quo or state planning, filling in gaps left by reform and building new organizational forms to promote reform.

### *Maintaining a Planned Economic System*

In the first round of reform (1978–92), emphasis was placed on rural areas and the goal was to establish an economic system called 'giving first place to the planned economy and second place to market regulation' (*jihua jingji weizhu, shichange tiaojie weifu*) (G. Fan 1994). At this stage, the government devolved limited autonomy to directors of SOEs, and initiated within selected enterprises experiments in reforming the labour system. However, throughout China the labour system remained substantially unchanged both at the macro and micro levels.

A major element of this early reform started from what turned out to be a successful attempt to reduce youth unemployment created by returning youth from the countryside after the end of the Cultural Revolution.[8] In August 1980, the central government instituted a 'three-in-line' employment policy in urban areas. This policy stated that, within the context of central planning and guidance, employment could be based on the recommendation from any one of state-run labour service departments, the provision of jobs by voluntary organizations, or by individuals who find work for themselves.[9] This guideline marked the beginning of Chinese employment system reform,

---

[8] During the 'Cultural Revolution' (1966-76), about 17 million urban youth were sent to the countryside to receive 're-education'. From 1976, most of them returned to their resident places which led to unemployment pressure nationwide.

[9] *Wanshan chengshi jiuye gongzuo* (Perfecting the employment work in urban area) (Department of Policy Studies, State Bureau of Labour 1981:5-14).

and one in which the previous job allocation system was abolished, in which the government had allocated jobs to new entrants to the labour force in urban areas. However, this excluded university graduates and demobilized soldiers, who were still allocated to jobs. The government wanted to maintain control over university graduates in which the education system had invested considerable sums of money, and such persons were directed to key industries and government jobs. Demobilized soldiers needed help in finding jobs, and the government was keen to avoid any discontent among military personnel arising from possible problems retirees faced in the new open labour market.

During this period, the central government introduced several trial schemes in certain locations to gain experience to help prepare for further reform. For example, in the 'Proposed Measures on Labour Wages Planning and Labour Force Management in Special Economic Zones' jointly issued by the Ministry of Labour and Personnel and the State Commission of Planning, the government explicitly stated that it would no longer assign labour and wage quotas in special economic zones (Ling and Sun 1992: 37). From the beginning of 1984, an experiment in changes to the labour planning system was conducted in several cities and counties but, until 1992, the experiment was limited to no more than 89 cities and counties in 18 provinces throughout China (Ling and Sun 1992: 39).

Prior to early 1993, public enterprises had virtually no autonomy in wage and employment decision-making. The government maintained tight control over labour recruitment and the total wage bill of enterprises. Through state places and the maintenance of an administrative system, government agencies allocated mandatory quotas for the number of employees in each work unit and their wage bills to enterprises. Although the government had realized that an over centralized, excessively rigid planning system might not be compatible with some reform measures being undertaken more generally within enterprises, those two sets of plans were left practically untouched until the end of 1992. During this period, local governments were allowed only marginal flexibility to adjust their own plans within the context of fulfilling state plans.[10]

Compared with SOEs, joint venture enterprises enjoyed more autonomy. In 1980, the enterprise's board of directors determined all their own wage standards, forms of wage payment, bonuses and level of subsidies. However, at that time, the recruitment of all employees into joint venture enterprises

---

[10] For example, according to the document: 'Some Temporary Provisions about Improving Planned System', issued by the State Commission of Planning and Economy in October 1983, when the number of newly recruited labourers does not meet production and development needs, each province, autonomous region and municipality directly under the Central Government could recruit up to 5 per cent above the state planned quotas (Zhuang et al. 1988: 98).

was still included in the state plan, and thus determined by the government.[11] With few exceptions (such as graduates from national universities), recruits were drawn from the locality in which the enterprise or work unit was established. However, in 1984 joint venture enterprises were allowed to hire technical and business managerial personnel nationally if they could not find enough or suitable persons locally, although such recruitment was still subject to the approval of the local labour administrative agency.[12] It was not until 1986 that foreign-invested enterprises (FIEs) could recruit employees in accordance with their production and operation requirements,[13] and only in 1988 were these enterprises exempt from gaining approval from the labour administrative agency to recruit employees from other localities.[14]

## Filling in the 'Gap' between Two Systems

Nevertheless, a gap emerged between areas of state control and those workers being regulated independently by managers and the market more generally, and this was particularly striking in the case of the growing private sector. Even in SOEs, Lee (1999) argues that social security provisions varied for those employed via central planning and those recruited by other means, although it appears the differences covered a number of employment areas in addition to welfare, creating dual employment tracks within enterprises. As this gap opened up, the government embarked on a second form of labour control, as it began to attempt to fill in this gap by instituting a number of administrative measures, which in turn became a highly important government function during the second round of reform. At a conference attended by the directors of provincial labour departments, the former Minister of Labour (MoL) spelled out this function clearly as follows:

> Labour administrative departments, especially those at province and central cities levels, must make efforts to establish and perfect a macro-

---

[11] Regulations on Labour Management in Joint Ventures Using Chinese and Foreign Investment' was promulgated by the State Council on 26 July 1980 (Department of Overall Planning 1989: 567-70).

[12] 'Implementing Provisions of Ministry of Labour and Personnel for Joint Venture Labour Management' was promulgated by the MoLSS on 19 January 1984 (Department of Overall Planning 1989: 571-78).

[13] 'Provisions on the Right of Autonomy of Enterprises with Foreign Investment in the Hiring of Personnel and on Wages, Insurance and Welfare Expenses of Staff and Workers' was promulgated by the MoLSS on 10 November 1986 (Department of Overall Planning 1989: 579-81).

[14] 'Opinions on Further Implementing the Right of Autonomy of Enterprises with Foreign Investment in the Hiring of Personnel' was promulgated by the MoLSS on 25 April 1988 (Department of Overall Planning 1989: 583-84).

control mechanism over labour and wages which can be compatible with the operation of the market. On the one hand, resorting to the market as a means to allocate the labour force; on the other hand, employing the plan, by taking its advantages of overall balance and [emphasis on the] long-term, to compensate for the absence in the former. (Ruan 1996: 50–66)

The government engages in a number of 'filling-in' micro-control policies. These policies were usually applied to the SOEs and public institutions, which in turn also had some 'role-model' effect to POEs. For example, by the end of 1992 the central government instructed SOEs to maintain a link between the total annual wage bill and the enterprise's economic efficiency. Thus, whilst SOEs took responsibility for their wage costs, and state-directed wage plans disappeared, a strong degree of control was maintained. At the end of 1993, the MoL put forward a new policy under which the enterprise can:

In the perquisite of maintaining a growth rate of the gross payroll below that of its economic returns and maintaining a growth rate of the average wage increase below that of its labour productivity, determine its wage levels in the light of the changes in the labour market and the requirement of government policies.

This policy ended the approach of 'macro-control on wage bill by state plan' (Zhu 1996a: 89–101). This not only controlled inflation but also acted to provide benchmarks for wage setting in joint ventures and the private sector more generally. Another policy attempted to 'guide surplus rural labourers to rational shift and orderly migration', which allows all types of enterprises in urban areas to recruit rural labourers. However, in line with regulating this shift and with controlling competition within the labour supply side, recruitment is usually restricted to menial or dangerous jobs, and ones that the urban residents are less likely to apply for. At the same time, rural (migrant) workers have to apply for work permits from the local government before they can legally move into cities to look for or take up these jobs. This policy to some extent prevents the uncontrolled migration of rural people to the cities and alleviates some of the potential competition for the urban unemployed.

## *Function of Establishing Market Mechanism*

From the start of the second round of reform in 1993, apart from filling-in policies, the government developed active policies to establish market mechanisms. Largely, this was part of a renewed emphasis on promoting economic reform, aimed at increasing enterprises' economic efficiency and gradually withdrawing itself from the internal labour relations of enterprises. This was undertaken through three main policy initiatives.

First, when establishing market institutions the government was keen to see this enhancing some notion of social development at the same time. For this reason, the government continued to use a substantial degree of planned economic methods to direct labour relations as well. This can be seen in the 'Decisions on Some Issues of Establishing a Socialist Market Economy', passed by the Third Plenum of the 14th CC-CCP in 1993, which worked on the principle of 'reforming the labour system and establishing a labour market'. So far, the concept of the 'labour market' has been defined by the MoLSS (formerly, Ministry of Labour),[15] as a 'labour force employment market' (*laodongli jiuye shichang*), a simple market providing employment information for parties wishing to buy and sell labour. This understanding of the labour market precludes all market regulators, such as trade unions, collective bargaining and so on. As a result, there were no effective means to address the growth of labour conflicts. For example, the long-term re-emergence of high levels of unemployment appears to have puzzled the government. The central government responded to unemployment by issuing a number of documents, focusing attention on how to equalize the balance between the supply of and demand for labour in recent years. These documents include establishing of an employment agency system in urban areas, and encouragement of training in technical areas to establish a 'standard and modern labour employment market'.[16]

Second, the government has placed priority on increasing the economic efficiency of the state-owned sector, and this has been designated as one of the most important goals of Chinese economic reform. In the first round of reform, the government had partially delegated authority to SOEs for such matters as recruitment and wage distribution. Moreover, it initiated reforms to the social insurance system through a series of ongoing experiments in order to reduce the non-wage financial payments of SOEs. Whilst the central government proclaimed that the Chinese economic system was based on market regulation, with the aim of promoting the economic efficiency of enterprises, it was also concerned that state policies continued to 'interfere' in enterprise management. The MoL stated that:

---

[15] The MoL expanded to include central management of welfare during the 1990s and in 1998 the ministry was re-titled MoLSS. This state department is in overall charge of labour relations and employment affairs, whereas traditionally it only handled labour issues, cadres being controlled by the Ministry of Personnel.

[16] See MoL (1996b), MoLSS (1999).

The state-owned enterprises have not enjoyed their autonomy of recruitment and they have to settle their surplus workers within enterprises, their wage bills are still subjected to tight control, and the scope of social insurance reform is too narrow to meet the needs of floating labourers. (1996a: 610–12)

At the beginning of the second round of reform, the central government explicitly stated that one of its basic targets was to 'comprehensively allow the enterprises to enjoy their entitled autonomies in a variety of personnel management activities, covering recruitment of workers, employment styles, wage system, wage form and wage level' (Tang and Xi 1994: 167–72). During this period, the government's aim in developing labour reform policies and labour regulations was that these should increase the economic efficiency of enterprises (whether SOE or otherwise). To reduce the social burdens on SOEs, the government established an overall social security system in the 1990s and replaced the 'physical distribution' of public housing with 'monetary distribution' (thus stimulating a consumer market for housing).[17] For the same reasons, in the early stage of the second round of reform, the government placed considerable attention on monitoring and stifling labour disputes that occurred in enterprises, because of their potential to disrupt production.[18] However, by the end of the 1990s, the government appears to have been more concerned with dealing with the social and political aspects of such disputes and thus would be more likely to deal with worker demands more genuinely (see Chapter 7).

Finally, the government is attempting to reduce its direct intervention in the internal labour relations of enterprises. Early in 1987, the central government called for the establishment of individual labour contracts between workers and management in enterprises. In the second round of reform, these individual labour contracts were defined as the main means for establishing employment relationships and thus the government promulgated these nationwide. As Warner (1996a) argues, the government's keenness to use collective contracts indicates its intention to gradually withdraw from the internal labour relations of enterprises. Further, the government promoted the nationwide adoption of the collective contract system, with the aim of establishing a self-adjusting mechanism for labour relations in enterprises (MoL 1994a).

Since the initial stages of reform, the government has changed its

---

[17] 'Physical distribution' refers to housing constructed by the unit and directly allocated to workers and staff members for them to live in. Although nominally rented, the actual rent amount is negligible - it is so low that it does not even cover upkeep costs.

[18] On 2 July 1993, the State Council issued the 'Rules for the Handling of Enterprise Labour Disputes' and a department charged with handling labour disputes was established in the Ministry of Labour in the same year.

orientation towards enterprise-level employment relations from one of direct manager to an increasingly macro-level adjuster, with minimal formal involvement in enterprise affairs. Moreover, having established a view that the labour market is the primary mechanism through which labour is allocated to work units, the governments' role has become increasingly confined to macro-level supply management. The methods by which this role is carried out, however, sometimes draws the government back into the micro or enterprise-based industrial relations again, as will be discussed in the next section.

## METHODS OF GOVERNMENT REGULATION

Economic reform provides an opportunity for the government to withdraw from internal labour relations, and then to become a third-party actor, primarily concerned with labour market regulation. The employment relationship between the workers and government is shifting towards one between workers and management (Chang 1995b; Deery and Mitchell 1993; Zhu 1995). The methods of third-party regulator have become that of regulator, administrator and arbitrator.

## *Regulator*

The Government is playing a role of regulator by standardizing labour relations and seeking to balance the power between management and workers, whilst protecting its own interests in regulating the labour market. This can be seen through the establishment of a fairly comprehensive legislative framework.

### *Chinese labour law and labour law framework*
At an early stage in the reform, the government begun to draft the Labour Law, the first labour code in China. Drafting this law took more than 15 years, during which time it was discussed throughout the trade union system, industrial and economic planning system and government departments concerned. The final law was adopted at the Eighth Meeting of the Standing Committee of the Eighth National People's Congress on 5 July 1994 and came into effect on 1 January 1995. Following its promulgation, the State Council and the MoL and then the MoLSS, detailed the principles provided in this labour code through a series of 'administrative regulations' (Z. Zhang 1996: 141–8).

In the Chinese legal system, there is a hierarchy to laws, which include five different levels, all of which relate to labour regulation in one way or another. The Constitution of the PRC represents the highest legal form and provides the principles for regulating relationships between workers and management. The Constitution also provides that other forms of law should not conflict with it (Article 89[1]). The Labour Law comes immediately below the Constitution and details the principles concerning workers and management, providing a guideline for regulating labour relations in enterprises. Below these come administrative regulations, issued by the State Council and its ministries or commissions, which usually focus on certain aspects of specific labour issues. Below this, the local governments and people's congress or their standing committees at provincial, autonomous regional and municipals levels, or capital cities of provinces and other major cities specified by the State Council, promulgate local regulations. These law-making organs can formulate local regulations. Finally, China is a member state of the International Labour Organization (ILO). So far, the Chinese government has ratified 20 ILO conventions that have legal effect in enterprises within Chinese territory, although they are not independent regulations. Instead, they are enacted through domestic legislation and or administrative guidance.

The Chinese labour law framework was established in the 1990s with two main features. First, it set up a single set of labour standards to be applied to all forms of enterprises (whether publicly or privately owned) and categories of employees within Chinese territory. These united labour standards are applied to most aspects of labour relations, such as terminating labour contracts, working hours and holiday entitlements, methods of wage payment, occupational health and safety, social security and so on. The significance of these standards is to help reduce differences in workers' identities stemming from different forms of ownership and attempting to establish a felt principle of fairness in the labour market. Moreover, partly because of the aspirations to socialist principles and partly due to the attention paid to international labour standards and practice (Z. Zhang 1996: 141–8), the government set Chinese labour standards which usually match and even exceed the minimum standards in advanced industrial countries for some features, such as working time, minimum employment age and non-discrimination (Chang et al. 2001).

Second, the legislative framework has placed most emphasis on setting out substantive rather than procedural provisions. This shows a continuing inclination on the part of the government to wish to control labour relations in practice. By providing such vague procedures concerning bargaining and labour contracts (see Chapter 8), the Chinese labour laws actually do little to promote the independent development of labour relations. Instead, by placing emphasis on laying out detailed requirements and minimum standards for labour provisions, such as conditions for terminating labour contracts, laying off workers, the regulation of social security, the conditions of overtime and payment of overtime wages, the government is essentially deciding the outcome of labour relations. These provisions demonstrate that labour regulations do not allow much room for managers and workers to consult or negotiate with each other, but instead, for the most part, simply get them to acknowledge the leadership of the government and submit to the regulations the government requires. The problem arises, however, when one party, usually management, refuses to follow the procedure in the first place, or uses its power to force 'illegal' provisions in the collective agreements (as will be discussed in Chapter 8).

### Regulation concerning individual labour rights

Due to the restrictions on industrial democracy and unofficial organizations, individual labour rights and the individual labour contracts signed by recruits become the main component part of the Chinese labour law framework. Of the 19 articles in Chapter 3 of the Labour Law (entitled 'Labour Contract and Collective Contract'), 16 articles are concerned with individual labour contract provisions. For several years following the publication of the Labour Law, the MoL and then the MoLSS constantly adhered to its policy that the individual labour contract should be implemented first, and collective contracts later.[19] In the system of labour contracts, the individual labour contract is subjected to legal provisions covering the causes and procedure of terminating contracting, grievances and so on. However, these individual provisions give no role to collective organizations, such as the official trade union. For example, all causes by which the employer may revoke a labour contract are related to individual behaviour or some other personal events.[20] Even in the procedure of terminating the labour contract, the grass-roots union can only have the right to 'air its opinion if it regards [a case] as an inappropriate revocation of a labour contract by the management', without the right to deny these decisions (Article 30 of Labour Law). In terms of wages, the Labour Law explicitly states that employers are free to determine the method of distribution and level of wages according to law and based on the characteristics of its production and business and economic results (Article 47). These regulations minimize the possibility that the workers can, through their own collective power or through the unions, improve their working conditions and economic benefits.

---

[19] In accordance with a speech made by Zhu Jiazhen, the Vice-Minister of Labour, 'the labour contract system defines a legal labour relationship, to establish a labour relationship between two parties, and so it is at the first place. The collective contract system is to adjust labour relations on the basis of the labour contract. Therefore, it is at the second place' (Zhu 1996b: 99).

[20] Article 25 and 26, Labour Law.

## Regulations on collective labour rights

In the Chinese labour law framework, collective labour rights, including the rights of organization, collective bargaining and dispute, are discussed but are neither emphasized nor thoroughly established. Workers are given rights to be represented and to collective bargaining. Article 7 of the Labour Law and Article 3 of Trade Union Law (2001) respectively provide that labourers 'shall have the right to join and organize trade unions in accordance with the law'. However, the Trade Union Law (1982) established a monopolistic position for the ACFTU, outside which workers may not organize legally. This 'exclusive' qualification is reaffirmed in the amended Trade Union Law (2001), which states that 'the All-China Federation of Trade Unions and all its trade union organizations represent the interests of workers and protect their legitimate rights and interests under law' (Article 2). While guaranteeing the ACFTU's monopolistic status, two sets of laws prohibit workers from organizing their own organizations. According to the Trade Union Law, the establishment of trade unions at all levels, including the grass-roots unions in enterprises, must report to the trade union organization at the higher level for approval (Article 11). This provision means that workers cannot organize an association or union that is outside the control (approving authority) of the ACFTU, which is itself under the direction of the Party-state. As such, it is unnecessary to define the 'bargaining unit' and 'coverage of collective contracts' in the Labour Law because the ACFTU's system is the only recognized and legitimated organization to represent workers' interests. The only jurisdictional issue is between those who are eligible or excluded from union membership and especially the eligibility of managers to join (this will be discussed further in Chapter 5).

Chinese labour law provides incomplete regulations on collective labour rights. The Labour Law and the Trade Union Law do not address the possibility of strikes as a means of furthering or safeguarding workers' interests. In other words, the government continually avoids addressing the issue of 'the right to strike'. Nevertheless, it is the view of the authors that the Chinese government has in actuality neither criminalized nor legitimized strikes and other industrial actions (see Chapter 7), leaving it up to local governments and the police to decide legitimacy on a case-by-case basis. This situation has fuelled growing confusion and tension, as unofficial reports indicated that workers often resort to strikes and demonstrations in an attempt to obtain unpaid wages, receive delayed pension and avoid lay-offs. Some domestic scholars of labour law have called on the government to enact legislation protecting and defining the right to strike. [21] However, in the amended Trade Union Law, this right is still ignored. Article 24 of this law

---

[21] For example, Chang (1988a: 51-8) and Shi (1999: 54-6) have suggested the government should grant the right to strike to trade unions.

states that the trade unions have the right to suggest to the enterprise that the workers abandon a dangerous site on discovering a situation where the personal safety of workers is jeopardized. The content of this provision is supposed to apply to avoiding industrial accidents rather than providing a legal basis for industrial action, and even then it places the final decision with management. Moreover, the 'Provisions on Collective Contracts', issued by the MoL in December 1994, states that extremist actions taken by either party during collective negotiations are prohibited (Article 12). This provision would most certainly cover both strikes and lockouts.

### Agency and procedure of setting labour disputes

According to the Labour Law and the 'Rules on the Handling of Enterprises Labour Disputes' promulgated by the State Council on 6 July 1993, the government established a dispute settlement agency and procedure. A labour dispute conciliation committee is an agency established in each enterprise, which consists of the representatives from employees, management and the enterprise's trade union. The chairperson of a conciliation committee is a representative of the grass-roots union and the office of the committee is established in the union. In cases where the conciliation committee fails to resolve a matter brought before it by one or more aggrieved worker(s), or if the parties concerned prefer arbitration, they may directly apply to the labour dispute arbitration committee to settle their dispute. A labour dispute committee is established at county, municipality or district level under the jurisdiction of respective levels of municipal government. These committees comprise the representatives from local trade unions, the labour administration department and the comprehensive economic management department designated by the government. If a party disagrees with an arbitration award, that party may file a suit in the people's court within a period required by law.

In the regulations setting out the labour disputes procedures the principle of 'individualism' is dominant. In both the internal procedure for conciliation and the external procedure of arbitration, the workers, even if they have a common collective grievance, usually register and follow the relevant procedures in their own individual names and not as a collective group. The law places the trade union in the position of mediator and arbitrator, rather than representative of workers. According to the law, enterprise-level unions are not entitled to be partisan in a labour dispute on behalf of workers, but are allowed to offer their support and assistance to a worker in a case 'where a worker believes that the enterprise has infringed upon his or her labour rights and applies to the labour dispute arbitration committee for arbitration or initiates legal proceedings with a people's court' (Article 21, Trade Union Law).

## *Inspector*

Another method of regulation is to inspect employers as to their compliance with the regulations specified above. The Labour Law stipulates that labour administrative departments of the people's governments at or above the county level have a duty to inspect workplaces to ensure regulations are followed. The duties also include promoting government's labour policies and labour regulations, and supervising the employing units and managers to implement these policies. In pursuing their public duties, labour inspectors have the right to enter workplaces to undertake on-site investigations as they see fit concerning the implementation of relevant laws and regulations, and examine necessary data. Moreover, the inspectors have the power to stop any acts that run counter to labour laws, rules and regulations and to order rectification where appropriate.[22]

## *Damage Control*

Whilst the government has embarked on a course of stimulating economic reform and establishing labour market mechanisms in different periods, labour policies play the role of either promoting reform or maintaining social stability. Most policy and regulatory formulation and implementation discussed so far refers to either promoting reform of employment practices or limiting the autonomy of industrial relations in enterprises. These practices fall generally in line with an argument that the government wishes to improve economic efficiency whilst retaining control of the political economic system, albeit from an increasingly macro level. However, some reform measures cannot be undertaken through such balancing methods, but fall into the category of 'damage control', whereby the government seeks to limit the potential for social unrest brought about by economic reform measures. A prime example of this is in the second round of reform, when the government introduced a series of policies aimed at 'increasing efficiency by downsizing staff' (*jianyuan zengxiao*).

From the early 1990s the central government identified 'surplus workers' as an impediment to raising the economic efficiency of the public sector and especially SOEs, and so adopted a policy of 'increasing efficiency by downsizing staff'. From then on, SOEs have been laying off their surplus workers in ever increasing numbers. Managers, whether from loss-making or profitable enterprises, have to fulfil quotas for lay-offs assigned by their senior agencies (Niu 1999; Li 2000). These lay-offs consequently threaten

---

[22] Article 85 of the Labour Law; Article 6 of the 'Measures Governing Labour Inspectors', issued by the MoL on 14 November 1994.

workers' interests, as public sector workers had traditionally accepted lower incomes in exchange for high job security (Li et al. 2000). To maintain social stability, the central government launched a parallel programme called 're-employment' to settle the laid-off workers. At the start of this programme, the government mainly provided financial assistance to the unemployed and laid-off workers to help them cover the costs of retraining and to provide guidance in finding new employment (that is, providing up-to-date employment information and guidance on choices of occupations). Where an enterprise was made bankrupt, the government organized the workers to use their settlement allowance (redundancy payments) to cover their living expenses and to help them try to start up co-operative enterprises with the money, or found other enterprises to employ them. In these activities, the laid-off workers were still officially tied to their enterprises; in other words, they maintained their status as SOE workers and were referred to as '*xiagang* workers' in recent years.[23] In this way, the government both forces change which creates the potential for worker unrest, and then engages in damage control to try to 'pacify' the affected workers.

In the course of implementing these labour policies, the government usually takes the role of proposing and leading reform. As the representative of state assets, implementing the policy of 'increasing efficiency by downsizing staff' can be seen as a method used by the government to increase the economic competitiveness of the state sector. However, the consequences brought about by lay-offs and the discontent from workers has led to a series of social problems that are beyond the scope of management to cope with. The government then steps in, in an attempt to solve these problems. However, from 1997 rising numbers of laid-off and unemployed workers fuelled social discontent across the country and brought about a renewed threat to social stability which required a direct response from the government.[24] Thus, the government adopted more proactive administrative measures to initiate such activities as a 're-employment project' in order to prevent *xiagang* from becoming a catalyst for major civil unrest. In May

---

[23] In the 'Notice of Strengthening the Management of SOEs' *Xiagang Workers* and Establishing Re-employment Centres', issued by the MoL, the SETC, the Ministry of Finance, the Ministry of Education, the State Statistical Bureau and the ACFTU on 3 August 1998, '*xiagang* worker' is defined as 'the person who has his or her name on the payroll of the enterprise, who has left his or her own job post because of the problems of production or operation of the enterprise, who still keeps labour relations with enterprise and cannot find another job in the society'.

[24] According to a survey in six cities (Beijing, Shenyang, Guiyang, Xian, Zhuhai and Luoyang) in February 1997, among 1510 families sampled, 53.3 per cent viewed Chinese society as stable, 36.5 per cent viewed it as less stable and 10 per cent believed it to be unstable; of the 13 factors that brought a negative effect on social stability, 'increasing unemployed workers' ranked the third, after 'corruption' and 'public security' (Wang C. G. 1999: 121-32). Recent indications are that the government may even be slowing down the pace of redundancies because of fears of social instability (Lim and Forsythe 2002: 11).

1998, the CC-CCP and the State Council held a conference to discuss how to guarantee the basic living standards for *xiagang* workers and on how to implement the re-employment project. In the 'Notice of Doing Best in Guaranteeing the Living Necessities for *Xiagang* Workers and Implementing the Re-employment Project' published after this meeting, the central government required the establishment of 're-employment centres' at all publicly owned enterprises where there are a large number of laid-off workers. These centres then attempt to guarantee basic living expenses and provide assistance for those seeking re-employment (*Xinhua yuebao* 1998 No. 7: 164–6; State Council 2002).

By implementing these policies, the government hopes to reduce tension whilst continuing its drive to further economic reform. The hope within the government is that once the market economy matures, the labour market will adjust itself autonomously (as it is supposed to do in capitalist economies) Whilst there are few restrictions on the private sector in labour market adjustment, the public sector, and particularly the SOEs, have wider functions than simply as economic units (see Chapter 3). However, without a readjustment to market 'rationality', the state sector cannot compete fairly with the private sector. In fact, from the middle of the 1990s, SOE managers were no longer responsible for finding new job positions for their surplus workers within their or other enterprises.[25] The government requires that the redundant workers leave their employers and enter the 're-employment centres'. This means their employment cards will be physically removed from the SOE administration offices and placed in the centre. This is much more than a symbolic gesture, it is a real change in status and almost invariably means the worker affected will never work in the same enterprise again. The redundant workers will become (completely) unemployed after two years if they cannot find a job or refuse to take a job or refuse to take a job offered to them by their re-employment centre. In 1999, the MoLSS declared a new market-oriented policy, which has meant the government will abandon the concept of '*xiagang*' altogether from 2002; laid-off workers will become 'unemployed' and have to enter the labour market directly (Z. Zhang 1999). The implication behind this policy is that the government will not continually keep the identity of 'national workers' for these laid-off workers. In other words, the state will be no longer be their employer, which further reinforces the previous action of removing the redundant workers' employment cards from their employer's possession. The high degree of worker unrest in the spring of 2002 means this policy is likely to be softened

---

[25] In the 'Provisions on Settling Surplus Workers and Staff in State-owned Enterprises' issued by the State Council 30 April 1993, it required that 'internal settlement within the enterprises' should be the main channel to settle the surplus workers and staff (Department of Policy and Law 1994: 253-5).

in some way (for example Lim and Forsythe 2002), but it is too early to tell yet.

## *Mediator and Arbitrator*

One exception to the government's emphasis on substantive provisions in its labour legislation is the establishment of procedures to deal with conflicts that arise in the workplace. Early in 1987, a formal procedure was established in SOEs, and this was extended to all types of enterprises in 1993.[26] This involved the establishment of arbitration committees at all levels to arbitrate and mediate labour disputes and to make arbitration awards.[27] However, the government, through the MoLSS and the ACFTU, has maintained a central position in such procedures (See Chapter 8).

There are numerous conflicts resulting from both the practice of economic-based employment relations and the process of reform itself. Tensions between workers and management often take the form of internal or workplace conflicts, when workers lose income or job security resulting from management strategies associated with responding to reducing financial deficits, mergers, government lay-off quotas and bankruptcy. The most explosive conflicts occur when workers perceive, or endure, the illegal activities of managers, such as delayed wage payments, unpaid bonuses or allowances, or other behaviour that violates labour regulations. However, workers often express their dissatisfaction by engaging in some form of collective action outside their enterprises, which are often directed towards the government. These include surrounding the local government offices, asking for direct communication with senior government officials and the like. The workers' logic is that it is the responsibility of government to remedy workers' grievances because China claims still to be a workers' state (Wang 2002), and in the case of SOEs, the government is still the owner. Workers hope the government, in turn, will exert pressure on the management of their enterprises, or refund the delayed paid wages, medical expenses or pensions directly if the enterprise is unable to do so. The government at all levels (from national to township) has responded to what are euphemistically called 'collective events' (*Fuanti shijian*). On the one

---

[26] In 1987, by promulgated the 'Temporary Provisions on Settling Labour Disputes in State-owned Enterprises', the State Council established both the mediation and arbitration procedures; in 1993, the State Council promulgated the 'Rules on Handling Enterprise Labour Disputes in Enterprise' and applied these two procedures to all types of enterprises.

[27] According to the 'Rules on the Handling of Enterprises Labour Disputes', the arbitration committee consists of the representatives from the local trade union, the labour administration department and the comprehensive economic management department designated by the government.

hand, they issue policies to require the enterprises in their jurisdictions to 'ensure a timely and full payment of the retirement pensions for retirees and guarantee the basic living expenses of laid-off workers' and so on (State Council 2002). On the other hand, they send representatives to appease workers as well as collect some money to meet part of the workers' demands when conflicts occur. Thus, whilst the state has sought to distance itself from industrial relations, and to position itself as the third-party macro manager, workers in many cases have successfully pulled the state back into direct employment relations.

## STATE RELATIONS WITH OTHER ACTORS

The government, as an actor in industrial relations, must seek to fulfil its objectives through various forms of relationships, with workers, the ACFTU and employers, as well as its direct relations with managers employed in SOEs. To some extent, the nature of these actors is a manifestation of state policy and thus the state continues to wield at least a 'parental' authority over them. Yet, once formed, each actor or party has opportunities to develop autonomy relative to state acts and omissions. The one exception to this parent-child relation is the workers, who helped in small part to form the CCP and the Chinese Communist state in the first place. A mixture of Chinese cultural values of patriarchy, respect for authority and the legacy of neo-corporation discussed in the last chapter act to extend the value of this 'parental state' model to all the other actors, although to ever diminishing degrees.

### *The State and Workers*

Even though the overall contribution to production of the public sector has been declining ever since the reforms began, publicly owned enterprises remain the industrial backbone of the Chinese economy (see Chapter 4), and the largest employer in China (as in most countries) is the state. Under the guideline of 'managing large enterprises well, while relaxing control over small ones' (*zhuada fangxiao*), the central government maintains control over strategically important and most very large SOEs. Controlling these large enterprises allows the government to maintain some macro-level control over the economy, whilst also seeking to improve the efficiency of key SOEs. For other SOEs, the intention has been dramatically to reduce direct intervention in all aspects of decision-making whilst ensuring such enterprises follow government regulations. As part of these changes the non-strategic SOEs are gradually being privatized or corporatized in some form or another in an attempt to ensure they have similar levels of autonomy to private sector enterprises.

Both the specific reforms to increase the autonomy of the sector and the more general changes to the labour system create a considerable cleavage between the interests of the state and those of workers (R. Jiang 1996; Qi and Xu 1995; Zhang 1997). On the one hand, after acquiring increased authority as well as economic responsibility, managers in the state sector can design their management objectives based on economic considerations. These objectives include reducing production and resource factor costs, increasing profit, expanding market penetration and so forth (Groves 1995; Tang et al. 1996; Zhang 1997; Zhao and Nichols 1996) with much less political and social consideration than before. On the other hand, workers have become both increasingly conscious of and worried about their own interests because of the reform measures, and have particular concerns over job security, wages and welfare (Change 1995a; Qi and Xu 1995; Zhang 1997). In these changes, the government is unable to continue its dual roles of representative of state assets as well as workers' interests and those of employers. Moreover, as the state remains the employer for a proportion of Chinese workers, these conflicts are internalized to the state itself. The policy of increasing efficiency by downsizing staff has demonstrated that, as the representative of state assets, the government has given priority to the interests of employers. Given the reality of conflicts of interest there is some doubt (Cheng X. 2001) that the state can define its role clearly, either as a direct employer or as a third-party arbitrator of labour relations.

## Relations with the ACFTU

The monopolistic status of the Party-state and its strong desire to maintain unitarist control has meant that organizations which may be thought of as making up the loose concept of 'civil society' are largely absent in China (Zweig 2000; 139), although market reform may be leading to some space for their formation (White et al. 1996). The very existence and status of the ACFTU is that which has been granted to it by the CCP, which in practice has meant the ACFTU has often been expected to play the role of a specialist 'arm of the Party'. Historically, the ACFTU was assigned with function of 'transmission belt' and the responsibly to transmit government's policies, assist management in meeting production targets and to promote the welfare of workers. At various times in its history, especially during the later half of the 1980s, the ACFTU had tried to free itself from the control of the CCP and to become more independent, but it failed to do so (Jiang K. 1996). In the second round of reform, the government has assigned the official trade unions, which make up the ACFTU, the function of promoting reform and maintaining social stability (Hu 1993: 598–607). Thus, the clear implication is the role is still defined as that of an assistant to the government. On 27 October 2001, the 24th Session of the 9th National People's Congress Standing Committee adopted an amended version of the 'Trade Union Law'. The amended 'Trade Union Law' states that the trade unions shall abide by the leadership of the CCP, and conduct its work independently and voluntarily in accordance with the Trade Union Charter (Article 4) and provides that 'the trade unions shall, while defending the overall interests of the whole nation, safeguard the workers' legitimate rights and interests' (Article 6). Moreover, the amendment requires that the trade unions 'shall, at the same time as participating in the management of national and social affairs, assist people's governments to conduct their work' (Article 5).

From the perspective of government, whether the role is to maintain social stability or promote economic reform, the trade unions can only play the role of assistant. The position of the ACFTU can be illustrated by reference again to the plight of *xiagang* workers. First, the trade union system of the ACFTU, and especially the local unions (the industrial unions and enterprise-level unions), can exercise little power in determining the issues of how and who should be laid-off, but instead management unilaterally makes these decisions. The grass-roots unions cannot, on behalf of workers, respond to the decisions made by managers when these decisions directly threaten the job security of their members but instead, in an attempt to fulfil CCP interests to maintain social stability, the unions should either remain silent or try to persuade the affected workers to submit to management decisions. Second, even in dealing with the problems of laid-off workers, it has already been shown that it is the government that plays the leading role, assigning the ACFTU the role of assistant. In a document issued by the central government stipulating six ways of guaranteeing basic living expenses for laid-off workers and re-employment, no mention is made of the trade unions' role (*Renmin ribao* 23 June 1998, [1]) for example.[28]

The legislative direction and process both subordinate the role of the ACFTU to the government. First, the detailed substantive provisions of labour laws and policies bring about a 'substitution' effect, in which a trade union's ability to negotiate for members' terms and conditions of employment are substituted by the detailed provisions laid out in the government-made regulations. Whilst the ACFTU assists in drafting these laws, once implemented they allow little room for trade unions to strive for any more for their members. Moreover, it creates the impression that the

---

[28] The six ways include: standardized procedure for lay-offs, establishing 're-employment service centres', increasing job opportunities, perfecting the social security system, strengthening occupational training and promoting ideological and political education of workers.

government implements a set of labour standards which act as both a minimum and a best practice, implying terms better than those stipulated in the regulations are neither necessary nor in national interests. Lacking political and economic power, the trade union will not be the workers' first choice when they meet trouble. This explains the main reason why aggrieved workers prefer to present their petitions directly before government in recent years.

Second, the government does not provide the trade unions with a sole right or exclusive status to represent the interests of worker. Theoretically, the managers of SOEs, the government at all levels, the Party organs and other official organizations that workers may have joined can take the role of workers' representatives and each has some legal and political rights to do so. In fact, at least nominally, besides the trade unions, the workers can resort to many measures to protect their interests when these come under threat.

Third, the trade unions have inadequate means available to safeguard their members' interests. Whilst the Trade Union Law and the Labour Law stipulate that the ACFTU should represent legitimate worker interests, they are prohibited from using instruments or means that are confrontational, but are required to follow rather weak administrative procedures. The unions must pursue initiatives or claims that safeguard their members' interests through direct or indirect communication with management and government. In direct communication with management, the grass-roots unions can put forward their 'demands', opinions and suggestions to the employers to ask them to respond but they can do no more than this. [29] In indirect communication, through reporting to the government agencies concerned, the trade unions at all levels can ask these agencies to take up their concerns. [30] In the former mechanism, the unions have no authority or sanctions to pressure management to respond favourably. In the latter case, the management determines whether to accept these requirements, opinions and suggestions. This procedure in the end amounts to the unions appealing to government agencies to put pressure on management. Even if this proves successful, the workers will not credit this to the trade union but to either management or the government.

Consequently, although unions in China at present have been entitled to represent and protect the interest of workers, in practice they have to subordinate their activities to the Party and government at different levels. As a result, it has been difficult for unions to establish a positive representative image among workers. Moreover, it has meant that the unions themselves tend to focus their attention upwards and outwards rather than towards members. 'Upwards' means the union cadres tend to rely on the vertical

---

[29] Articles 17, 19, 23, 24 of Trade Unions Law.
[30] Articles 16, 23, 24 of Trade Unions Law.

chain of command to receive instructions and guidelines from above, with the ultimate authority in Beijing, where at least the ACFTU can assist the government in drafting legislation and policies favourable to its own and its members' interests. 'Outwards' means the unions tend to look to the Party, MoLSS or other government agencies horizontally to seek help in promoting their own interests and to help fulfil the tasks assigned by higher levels in the hierarchy.

As a general consequence of the ACFTU not being recognized by workers as their representative, the central government also seems not to have relied on the unions to represent members. For the same reason, the government has never relied on the ACFTU as an organization to control workers either. Except during periods when the ACFTU showed some tendency towards independence, the central government has never issued policies to regulate its relationship with the ACFTU. Therefore, we would argue that there is little chance the Party will seek to develop a 'state-corporatist' relationship with the ACFTU.

## Relations with Employers

In order to activate the dual goals of promoting economic reform whilst maintaining political stability, the government has remained intimately entwined with workplace industrial relations. The central government has been trying to maintain control over labour relations in different types of enterprises, but it has done so through a mixture of general and specific provisions. Li (2002) argues that the government works mainly in the interests of employers when making policies but once it finds reforms endanger social stability, it will formulate some 'repairing' policies to restrain the power of employers and managers and compensate workers in some way in order to head-off social unrest.

Compared with the central government, local authorities take a more strategic stance, which we may label 'limiting intervention in labour relations'. Limiting intervention is basically trying to reduce interference by outsiders and promote managerial and employer interests up to the point that government officials think workers' (and others') interests are subordinated to a bare minimum without disrupting social stability. In some cases, the alignment of interests between local officials and entrepreneurs can be so close that even social instability is not a restraint, sometimes leading to purges from more senior government organs when widespread unrest does not occur. In adopting this approach, a slight twist of meaning occurs, from that of maintaining state or government interests, to promoting the officials' own interests. To understand this we must examine the relationship between the local officials and private employers, and how their interests overlap and sometimes converge. Whilst there is an old saying that the 'hills are high and the emperor is far away' (*shangao huangdi yuan*) to refer to provincial government autonomy in the huge and complex geography of China, decentralization of power has been promoted as part of the reform process. This provides local governments with opportunities to establish mutually dependent relationships with private owners in their jurisdiction. In return for fiscal revenue from private enterprises, the local bureaucracies often offer preferential treatment to these enterprises and assist them in their profit-seeking goals. It is not surprising that local officials will support and protect the private owners' profit-seeking behaviours (Yi and Li 2000), and tolerate, acquiesce or turn a blind eye when labour law violations occur (F. Chen 2000; Chan 2001).

The reasons for local cadres to favour employers are not only selfish, in promoting their own chances to pocket a bit of extra income before retiring, but stems from the reform process itself. The development of private enterprises, especially the introduction of foreign investment, is usually taken as an important standard to evaluate the achievements in local officials' careers. Therefore, so long as social stability can be maintained at a minimum level and no serious unrest occurs, the local officials would make their effort to keep these private enterprises operating in their jurisdictions. Moreover, as increasing numbers of public sector enterprises face financial difficulties, revenue from them becomes less certain. Whilst the private sector has been unwilling and sometimes unable to replace the economic and social contribution that the public sector has traditionally fulfilled in urban areas, it appears to be the only hope in the eyes of many local government cadres to sustain the government in the future. Certainly, this also provides golden opportunities for some cadres to make personal gains at the same time.

The mutual favours and overlapping interest (and at township and village level even blurring of identities) between local officials and private owners can sometimes mean the interests of local governments and the central government are quite different as regards industrial relations. Some local officials or their relatives often openly or surreptitiously register private enterprises or invest in existing enterprises, while in others they are invited by the owners to be paid 'consultants'. Wearing these two hats, the identities of some local officials share exactly the same economic interests as private capitalists. Within the hierarchy of the Chinese government, such merging of interests is more popular among the officials at the lower levels because there are more changes of accessing private enterprises. Oi (1999) called this system 'government corporatism', one in which both parties exchange power and money, but one in which workers' interests are absent.

One result of this exchange is that workers, especially migrants from remote areas are often denied the protection provided by law, or remedy when employers with such close ties to government infringe their legal rights.

As such, labour laws are commonly ignored in these enterprises, with the tacit or active endorsement of local of officials. This system is perpetuated because of the strong degree of 'hierarchical structure' in the Chinese bureaucracy. A junior official with such discretion to enhance personal interests may be allowed to do so, so long as officials that are more senior gain some benefit also. More importantly, if the head of a section or agency were given the opportunity, subordinates would not report this to superior organizations because their leader is likely to share such illicit benefits with them. Law enforcement and labour inspectorate officers will obey their superiors to avoid chosen enterprises, and in return the superior will often be 'generous' to their subordinates when the opportunity arises. In theses cases, the market economy has corrupted the political system to varying degrees and the value of money as political capital has dramatically increased.

The different roles and attitudes toward labour relations between the central government and local authorities contribute to a 'dual policy on labour relations'. In some large-sized SOEs directly controlled by the central government, the unitary labour relations model that was created under the planned economy continued to characterize the internal labour relations for many years after reform, and in some cases can still survive today. The government maintains its dominance over industrial relations and there are no clear boundaries between the identities and interests of workers and senior managers, whilst the government also retains a strong presence as the employer. To the private-owned, foreign-owned enterprises and some medium-sized and small public enterprises that have been privatized, the local governments have shifted their strategies towards a laissez-faire basis and tolerate, if not actually underwrite, the employers' control over labour relations. These kinds of strategies contribute to market-individualist driven labour relations in private enterprises. In these enterprises, there are clear identities and divisions of interests between employers and workers, with little intervention from government. Moreover, the actual enforcement of labour laws and regulations is questionable. Generally, the Labour Law can help establish a legal basis for workers' interests, but little significant progress will occur without major government support. Thus, the solution as well as the problem to some degree lies with the way the central government has developed its relations with the other industrial actors, including local governments.

## CONCLUSION

There can be little doubt that the government still plays a very active role in the unfolding patterns of industrial relations in China, as a regulator, arbitrator and inspector. However, the government has been unable to move itself completely from the position of direct employer, sitting across the table as it were from workers, with managers and trade unions acting as its agents, to that of a third party as it would wish. The process of marketization and privatization has not enabled the government to find an effective way to adjust labour relations without creating the potential for widespread social unrest. Whilst the government has allowed both public and private enterprises greater autonomy to increase efficiency in the allocation of resources, the government has no interest in doing this if such a process threatens its own interests, those of an authoritarian Party-state. The 'dual labour relations' structure discussed in the previous section stems from the different strategies central and local governments have, and shows that even the government structure itself in China has different interests, and this poses particular dilemmas for the central government. On the one hand, ceasing directly to intervene in enterprise-based industrial relations will lead to an uncontrolled exploitation of labour and then social chaos, because Chinese urban workers will not tolerate such abuses for long. On the other hand, continued intervention makes it difficult to establish a system of labour allocation based on market regulation, a labour market, which is in the interests of capital. Until now, the government has not found a way to overcome this dilemma. Therefore, the role of the government still remains undefined. What is certain, however, is the continued pre-eminence of the state in defining and shaping the development of industrial relations in China. All other actors, and all industrial relations processes, act either with a relative autonomy permitted by or neglected by the state, and have as their primary relationship the state in some form or other. As such, the state continues to dominate industrial relations in China, sometimes actively and sometimes reluctantly.

# 3. Enterprises and managers

At the formal level, there has been a rapid and ongoing transformation in the employers' side of the industrial relations system in China. New forms of ownership emerged and control has continually been realigned to meet state objectives of economic reform, whilst simultaneously attempting to maintain stability of the existing political structure. At the informal and practical level of daily management in China, change in industrial relations management has been more complex and often contradictory. Relations with workers are constantly being renegotiated at a number of levels. Relations with the state are also being both formally changed and informally negotiated, but with considerable blurring of state-enterprise interests being maintained, even as a growing number of enterprises become primarily economic organizations.

It is popular to see two phenomena among Chinese employers as a result of enterprise reform: the growth of new forms of capitalist or quasi-capitalist employers, and the growth of the professional manager as a distinct category, separate from the Party-government cadre. A fundamental issue in the study of enterprise reform concentrates on whether the communist-constituted enterprise and new capitalist organizations are able to behave in rational-economic terms within the context of marketization, or whether they are constrained by government interference and/or organizational capacity (for example: Knight and Song 1999). Studies of management examine much the same issues as do studies of enterprise reform, but from the viewpoint of management ideology, capacity and motivations. Under the planned economy, managers were given the identity of cadres, signifying a highly politicized bureaucrat who has been responsible for the production and distribution of goods and services in the Chinese communist political economy. The cadres carry a broad range of responsibilities but also have clear political missions to uphold the interests of the CCP. Confusion that does arise for the role of the cadre does not come so much from themselves as individuals or jobholders but from the conflicting signals sent out from the CCP. This has been discussed in the last chapter in relation to multiple government expectations on cadres, but also reflects a broader concept of cadre than manager.

This chapter will outline the different forms of enterprise that have developed, providing some historical location in which to understand current tensions in enterprise reform. The chapter will then examine who controls these enterprises, through examining enterprise governance. This will draw on the idea of the interests and control of different stakeholders to identify the interaction between the owners and managers in the corporate governance of enterprises. Then, the chapter will explore the position of the 'manager'. In contrast to previous discussion, we will develop a number of contrasting types of management orientation that appear to have emerged in China. This will show that, whilst there is an objective managerial class of sorts forming, because of objective differences of interest and subjective orientations to reform, the class remains fragmented. Taken together, the sections will provide an introductory understanding of how complex and often contradictory the employers' side of different types of industrial relations has become in China.

## FORMS OF ENTERPRISE

There is now an array of different types of employers in China, but the two primary forms of urban employment remain SOEs and COEs. SOEs are enterprises that are 'invested, owned and controlled by the state' (R. Zhao 1999: 230–1) and 'the ownership of state-owned assets in the enterprises belongs to the state; the enterprises, as legal entitles, possess all rights over the assets and enjoy rights and shoulder responsibilities under civil law' (CC-CCP 1993). There are many different types of SOEs, according to size, strategic importance and industry, and each reports to one of the state organs. A process of developing new forms of more commercially orientated enterprises has taken place, within a context of gradualism, experimentation and adaptation.

Table 3.1 below shows the number of industrial enterprises formed under different types of ownership since the mid-1980s, showing that SOEs at the beginning of the period were numerically the most significant form of enterprise.

The private sector, mainly in the form of POEs, is by far the most numerous employer in urban and rural areas. Whilst the data is very unreliable, the government claims that during the ten-year period from 1989 to 1999 the number of POEs grew sixteen fold (Department of Information 2001).[31] Another category of POEs are the numerous individual employers

---

[31] However, there is a slight decline in industrial POEs over the same period. The difference is accounted by excluding non-industrial POEs. Moreover, Table 4.1 indicates in excess of a twenty fold increase in employment in POEs over the period.

*getihu*. Individual employers roughly equate to sole traders in Western business law and are made up of a large number of small employers, with fewer than eight employees, and are often family businesses. Probably many of these *getihu* had existed as family firms for several generations, but had been forced to reduce their emphasis on 'business' during the 1960s and 1970s. The number of *getihu* grew ten fold in the decade up to 1999, and total employment grew 340 per cent over the period (see Chapter 4). In practice, the distinction between POEs and *getihu* is not as clear-cut as the legal definition of employment size might suggest. Taken together, POEs and *getihu* make up by far the fastest growing sector within China.

*Table 3.1 Number of industrial enterprises by ownership (x 100)*

| Year | SOEs | COEs | TVEs | SHEs | POEs | HTWs and FIEs | Others |
|------|------|------|------|------|------|---------------|--------|
| 1978 |      |      | 15 242 |    |      |               |        |
| 1980 |      |      | 14 246 |    |      |               |        |
| 1985 |      |      | 122 245 |   |      |               |        |
| 1986 | 968  | 18 230 | 151 530 |  | 47 845 |             | 24     |
| 1987 | 976  | 18 193 | 175 024 |  | 55 533 |             | 39     |
| 1988 | 1023 | 17 470 | 188 816 |  | 61 242 |             | 54     |
| 1989 | 1023 | 16 685 | 186 863 |  | 61 242 | .           | 72     |
| 1990 | 1044 | 16 685 | 185 040 |  | 61 760 |             | 88     |
| 1991 |      |      | 190 888 |   |      |               |        |
| 1992 | 1033 | 16 406 | 209 162 |  | 68 540 |             | 142    |
| 1993 | 1047 | 18 036 | 245 290 |  | 79 712 |             | 321    |
| 1994 | 1022 | 18 630 | 249 447 | 46 | 80 074 | 300       | 445    |
| 1995 | 1180 | 14 750 | 220 267 | 59 | 56 882 | 540       | 603    |
| 1996 | 1138 | 15 918 | 233 633 | 83 | 62 107 | 443       | 702    |
| 1997 | 986  | 17 723 | 90 750 | 131 | 59 747 | 438       | 773    |
| 1998 | 647  | 17 978 | 200 400 | 114 | 60 338 | 625      | 857    |
| 1999 | 613  | 16 592 | 207 090 | 142 | 61 268 | 623      | 918    |
| 2000 |      |      | 208 466 |   |      |               |        |

Note: SHEs: share-holding enterprises; HMTs: enterprises invested by people from Hong Kong, Macau and Taiwan.

Source: NBS, *China Statistical Yearbooks* (various years 1996–2001).

Another type of private investment has come from foreign capital that entered China, mainly in the form of setting up FIEs during China's market-oriented economic reforms.[32] There was a large growth from the opening of

---

[32] In China's own categorization, there are three main forms of FIEs: *duzi* (wholly foreign-owned enterprise), *hezi* (equity joint ventures), and *heying* (contractual joint ventures).

the first FIE in China in 1980, to more than 380 000 FIEs registered by 2000,[33] with about 90 per cent of these being located in coastal areas. More than 70 per cent of FIEs are labour-intensive manufacturing firms, with the investment coming mainly from East Asia's newly industrialized economies such as Taiwan, South Korea and Hong Kong. These FIEs from newly industrializing economies employed 6.42 million workers in 2000, an increase of about 49 times compared with 1986 (see Table 4.1). The geographic concentration means FIEs have a disproportionate influence on China's economic development, and the few among them with advanced technology increase the impression and desire for them to influence China's development. However, overseas Chinese and foreign investments accounted for only 4 per cent of urban employment in 2000. Moreover, there are about 100 times as many POEs as FIEs, with almost four times the total urban employment (see Table 4.1). Furthermore, whilst the number of POEs declined between 1996 and 2000, their employment more than doubled, whereas employment in FIEs grew by less than 24 per cent in the same period. Thus, the domestically owned private sector economy of China is by far the fastest growing sector, and FIEs need to be understood as a relatively minor player within the overall framework of emerging industrial relations in China.

Township and village enterprise (TVEs) were originally a kind of COE in rural areas initiated during the Great Leap Forward (1958) when People's Communes and brigades were encouraged to establish enterprises as part of a movement to increase industrialization in the rural areas of China. Due to the failure of these movements the central government soon limited the development of such ventures,[34] and it was not until 29 September 1979 that the CC-CCP stated that the commune and brigades should develop enterprises rapidly again, and instituted favourable policies towards this end. In 1984, the central government required the governments at all levels to support these enterprises and renamed them 'township and village enterprises'. Thus, whilst the number of COEs remained quite stable during the reform period, the number of TVEs grew rapidly, especially in the early phase of reform period, the number of TVEs grew rapidly, especially in the early phase of reform. Some of these enterprises were contracted and leased to individuals (political or government cadres, existing managers or

---

[33] The total contracted investment reached US$726 billion and the total accumulated utilized foreign investment reached US$380.8 billion in 2001 (*Renmin ribao* 15 October 2001).

[34] In 1962 the State Council prohibited bridges and communes from running industrial enterprises, except for some small-sized factories to manufacture and repair agricultural machines and equipment. Moreover, the government stressed that these factories could not compete with SOEs in terms of raw materials, market or labour force utilization (Tan 1998). At the end of the 1970s, when the commune system was confronted with crisis and reform, the government removed these limitations.

entrepreneurs) from the second half of 1995. The ownership of these enterprises at the township and village levels has been changed because of the market difficulties they faced. Now, besides a few profitable and large-sized TVEs that are still controlled by the township government, many other TVEs have been privatized.[35]

This section will now examine each of these three main types of enterprise: public, private and foreign. They will be analysed within an historical context in order to understand their role within the post-planned economy of China, and to allow us to better understand how these contexts influence their governance structures, which will be explored in the following section of the chapter.

## *The Publicly Owned Sector*

The most prominent urban employers during the planned period were the state-owned enterprises, which were initially modelled on the Russian state enterprise structure. In the late 1940s thousands of Russian technicians and managers were sent to China to help develop the technical, managerial and organizational capability of these enterprises, which in turn became the dominant productive organizations of the planned economy. SOEs, whether large or small, became the main productive units for fulfilling national plans. The central government and its ministries directly controlled the largest SOEs. These ministries also organized geographically to manage medium-sized and smaller SOEs at the provincial, city and township levels. The managers of Chinese SOEs had comparatively little authority in determining their own allocation and distribution decisions. Not only were the levels of output and the amount of key inputs set by the state plan, but the prices charged for their productions, and the wage rates paid to the workers were also set according to government decrees (Fan Q. 1994; Tang et al. 1996; Zhou 1994). The SOEs' role in that period was not to emulate the profit-maximizing behaviour of firms in a capitalist society or to compete in the international market place, but to fulfil the strategic industrial goals of national economic policy. These goals changed over time, but included adoption of Russia's model in the 1950s and independent technological development in the 1960s.

Within the planned economic system, SOEs were not only economic organizations but also basic units of social organization in the urban areas as well as the primary units for organizing the political power of the CCP (Walder 1986). Lu and Perry (1997b: 8–12) state that, in addition to the economic function of the workplace, *danwei* were political and social units

---

[35] For example, in Wu County, Jiangsu Province, by the end of 1998 among 3 135 TVEs, 2 438 were reconstituted as POEs or *getihu* (Lu 2002:175).

which bound individuals' lives into the administrative system.[36] The social function refers to the SOEs' responsibilities to provide workers with social services, such as education and welfare, which in a market economy is usually either provided by the state or acquired through market changes. SOEs formed an important part of the administrative system of China. They were not autonomous units regulated primarily by the invisible hand of the market, but administrative units fulfilling bureaucratically arranged plans. Being administrative units, SOEs had duties to carry out the policies of the CCP and the state. According to liberal critics, it was this subordination of their economic activity to their political functions that undermined the overall economic efficiency of SOEs.

Drawing on Mao's experience of early war production (Hsu 1982: 652–8) , the development of collectives was promulgated as the main means to develop the rural areas, to replace feudalism in the countryside and to bring women into the labour force. Collectives [37] organized as self-sufficient economic units producing food, farm tools, construction material and so on, and organized up to 9000 rural households, covering 99 per cent of peasants by the late 1950s (Denigan 2001; 217). The collectively owned enterprises were also established in urban areas, and eventually developed into quasi state-owned enterprises before reforms began. Most of them were under the leadership of local government and their senior managers were still appointed by the government. Like SOEs, these COEs had to fulfil the plan designed by the local government and had obligations to look after their workers, including the provision of medical care, training, pensions and, if possible, housing.

Thus, the planned period provided two main forms of enterprise, SOEs and COEs, as well as the forerunners of more commercially orientated enterprises, such as TVEs. Both are very complex organizational forms, with a diversified range of production and a strong sense of near self-sufficiency. In terms of industrial relations practices, they are almost identical. To a large extent, these forms of enterprise became closed systems, only opened up by occasional politicization drives by Mao and his followers (such as during the Cultural Revolution), which will be discussed below. The main differences between SOEs and COEs were the strategic role given to SOEs, and much better employment conditions provided in the urban areas. Moreover, the key SOEs came under close scrutiny by government and Party alike. SOEs formed not only the means of achieving economic plans, but also the experimental laboratories for designing modern industrial socialism. Unlike

---

[36] Bian (1992: 48-52) uses the term 'administrative' instead of 'social'.

[37] The original meaning of collective was 'commune' but almost all COEs were organized from outside the community by the government, and this defeats the self-determining principle of communes.

the community-based COEs, the SOEs were and are specifically productive organizations and thus the social and political mobilization of their members, especially the workers (Boisot and Child 1990), became and has continued to be a major concern for the CCP.

## Reforming Public Enterprise

The CCP, headed by Deng Xiaoping, established a very clear set of objectives for SOE reform, which was the separation of government and enterprises and strengthening the economic function of SOEs to increase their economic efficiency. This goal has been maintained for the past 20 years in a continual series of reforms directed towards SOEs. SOE reform has gone through three phases over this period, including a pilot or experimental phase to expand decision-making autonomy, establishing a contractual responsibility system and finally establishing the 'modern enterprise system'.[38]

On 13 July 1979, the State Council issued its first five policy documents related to SOE reform, the most important of which was the 'Regulation Concerned with the Expansion of SOEs' Managerial Autonomy'. In this document, for example, the central government allowed enterprises to plan their production on condition they fulfilled the state plan, introduced a profit-retention system and linked employee rewards to realized profit (Liu and Zhou 1992: 133–4). On 20 May 1981, ten government agencies[39] jointly issued a detailed policy called the 'Interim Specific Procedures to Implement and Fulfil State Council Documents Concerning Power Expansion and to Consolidate and Improve Power Expansion'. In this document, the autonomy of SOE managers was categorized into twelve aspects, including production planning, profit retention and utilization, purchasing, export and retention of foreign currency, pricing, bank loans, organizational structure design and personnel management (Department of Policy and Law 1983: 16–25). During the five years from 1979 to 1983, the management in SOEs was largely unable to take advantage of the authority granted by these provisions because various reform measures lacked key enabling components (Zhou 1994). After reviewing five years of trials in expanding decision-making powers, on 10 May 1984, the State Council drew up the 'Interim Provisions for the Further Extension of Scope of Autonomy in State Industrial Enterprises'. This

---

[38] The division into different phases of SOE reform is a matter of opinion (see Coll 1993; Child 1994; Q. Fan 1994; Liu and Zhou 1992; S. Wang 1998; White et al. 1996; Wu 1994).

[39] These included: the State Commission of Economy, the State Council's Finance and Economic System Reform Office, the State Commission of Planning, the Ministry of Finance, the Ministry of Commerce, The MoL, the Ministry of Foreign Trade, the General Bureau for the Supply of Raw Materials, the General Bureau of Prices and the People's Bank of China.

granted enterprises autonomy in ten areas, including: production planning, product sales, pricing, supplies, the use of capital retained from profits, disposal of unnecessary assets, management of labour and personnel, organization design, rewards and wage setting and the formation of industrial groups among enterprises (Department of Policy and Law 1985: 49–51). While expanding management autonomy, the CCP and the State Council promulgated the 'Regulations on the Work of the Factory Directors of Industrial Enterprises Owned by the Whole People on 15 September 1986, which enabled the directors to become the sole leadership of SOEs and, at the same time, undermined the power of Party organs (Liu and Zhou 1992: 186–90).

The second phase of SOE reform began in 1987. In accordance with the principle of separating ownership and management authority, the government tried to establish a management mechanism combining rights, responsibilities and profits in SOEs. On 27 February 1988, the State Council promulgated the 'Provisional Regulations on the Contractual Management Responsibility System for Industrial Enterprises Owned by the Whole People'. Through the Contact Management Responsibility System (CMRS), the central government defined the relationship between government and enterprises in terms of duties and rights, and allowed the enterprises to operate with autonomy and to be solely responsible for any profits and losses (Liu and Zhou 1992: 201–11). The major strands of the CMRS may be summarized as covering two main points. First, following the principle of integrating duties, rights and profits, the system specifies various management authorities and legitimates the interests of enterprises. Second, in accordance with the principle of ensuring payments to the state, retaining the extra profits and making up for any losses incurred, the system defines the distribution relationship between the state and enterprises. Through the CMRS, the government, as the owner of SOEs, signs a contract with the director of the enterprise (or all the workers and staff, represented by the director). The contractors, while having their authority regulated by the contracts, are restrained by an agreed profit figure they must contribute to the state. If the profit exceeds this figure, the surplus can be retained by the enterprise; if an enterprise falls short of the profit base figure stipulated in the contract, it should make good and difference. CMRS differs from the former of 'decentralizing power and giving up profit' (*fangquan rangli*) in that the directors are able to retain profits made in excess of that contractually required by the government. In this case, the contractors, or all of the workers and staff represented by the director, are eligible to share the surplus profit (Wu 1994). In addition, the relations between the state and enterprises are set out as a contract, which allows the managers to have greater autonomy in routine management and in using assets, thus avoiding, at least formally, administrative intervention (S. Wang 1998). In this stage of reform, the government attempted, in accordance with the principle of separating ownership and management authority, to institute a management mechanism combining responsibilities, authority and interests.

From 18 January to 21 February 1992, Deng Xiaoping inspected two southern cities and made several speeches concerning urban reform. Deng's tour exerted the heaviest influence upon deepening SOE reform into a third phase, which saw the State Council instituting a 'modern enterprise system'. In his speech at the 14th National Congress of the CCP, Jiang Zemin, the General Secretary of the CCP, put forward the concept of establishing a socialist market economy (*Xinhua yuebao* 1992. 10: 7–19). On 14 November 1993, the Third Plenum of the 14th CC-CCP passed the 'Decision on Some Issues Concerning the Establishment of a Socialist Market Economic Structure', which claimed that establishing a modern enterprise system was a necessary requisite for developing 'socialist mass production and the market economy' (*Xinhua yuebao* 1992. 11: 6–13). This then provided the ideological foundation for further reform. Wu (1994) argues that the so-called 'modern enterprise system' is the corporate system which has developed from the end of the nineteenth century, and is currently the dominant from of business organization in industrialized countries, implying that China had adopted capitalism. In this third stage, in stressing the establishment of the modern enterprise system, the central government called for transforming the traditional SOE status into autonomous legal persons in accordance with company law. These forms include 'limited liability companies', 'limited liability stock companies' and 'state wholly owned companies'. The modern enterprise system defines the state as the investment organization of state-owned property and the enterprises as the operating bodies of state-owned property authorized by the state, to separate government administration from enterprise management (ownership from control), although some ambiguity remains (Ho 2001).

After 23 years of reform, SOEs are gradually being transformed from 'workshops of government-directed production' to production organizations in a market economic system (Wu 1994). Profound changes, at least in theory, have taken place in the management system and operational mechanisms of SOEs. The relations over property rights between the SOEs and the state are now clearly defined. The state is attempting to change its status into an investor and owner of assets, while at the same time striving to decrease or abandon its control and direction over the production and management of SOEs. In this context, the SOEs are treated as economic organizations with authority over production, just like other forms of enterprise ownership in a market, and in theory at least, no longer need to fulfil political or social functions for the state.

## New Forms of Enterprise

The early stage of reform concentrated on decentralizing some decision-making within the existing enterprise structures. This took two primary forms, increasing autonomy of decision-making to enterprise directors and the introduction of limited but strategic joint ventures with foreign capitalists. A flurry of joint ventures took place, mostly in coastal areas, during the 1980s. The strategic objectives from the Chinese side were to boost the importation of technology and 'modern' management practices, as well as to earn foreign exchange from exports. Foreign investors often introduced technology as collateral, and whilst market penetration in China was a major objective initially, cheap resource costs for export items became rationales for continued investment (Chiu and Taylor 2001a). It appears that these joint ventures were to be milked for their benefits to Chinese development and profitability was continually renegotiated, so that foreign investors frequently had to downscale their expectations. The upside for the foreign investors in the long run was that the networks they established penetrated deep into the Party and government which both ease political restraints and enhances access to state regulated markets.[40] For their part, Chinese officials frequently made personal gains (Ding 2000) as well as prestige in working in or with these early joint ventures and sought to protect them from further competition by limiting the entry of new foreign (and sometimes even local) firms. In the 1990s, the restrictions on foreign ownership were eased, and an increasing number of foreign investments have been wholly foreign-owned (Walsh et al. 1999: 70).

This attraction of foreign investment was paralleled by the growth of the private sector. The POE sector is a collection of different types of enterprises, which in many instances include organizations that are formally categorized under the types of enterprises already discussed in this chapter. Until the early 1990s the Chinese government had no category for private enterprises, referring to them under the category of 'other',[41] 'other' being the residual left over after accounting for government, SOE, COE and joint ventures (which included wholly foreign-owned) work units. However, in the 1990s particularly, the number and variety of private enterprises mushroomed. They include small family firms as well as spun-off businesses from state and collective sectors, which raise capital from the equity markets and borrowing

---

[40] However, an interesting problem has developed, in which increased market competition, and increased competition among regional governments to attract potentially lucrative FIEs, has meant these guarantees can be undermined over time. An example may be seen in the auto industry, where Beijing Jeep is being affected by Shanghai's developmental policies to promote its Volkswagen Joint Venture.

[41] For example, see any of the relevant NBS data published before 1992.

(including those discussed in Table 3.1). The development of private ownership experienced a tortuous road in defining its status in the Chinese economic system. The 1988 Amendment to the PRC Constitution defined private ownership as a supplement to socialist public ownership. In 1989, private became an independent category in the national statistics. At the 15$^{th}$ National Congress of the CCP, private ownership was officially endorsed as 'an important component part of China's socialist economy' (*Renmin ribao* 22 September 1997) and the Constitution was amended following this principle in 1999. Finally, private ownership in China has gained an equal status to public ownership (Dai 2001a). Whilst some POEs have become large successful business, most form a kind of twilight zone of semi-legal, often informal activity, prone to bankruptcy and illicit activity.

Thus, there has been a growing number of types of enterprises in China from the former planned period of SOEs and cooperatives. However, in practice they analytically fall into two main groups: publicly and non-publicly owned. This division is complicated in practice, and the next section will demonstrate this by exploring the interplay between the public and private sectors.

## Corporate Governance

As discussed previously, it has been popular to claim that ambiguous property rights have contributed to the supposed low efficiency of the public sector (Gao 1998: 372–3; Choi and Zhou 2001). Therefore, establishing a 'modern enterprise system' and defining property rights became central concerns of the second and subsequent stages of urban reform. From the second half of the 1990s, these reforms have not only been carried out in the public sector, but also in POEs and TVEs.

### Control

Whilst influenced by the Soviet Union in the early period of planning, the Chinese SOEs were arranged slightly differently even from the beginning of their establishment in the 1950s (Jin 1997). Using the rhetoric of universal ownership by all the people, and the government as the people's 'representative', Chinese SOEs placed a greater emphasis on elements of democratic management than in the Soviet Union (Clarke 1995). In this vein, the SOEs were political instruments for the Party to meet national goals, as well as a primary means for maintaining social stability. Therefore, the special characteristics of SOEs have determined that the problems of their low efficiency should not be resolved by defining their property rights. In other words, even if their property rights are clearly defined, they are still restrained from behaving as capitalist firms.

The government, using its position as the self-proclaimed representative of the whole people, has not released control over SOEs after more than 20 years' reform. According to information from the State Commission of Economy and Trade (2001), it has decided to control directly 514 so-called 'backbone' (strategic) SOEs. Following this model, all provinces, autonomous regions and municipalities directly under the central government have designated their own strategic enterprises as well. As such, even in the last round of reform, the state maintains control over several thousand very large and strategically important SOEs all over the country. A good example of continued control can be seen in the appointment system for the leading body (*lingdao banzi*) of these SOEs (N. Sun 2001; Chen and Huang 2001). On 1 December 1999, the CC-CCP issued the 'Notice of Establishing a Working Committee of Enterprise and Some Related Issues' that stated the directors of 39 SOEs of strategic importance would come under the direct control of the CC-CCP. Another example is that the system for making senior management appointments changed little. The result of a survey in 1993 showed that 92.9 per cent of SOEs' directors and senior general managers were appointed by the senior agencies, and this figure was 73.37 per cent in 2000, a decrease of less than 20 per cent after eight years (China Enterprise Confederation and China Investigation of Entrepreneurs 2001). The procedure for appointing senior directors means candidates would first be examined by the CC-CCP and then appointed by the State Council while the candidates at other national backbone SOEs shall be examined by a 'Working Committee of Enterprises of the CCP' and appointed by the Ministry of Personnel, the ministry responsible for civil servants (CC-CCP 1999). This provides a clear indication of the continued administrative control over management in a significant number (several thousand) SOEs, as local government will follow this model when it selects and appoints the directors of the core SOEs under its jurisdiction.

SOEs are primarily politically constituted organizations. Their function from their inception was to carry out the political will of the Party-state. Whilst it is undoubtedly true that they are increasingly required to perform according to market economic rules and capitalistic notions of rationality, because they are politically founded organizations, the market imperative is both constrained within political bounds[42] and mediated by other political responsibilities. These responsibilities are reflected through the Party organs and grass-roots unions within SOEs.

---

[42] Therefore, it is simply not possible for managers to behave as capitalists. For example, they cannot pay themselves salaries comparable to FIEs operating in China, let alone comparably sized firms overseas.

At the beginning of reform, the status of the Party organs was threatened.[43] This situation lasted until June 1989 when the SOEs were ordered to reinstate the powers of the Party secretaries. On 22 September 1989, Jiang Zemin, the new General Secretary of the CCP, stated that the CCP should step up efforts to strengthen Party building in SOEs, to ensure the smooth progress of reform (*Renmin ribao* 23 September 1989). In order to restore the Party's status, on 28 August 1989, the Political Bureau of the CC-CCP issued the 'Circular on Strengthening Party Building', in which the grass-roots Party organs in SOEs were assigned the role of 'political core' (Liu and Zhou 1992: 573). The 'Resolution on Several Important Issues about the Strengthening Party Building', passed at the Fourth Plenum of the 14th CC-CCP on 28 September 1994, marks a further increase in Party organs' status. In this document, the Party organs are required to examine carefully the experience of participating in decision-making, supervising and guaranteeing the implementation of the principles and policies of the Party and the state (General Office 1997: 138–53). These requirements have re-established the authority of Party organs to intervene in the decision-making of SOEs. On 24 January 1997, the CC-CCP issued the 'Notice Regarding Strengthening and Improving the Party Building in SOEs', in which the Party organ's status of 'political core' is further raised to 'political leadership' (*renmin ribao* 11 March 1997). Thus, signifying that the Party's role is to guide and coordinate power within the complex organizational structure (of Party committees, Workers' Congress [WCs] and, where appropriate, congress of shareholders, board of directors and supervisory boards) of SOEs. In this document, perhaps more important, the CC-CCP re-emphasizes the principle of the 'Party controlling cadres', declaring:

> The Party committee is empowered to nominate the candidates of middle-level or senior managerial personnel... The candidates should undergo the investigation of the Organization and Personnel Department of Party organs and pass the group discussion of Party committees before being appointed by the director.

---

[43] In October 1984, the CPC adopted a policy document concerning reforming of China's economic structure, in which it called for a system whereby directors or managers assumed full responsibility over enterprises. Under this system, the Party committee in SOEs no longer served as the leading organ of control. Instead, the director of SOEs assumed a position of unified leadership. In the 'Regulations on Deepening the Reform of Enterprises and Improving Their Vitality', promulgated on 5 December 1986, the State Council claimed to implement the 'Director Responsibility System' (DRS) in SOEs. This replaced the former 'Director Responsibility System under the Leadership of Party Committee' (*danwei lingdao xia de changzhang fuzezhi*) and made the director the 'primary figure' (Liu and Zhou 1992: 204-6). In order to ensure management authority, an experiment in a number of factories was conducted to restructure the Party's command system, removing the Party organs from its vertical and sectoral bureaucratic agencies to the Party's local offices (Wu 1997).

Even though the status of the Party has not been restored to the degree in which the Party secretary is the 'primary figure' (*yibashou*), its current power and status is strong enough to limit the discretion of directors. Lu (1989) argued that the Party is well placed to maintain political power in SOEs, using this to intervene in the management of an enterprise, without the necessity to rely on formal or legislative procedures. Ji (1998) argues that the essence of Party building is to create institutional channels to enable the Party system to manipulate management.

Another way in which Party influence is maintained has been through well-orchestrated participative democracy. Under the planned system, overall targets, both economic and political, came from the superior ministries and government agents. However, overt political manipulation of enterprises could come from below as well. Mao and others used the media and the Party structure to 'agitate' policies through the WCs, among workers and junior managers inside enterprises, and this acted as a powerful alternative means to control enterprises. Following the trials of the 'Gang of Four' after Mao's death, this form of politicization largely disappeared. One of the lasting repercussions of the Mao period has been a widespread distrust of these organizations. As such, in the enterprises the WCs have been unable to perform meaningful participation in management.[44] To illustrate the problem let us briefly re-examine the appointment of directors. In SOEs and all enterprises that have a WC, these organs should select the plant director (the head of the enterprise) by election of congress members. However, the superior agency and equivalent Party branch[45] would select the candidate or candidates to be considered by the WCs. in other words, it is not the WC but the superior organizations (Party or state bureaux) that draw up the shortlist. In this way, the WC does not select but merely endorses the plant director's appointment. Thus, in a survey of 3629 senior Chinese managers across a range of enterprises it appears that about 4 per cent of directors were actually elected by a WC in China, and this was lower in the period prior to 1979 (only 2.3 per cent), whereas almost 80 per cent were appointed by superior agencies (China Investigation System of Entrepreneur 2000). Using this illustration, we can see that the government maintains a high degree of control over SOEs and that the WCs have only limited power.[46]

However, whilst the workers have little effective means to control management, it does not mean that management can ignore worker interests.

---

[44] Of course there were other reasons for workers to distrust WCs, not least being their ineffectual capacity to 'supervise' top management. Of course, there were other reasons for workers to distrust WCs, not least being their ineffectual capacity to 'supervise' top management (see Chapter 6).

[45] 'Equivalent' here means 'same rank'. Thus, if the SOE falls under the jurisdiction of the Shanghai government, the Shanghai Party committee will be involved.

[46] This will be discussed further in Chapter 6.

Both the collective will of workers, and their ability to call on the rhetoric of socialism, has ensured, with Party support, that a strong degree of welfare corporatism was maintained right up until the third phase of reforms, and still exerts a heavy influence on management decision-making. The result is that management autonomy is almost non-existent (Kagawa 2000), although managers are increasingly responsible for outcomes. In capitalist enterprises, managers have little discretion concerning objectives either – they must make profits. But in Chinese SOEs, because there are multiple objectives coming from different parts of the government which sometimes pull the enterprises in different directions, there is a degree of autonomy to negotiate objectives in a way not possible under capitalism. However, similar to the problems of managing non-governmental organizations (NGOs), the multiple and complex objectives mean that the policy, funding and other types of sponsors maintain a high degree of influence on how objectives are carried out. This is increasingly considered as interference by foreign (Blackman 1997; Zapalska and Edwards 2001) and domestic scholars (Gai 2002; Hou 2001) but this shows a misunderstanding of the political role of SOEs, which include a continued responsibility to the Party to maintain social stability.

Whilst the public sector generally faces similar pressures and competing stakeholders, there are differences, especially between the state-owned and collectively owned forms of enterprise (and particularly the TVEs). In theory, TVEs should face a similar complexity to SOEs but at a local level. Moreover, as the owners are the local community it would appear to make ownership interests more complex and immediate. However, since their inception the property rights of TVEs have been ambiguous. The initial investments founding TVEs come from township governments, village collectives or funds collected from individuals in a locality, and in recent years, whilst township or village administrations continue to own some, others have been contracted to individuals or privatized (Chen and Huang 2001; Chen and Rozelle 1999). Wong Hongling (2000) examined ownership changes among TVEs in Changzhou City, Jiangsu Province, finding that privatization in township-owned enterprises is slower than that in village-owned enterprises. Wang attributed this to differences in the nature of government at the town and village levels. Because the representative of the owners at the township level are formal officials (civil servants), being the lowest level of the bureaucratic system in China, they rely on these enterprises to support both economic and political objectives of the township, and when they are transferred or retired, their personal interests usually no longer coincide with the situation of these enterprises. However, the people who represent the property rights of village enterprises are not the formal officials of the government and it is impossible for them to be transferred or promoted to other government posts, once they retire from their current position as head of village or Party secretary. Instead, because they usually stay on in their community, their interests lie in direct or informal continued relations with these enterprises, and their economic performance will affect the retired cadres prosperity greatly.

According to Bao (2001), township enterprises that continue to be controlled by the township government can be divided into two categories. For the first, the township government appoints the directors, determines the distribution of profits and examines and approves the development and investment plans. This is a model of 'large government and small enterprise' (*Da Zhengfu, xiao qiye*). The second type is 'group corporations' (*jituan gongsi*), which have more autonomy over issues relating to management and business. Nevertheless, both forms retain the dual functions of increasing economic efficiency and promoting the interest of local officials and the government as a whole. Thus, similar to SOEs, besides their economic tasks, they have some social responsibilities to provide financial assistance to public works projects, providing job opportunities for local people and supporting other loss-making TVEs as and when required by local government (Wang Hongling 2000).

The private enterprises are by far the most simple governance structures, with objectives being only those of the owner-managers. Whilst it is well understood that managers are not profit maximizers (Watson 1980), they tend to grope in that direction, and this describes the objectives of China's POEs well. Most POEs in China are developed from individual business (*getihu*) in which the owner is the manager.[47] Once they become POEs, they tend to maintain governance structures centred on the original owners and their families (Ding and Zhao 2002). This is a structure established on the basis of both Chinese traditional cultural and the external environment facing POEs. Traditional culture elements have been a major concern of Western business scholars (Selmer 1998; Zapalska and Edwards 2001), but domestic scholars emphasize an environment in which there is a shortage of professionally trained managers and many policies that discriminate against private entrepreneurs (Yu 2001). One way to help overcome these problems is for POEs to register under different forms, such as cooperative share, joint stock or limited liability companies. A survey conducted by the National Association of Industry and Commerce in 2000 found that, among 3073 POEs, 1102 (35.9 per cent) were invested by one person. Of these, however, 4.6 per cent were registered as joint ventures, 15.3 per cent as limited liability corporations and 6.0 per cent as share-holding corporations (Dai 2001b: 71–2) Moreover, many POEs falsely register as COEs to avoid unfavourable policies towards POEs and to seek the benefits COEs enjoy, such as greater

---

[47] According a survey by National Industrial and Commercial Association in 1997, 38.2 per cent of POEs' owners were individual business owners before opening their private enterprises (Dai 2001b).

access to loans. However, the government neither controls these enterprises, nor does it consider them COEs in practice (Bao 2001).

Among FIEs, there has been both an historical change in governance structures and, relating to this, the emergence of wholly owned foreign enterprises. In the early days of reform, as already discussed, the government saw FIEs primarily as opportunities for hard and soft technology transfer. Thus, governance was strongly placed in the hands of the Chinese-appointed directors, and many state agencies and departments sought to regulate FIEs, in some ways more obtrusively than SOEs (Child and Yan 1999). Whilst the foreign partners' interests needed to be accommodated most of the time (which usually meant placing a lower priority on welfare provisions), FIEs were still seen as an element within the overall state economic plan. Moreover, as the standing of capitalistic practices rose and FIEs began to be seen as 'assets', many agencies wanted to improve their own political and economic fortunes by seeking to regulate FIEs in some way. This meant not only much 'interference' in FIEs but also much contradictory regulation. For the Western firms this was usually seen both as a sign of the weakness of the Chinese regulatory system (Huang 2001) and as a problem of doing business in China (Tan 2001). However, it also appears the more astute overseas Chinese opportunist investors could play agencies against each other and cultivate protectors among some sections of local Party-government not only to ignore outside influence, but even to insulate these enterprises from it. In many cases such local political leaders are given board membership or consultancy fees in recognition of their role in 'promoting' the FIE (Chen and Huang 2001).

In the first round of reform, the central government developed a broader view of FIEs in economic development, and the 'Law on Foreign-Capital Enterprises' was passed by the Fourth Session of the 6th People's Congress in 1986 to ease share ownership restrictions. Thereafter FIEs could be wholly owned and many in China have seen this, to some extent, as a new form of enterprise within the private sector. Allowing wholly foreign-owned multinationals has stimulated further reform among domestic enterprises, which some in China see as a good thing (Xu and Zhong 1997: 28–9), furthering the process of marketization and reducing governments' ability to control the market. These are supposedly unambiguously private enterprises, with profit maximizing goals and little or no direct interference from the government, except for legal provisions and taxation, although Sanyal and Guvenli (2001) argue old habits of other forms of 'interference' remain. At the same time, the ideological category of the wholly foreign enterprise has upset some conservatives (Chen 1990: 63), and the lack of indigenous ownership rights is seen as allowing both the good and the evil (depending on your point of view) of modern capitalist organizations. However, the evidence, limited as it is, does not seem to support this assertion. Whilst preference for sole ownership probably is evidence that foreigners wish to control these enterprises alone (Hezens et al. 2001), it may simply be that certain enterprises do not benefit much from the strategic alliances that mergers and joint ventures bring (J. Luo 2000; Taylor 1999b). Thus, whilst foreign ownership may pose an ideological problem for conservative Chinese, it is just one form of strategic decision for the foreigners (for example Weldon and Vanhoncker 1999). The ideological debate should really revolve around admitting foreign capital at all. Once admitted, the issue of control, as the case of Chinese practice shows, is quite another matter, with percentage share ownership being only one factor.

## Management autonomy and marketization

As in other countries, there are two main forms of management orientation in China: those directed towards economic efficiency and profit seeking, and those to promote some form of political agenda. We may equate these with the private and public sectors respectively, but that is overly simplistic. First, the split between public and private is not so clear, as the chapter has already shown, and the growth of new forms of ownership in the last few years is actually deepening the complexity of forms of ownership. Second, whilst there have been ideological reasons for separating politics and economics, in practice enterprises and their managers form an integral part of what is a political economy. Finally, we need to give some acknowledgement to the personal orientations of individual managers, based on their own career histories and future expectations.

The job of the manager has always been somewhat complex and contradictory. Both the diffusion of formal power among several agencies, and the clear geographical organization of the government, made the lines of command confusing for those who directed large enterprises. Prior to 2001, the CCP excluded private entrepreneurs from membership because they were an exploiting class, and tensions over their recent admission to the CCP remain among senior Party members (Dickson 2001). SOE cadres, on the other hand, were invariably CCP members, and it was only in 2000 that their official title changed from 'state cadres' to 'managers'.[48] Thus, up to that point it was implicit that managers of state enterprises should not have an entrepreneurial orientation. Moreover, the private entrepreneurs were not 'assets' of the country on whose expertise and interests the CCP should draw or whom it should seek to represent. Managers in all organizations with some degree of public ownership had to balance requirements from superior agencies to 'make the plan' and from employees' interests (and their own) to

---

[48] On 27 October 2000 the SETC declared that the managers of SOEs would be separated from the mainstream cadres and their treatment would no longer be in accordance with rank-and-file cadre. This is short-hand for decoupling SOEs from civil service conditions of employment.

gold-brick their tasks which, in turn, were possible because it has traditionally been hard for the superior agencies to have an accurate measure of enterprise efficiency. The market is supposed to do this, but it is notoriously unreliable, both because of its orientation to short-term profits over long-term growth (encouraging asset stripping) and susceptibility to manipulation (monopolistic tendencies). The government has sought to relieve managers of some of these contradictory pressures by introducing formal autonomy to state enterprises, supposedly to enable them to compete with private enterprises. Private enterprises thus serve the useful function of driving up the economic efficiency of the public sector.

*Table 3.2 Evaluation to the 14 autonomies entrepreneurs 'should enjoy' (%)*

|  | 1993 | 1994 | 1995 | 1997 |
|---|---|---|---|---|
| Decision-making about production | 88.7 | 94.0 | 97.3 | 98.3 |
| Fixing price of product and labourer | 75.9 | 73.6 | 85.4 | 92.0 |
| Selling | 88.5 | 90.5 | 95.9 | 96.8 |
| Purchasing materials | 90.9 | 95.0 | 97.8 | 98.8 |
| Importing and exporting | 15.3 | 25.8 | 41.3 | 54.0 |
| Decision-making about investment | 38.9 | 61.2 | 72.8 | 82.5 |
| Allocating profit-retention | 63.7 | 73.8 | 88.3 | 90.6 |
| Disposing surplus assets | 29.4 | 46.6 | 68.2 | 76.5 |
| Merging and joint venture | 23.3 | 39.7 | 59.7 | 61.4 |
| Recruitment | 43.5 | 61.0 | 74.8 | 84.3 |
| Personnel | 53.7 | 73.3 | 83.5 | 90.3 |
| Wage system | 70.2 | 86.0 | 93.1 | 96.0 |
| Designing won organizational structure | 79.3 | 90.5 | 94.4 | 97.3 |
| Rejecting unreasonable fee | 7.0 | 10.3 | 17.4 | 35.1 |

Notes: Multiple selections possible. Sample size: 2451.

Source: China Investigation System of Entrepreneur. 1998: 157–65.

For SOEs and COEs, a more proactive policy was taken to encourage autonomy, whilst reducing government support for the state sector (Lin and Zhu 2001). Reform of SOEs began from expanding the autonomy of managers. In 1992, the State Council issued a list of what is sometimes called 'fourteen autonomies' to encourage SOE managers to make market-based decisions. Informally, however, the Party, in its own name and partly through superior agencies and the trade unions, acted as regulator, sometimes promoting and sometimes restricting managerial discretion on these matters.

Table 3.2 lists the areas of autonomy and shows a measurement of just how dramatically senior managers perceive their autonomy has increased over all matters during the 1990s.

Table 3.2 examines perceptions of managerial autonomy, and the sample is heavily skewed towards the state (SOE) sector. The most dramatic increase in autonomy is in the area of new investment and mergers, followed by employment flexibility. [49] The change is so dramatic that research on management in China undertaken prior to 1995 is now probably too outdated to be a reliable reflection of the nature of management nowadays. This is unfortunate for Western scholars, because most of the comprehensive analysis of management presented in English precedes that date (for example Brown and Porter 1996; Child and Lu 1996; Korzec 1992; Ng and Warner 1998). However, there are important limitations to this change. First, given

*Table 3.3 Three most important external factors restraining management decision-making (%)*

|  | general | SOEs | COEs | TVEs | HTMs | FIEs | POEs | SHEs | Others |
|---|---|---|---|---|---|---|---|---|---|
| Law and regulations | 85.2 | 85.3 | 86.8 | 82.7 | 99.0 | 81.0 | 85.7 | 84.0 | 95.7 |
| Assessment system | 39.4 | 41.4 | 38.4 | 34.1 | 33.3 | 42.4 | 14.3 | 29.7 | 43.4 |
| Committee of directors | 33.4 | 27.6 | 30.5 | 41.8 | 58.3 | 75.9 | 71.5 | 55.4 | 47.8 |
| Party organ | 32.8 | 36.9 | 24.1 | 28.2 | 16.7 | 22.7 | 28.6 | 24.8 | 26.0 |
| Internal regulations | 32.5 | 29.1 | 33.8 | 42.2 | 50.0 | 33.7 | 85.7 | 43.7 | 26.1 |
| Trade union and W. C. | 25.0 | 27.6 | 24.7 | 18.5 | 16.6 | 15.2 | 0.0 | 16.7 | 34.7 |
| Superior agency | 23.8 | 25.4 | 9.2 | 24.3 | 9.5 | 9.7 | 0.0 | 18.2 | 13.0 |
| Public opinions | 17.2 | 17.6 | 21.2 | 14.5 | 8.3 | 9.6 | 14.2 | 16.2 | 9.0 |
| Social departments | 9.7 | 9.1 | 11.3 | 13.7 | 8.3 | 9.8 | 0.0 | 11.3 | 4.3 |

Note: Sample size: 3154.

Source: China Investigation System of Entrepreneur. 1997: 119-132.

that the directors of many SOEs want to, or are forced to, become more economically efficient in the short term, restructuring meant divestment and cutting down their organizations, but due to the implications this has for

---

[49] Lu (2002) provides similar findings, though slightly more conservative.

social stability, downsizing remains to some extent constrained. Second, the previous argument under governance of a number of competing stakeholders with control over enterprises, especially public sector ones, means control is more complex than regulations of autonomy may imply. In other words, being free to do something on paper and in perception, may not translate into practice because of other considerations. Whilst this is difficult to prove, we think some evidence of this can been seen in Table 3.3.

*Table 3.4 Effective supervising organs of entrepreneurs (%)*

|  | SOE | COE | POE | JOE | SHE | LLC | FIE & HTM | total |
|---|---|---|---|---|---|---|---|---|
| Superior agency | 31.7 | 28.3 | 11.3 | 7.1 | 12.4 | 14.8 | 9.2 | 22.2 |
| Committee of directors | 4.2 | 13.3 | 31.2 | 26.3 | 27.3 | 30.1 | 67.5 | 20.0 |
| Department of financial supervision | 21.8 | 22.1 | 24.3 | 12.1 | 13.8 | 15.0 | 13.0 | 18.5 |
| Workers' congress | 24.8 | 27.5 | 4.3 | 6.1 | 5.2 | 6.4 | 2.4 | 15.6 |
| Shareholder meeting | – | – | 20.9 | 36.3 | 26.6 | 17.4 | 4.8 | 9.2 |
| Party organ | 13.5 | 8.8 | 1.7 | 4.0 | 2.7 | 5.6 | 1.4 | 8.4 |
| Committee of supervisors | – | – | 4.3 | 7.1 | 8.4 | 7.4 | 1.4 | 3.0 |
| Dept. in charge of managing state assets | 3.6 | – | – | 1.0 | 3.4 | 2.8 | 0.3 | 2.7 |
| Media | 0.4 | 0.0 | 1.7 | 0.0 | 0.2 | 0.5 | 0.0 | 0.4 |

Note: JOEs: jointly-owned enterprises; LLCs: limited liability companies.

Source: China Investigation System of Entrepreneur. 2000: 92–102.

The regulatory environment is the most important restraining managers, decision-making, which reflects the argument made previously in the chapter, that a more comprehensive legal framework is replacing governments' direct regulation of enterprises. However, three other factors are also important. For private-sector firms, the board of directors is important, and to a lesser extent, this is true of public enterprises as well (Lu 2002). Directors are generally drawn from the owners, but also include Party officials,[50] trade union chairs and other stakeholders. The Party organs, either within the enterprise or in the locality, also exert a strong influence. Influence from the assessment system,

---

[50] For example, in a survey of 104 China's listed corporations in 1997, over 32 per cent of chairpersons of the board of directors was also the Party secretary, and in another 30 per cent the Party secretary was a board member (Gu et al. 1999).

however, may be one of the most obtrusive of the influences. This is because managers, especially in the public sector, are assessed annually to keep their posts. The assessment involves appraisal by the superior agencies (the owners) but draws on viewpoints from a number of sources. These include the Party, the union, other managers and some sentiment of the workers. If workers complain to the government about a plant director, especially in the public sector, the director or senior manager needs to respond quickly to resolve the problem. In some cases they may be able to isolate and remove individual 'agitators', but it is much more likely, especially if several workers have the same grievance, that mangers will seek to 'buy off' the workers in some way. This does not strongly empower workers, however, because they need to show a severe grievance, which can be clearly laid at the door of the plant director (as opposed to some systematic or political problem). Nevertheless, as a recent annual survey found, senior managers must be careful not to appear corrupt, to make platitudes of respecting workers as their masters and not to take their full salary, especially in times of economic hardship (China Investigation System of Entrepreneur 1997). Chinese culture, reinforced by Mao's leadership, has created a psychology that leaders are personally responsible for their performance. Most managers still believe that the main reason for the success or failure of an enterprise is its leadership

Thus, overall, the plant director or chief executive officer carries a tremendous personal responsibility for the enterprise they manage, and they know they will be judged, and that will form the basis of their future security. Table 3.4 shows that in SOEs and COEs the most effective supervising organs are superior agencies and workers' congresses.

Lurking at the back of these senior managers' minds is probably the haunting fear of political reprisals should the move towards capitalism in China be reversed. Whereas Reagan and Thatcher helped to restore the prestige of the capitalist manager[51] in much of the West, the manager in China may be increasingly rich and powerful but it is doubtful whether as a class they are able to take up the pre-eminent position as the ruling elite of China. Dressing in Party clothes remains by far the safest and most reliable road to membership of the elite in modern China (Lu 2002: 86–8).

POEs are almost fully autonomous, and thus owner-managers have a high degree of control over decision-making and finance (Dai 2001b). A survey of 1947 POE owners in 1999 indicated that 55.3 per cent of owners made important decisions and 49.7 per cent made general decisions alone (Yu 2001), and it is likely this grossly understates the reality for the reasons discussed in the previous paragraph. As discussed in Chapter 2, the government is moving towards macro regulation of enterprises, and the only

---

[51] Although the recent scandals in the US concerning the accounting practices of various large corporations may undermine this.

potential impediment to management autonomy is the workers. However, as will be discussed in Chapter 4, because many of the workers in POES are migrants, apart from high labour turnover, they pose few threats to managerial power (Chan 2001). In some privatized TVEs, sometimes the local workers can exert pressure on management by their ties of family and clan with owners and managers. However, P. Wang (2000) showed that after privatization, one of the measures taken by such owners was gradually to replace local workers and junior managers by migrants.

# THE MANAGEMENT AND THEIR ORGANIZATIONS

Having examined the forms and nature of employers, and the governance of these organizations, we now need to take a closer look at managers themselves. Managers in China are a post-reform development, drawn from the cadre class of the planned economy, whose interests were aligned or at least articulated through the Party structure. This section will examine first the orientation of different sorts of managers, and then look at management associations, which are supposed to represent their interests, much in the same way that trade unions purport to represent the interests of workers.

## *Manager*

The PRC has already recognized a separation of identity between workers and 'staff'. However, reference to this as a class difference was largely avoided. Since 1992 recognition has been given to a new kind of manager, the 'entrepreneur', which appears to cover both domestic business people and foreign managers, but again there is reluctance see them as anything more than a sub-stratum of society. However, a new and distinguishable management class *is* beginning to form within China (Lu 2002: 15–16), one with its own identity and interest. The development of special labour markets for managers, professional education opportunities and increasing projected social status (such as in the media) all provide opportunities for such class identity to develop. Moreover, rising incomes, benchmarking standards of living through international comparisons (enabled by exposure to foreign counties via direct contact and the media), and ambiguity of status within socialism will encourage greater cohesion of this class. However, at present, there are still probably four different kinds of managers, with a strong tendency towards convergence amongst them, but the differences are too important to ignore at present. We will now briefly discuss these four kinds of managers.

The first category is the cadre-manager who is both a government official and a business manager. This kind of manager is most common in public enterprises such as SOEs, COEs and TVEs owned by townships, but may also be found as the Chinese partners in joint ventures. Although the central government officially removed the title 'cadre' from managers in these enterprises, their identities have not changed substantially. As managers, their functions have changed greatly after reform, with heavier stewardship responsibilities to meet economic objectives. However, these cadre-managers owe their positions to the departments that appointed them, and thus must act within the interests of that particular government agency (Li and Chen 2000: 42). Moreover, because of this relation, many do not consider 'management' as their career. More than 20 years of reform made more of them qualified to be professional managers, but they can be transferred to government posts at any time. Mi (2001) states that among the first 20 'model entrepreneurs', who were elected nationwide in 1987, three stayed in enterprises, five were removed and six were promoted to be officials. Finally, the pay of such cadre-managers is generally low, with low income differentials between themselves and the workers they employ, compared to other types of managers. According to a survey in 1998, the average monthly wages for SOE and COE senior managers were respectively 1477 yuan and 2596 yuan, while that of the workers and staff were 635 yuan and 439 yuan NBS 1999; MoLSS 1999: 229, 339). The gap in SOEs was thus only 2.32 times, but it was six times in COEs.

In recent years we should make a further distinction between cadre-managers running large SOEs and those running smaller public enterprises. The latter have increasingly clear economic objectives and are more likely to have a higher degree of pressure to concentrate on either breaking even or making profits. The larger SOEs, however, remain very complex organizations, and the director is very likely to need to balance economic objectives with political concerns. Nevertheless, in general we have found that cadre-managers, especially those working in SOEs, have considerable empathy with the plight of workers, especially if their enterprises are loss making.[52] As we will see in later chapters, this often means many plant directors tacitly support worker demonstrations and conflicts directed towards the local government, both as an attempt to ease financial pressures on the enterprise and in recognition of the fact that these remain state employees. Moreover, as Tan (2001) indicates, these managers are likely to be 'risk adverse', preferring to avoid decisions which run a high risk of being

---

[52] A survey of 3 154 entrepreneurs in 1997 showed that 73.6 per cent of SOE directors would make increasing the income of workers one their first three goals of operation, compared with 58.5 per cent POEs, 47 per cent in FIEs and 53.3 in POEs (China Investigation System of Entrepreneur 1997).

criticized from workers, government officers or local CCP branch officials. These managers, especially those employed in SOEs, remain the most educated group of managers in China.

The second category of managers are the 'owner-managers', who have almost absolute managerial power in their organizations (Gregory and Teney 2001), generally without alternative power bases to compete with themselves. In their routine management, they need only bow to legal regulations and, as will be discussed in Chapter 8, this often leads to difficulties for the trade unions trying to implement the collective contract system, even though there is sharper labour conflict in such enterprises. This kind of manager exists in most private enterprises, and is often associated with the Chinese family firm (Tan 1999). Even though several POEs and overseas Chinese-owned FIEs have become large employers, the owner-manager style is often maintained.

The third category is the new 'professional manager'. Although these are often indistinguishable from the first category, we may think of these as a new class or orientation to managerial tasks, which is more akin to the capitalist entrepreneur who sees profits as the primary objective. These people will often still complete questionnaires that indicate political correctness but, in practice, they place economics in front of politics (Pistrui et al. 1999). These entrepreneurs not only work in POEs and FIEs but also in TVEs and other publicly owned enterprises, although in fewer numbers. Tan (2001) argues that, irrespective of ownership, the smaller-sized enterprises are more likely to be managed by these entrepreneurially orientated managers. We cannot know their number, and this is of great concern to Mainland scholars. There have been various attempts to examine this category of manager, but it is almost impossible. For example, in 1994 and 1998 11.4 per cent and 6.2 per cent respectively of directors of all types of enterprises obtained their positions either through internal bidding (*neibu toubiao*) or were recruited through the open market (China Investigation System of Entrepreneurs 1999). Whilst there is no data, many graduates leaving further and higher education institutions in China are entrepreneurially orientated. Being younger (Tan 1999), and having grown up in the post-Mao era, they are more likely to want to earn higher personal income and seek greater autonomy than the older generation of managers (China Investigation System of Entrepreneur 2000). However, it is unclear if this is a changing generation or merely that samples capture interests at different life stages (younger – more ambitious, older – more conservative). Thus, when these young managers get older, they may be more likely to be more communitarian and less individualistic, but we just do not know. Moreover, if we examine the age of enterprise directors across different types of enterprises, whilst directors of SOEs are on average older, COEs in general have younger managers than in the non-state sector (China Investigation System of Entrepreneurs 1993). Further, the most highly qualified managers tend to continue to work in SOEs and to a lesser extent FIEs (China Investigation System of Entrepreneurs 1999). Thus, rather than looking for a demographic characteristic of these managers, who form a new entrepreneurial class, it is better to consider them as having a capitalistic management orientation, which we will now examine through analyzing managerial consciousness. Whilst not as well educated as SOE managers, these younger entrepreneurs are likely to have significant knowledge and belief in Western human resource management practices, although not to the extent some North-American business school professors would wish (for example Harwit 2001; Lau and Busenitz 2001: 15).

The fourth type of manager is the 'foreign expert', and we will discuss their attitudes, and attitudes towards them, in the next section in more detail. The foreign manager is, however, largely absent from industrial relations. In smaller Japanese and South Korean firms and among the myriad of 'overseas' Chinese firms, formal procedures and institutions of industrial relations regulation are generally avoided. This includes avoiding establishing unions, accepting high labour turnover, suppressing overt conflict and dismissing 'troublemakers'. Despite their honoured position as welcome guests in China, most research shows considerable disappointment among local managers in the foreign 'experts' and a good deal of tension appears to exist between them (Ahlstrom et al. 2001; Peng 2000; Walsh et al. 1999). More significantly for us, except for those invested by 'overseas' Chinese, foreign managers usually do not get involved in human resource management or industrial relations (Taylor 1999b) at all.

## Management Associations

Employers' unions or associations have a long and influential history in the development of industrial relations in industrialized countries. The development of tripartite national labour policies and industrial relations regulation common in Europe are built on the view that employers have their own members' interest, just as labour unions represent workers. In the reform period of China there was initially a great resistance to allowing employer organizations, but latterly the state has attempted to organize such associations, much in the way it controls the trade unions in China. As a result two types of employers' associations have been formed: the official, with legal status, and the informal, with ambiguous legal status.

The government established the China Enterprise Management Association (CEMA) (renamed the China Enterprise Confederation (CEC) in April 1999) and the China Enterprise Directors Association (CEDA) under the leadership of the SETC, a central government organ. CEC and CEDA are organized geographically, and whilst initially they mainly included public sector enterprise directors, they now organize private sector entrepreneurs as well. Their function is to provide advice and information to the government on employer interests in the locality, and to educate member organizations about state policies and regulations.[53] An important element of many of these associations has been to engage in training courses for managers, and in some respects, these associations resemble state-owned management consultancy bureaux. However, it is possible their role will change, as the MoLSS is presently encouraging the development of tripartite industrial relations across the whole of China with the eager support of the official trade unions. However, it is pure speculation to guess whether this will change the basic dynamics of these organizations. This depends on the scope of tripartism, whether the ACFTU is granted more autonomy from the government and party, and whether the private sector enterprises submit themselves to the authority or actively seek to influence the employer associations. Evidence suggests change will be minor, as Zhou (2000) suggests CEC-CEDA is declining in importance, mainly because the government progressively re-imposes strict control over these organizations.[54]

Another kind of informal association enjoys a dubious legal status, and so has been virtually impossible to research. These are the numerous 'social clubs' among private and especially foreign-owned enterprises, where employers from the same nationality within a close geographical proximity form clubs or associations. Japanese, Singaporean and Taiwanese managers and employers usually join such associations (Taylor 2000; Fu et al. 2001), but why? We are told that they are social clubs, to play golf, drink or even to allow wives to meet (in the case of some Japanese enterprises, but also probably others) to support each other in coping with a different living environment than they are used to at home. However, they often discuss business practices to a degree that should be thought of as strategic cooperation. This likely includes systematic sharing of employment practices but also probably extends to wage fixing and policies for dealing with unions.[55] A sceptical view would ask why competitors in product markets should cooperate on labour issues. The answer is the same as for those in capitalist countries. First, this simplifies the job of managing people in a strange environment, so mutual support of what is after all a low-cost item (labour), but potentially a political hot potato if you make a mistake, is very helpful. Second, by agreeing common practices, employers attempt to

---

[53] CEC and CEDA. The Constitution of CEC and CEDA. http://www/cec-ceda.org.cn/china/zc.htm.

[54] There is still a good deal of confusion over the degree to which such orgnisaiotns are independent from state control. For example, Ogden (2000) conflates normative and descriptive elements in claiming that such organizations are both necessarily increasingly independent of state control and this is necessary for overall development (along an implicit liberalist path). There is no evidence that economic reform leads to the development of forms of civil society in which non-governmental groups gain more independence and political space.

[55] This may include no-poaching agreements, whereby another employer covered by such agreements will not recruit a worker who resigns from one firm.

regulate the local labour market, to manage (not necessarily minimize) costs. Such cartels not only regulate common minimum standards, but also reduce pressures to improve standards. Trade unions know this well, and often seek out the most prominent foreign firm of a certain nationality in the locality to get them to agree to some new union policy, such as collective bargaining (see Chapter 8), in the knowledge that once the 'leader' has agreed the other firms will likely follow. Third, for FIEs, especially those from advanced industrial countries, operations in China represent something of a public relations concern. Informal employers' associations, drawing on links to such legal institutions in their home countries, seek to influence both unions and the public at home that they are good employers (Fu et al. 2001). However, because these organizations have no legal constitutional basis, they cannot act directly in industrial relations, and labour being a sensitive issue, it is highly unlikely much will become known about such employers' associations for the present.

## CONCLUSION

There are three points worth reiterating in relation to the significance of employers in understanding the emergence of industrial relations in China. First and most obviously, there is strong segmentation between the public and the private sectors. This is historical both in the formal structure of ownership, but also at the less formal level of balancing pressures or responding to demands to meet political interests and/or market signals. Whilst it is undoubtedly true that the public sector, especially SOE managers, face the greatest pressures, other forms of ownership also need to balance these pressures because of the complex nature of stakeholders, and for the personal career interests of Chinese managers. Some TVEs, POEs and foreign firms, however, have been able to reverse the logic, and use local connections to allow them to exploit the authoritarian political system to serve their private economic interests.

Second, by far the most common form of employment in China is not in large SOEs and FIEs but in small enterprises. Something of a dual economy is emerging, with large enterprises and smaller businesses with different forms of ownership, but also perhaps with increasingly similar problems in their power relations towards the political economy of the market and relations with the Party and government. This is not simply that the large are powerful and the small are weak, it is more complex. The large have power (and authority in many cases) to manipulate the market but they also act in a 'goldfish bowl' in which they must cultivate a good political image. The small firms may have less official power and lack economic stability, but they have two advantages over the large or high-profile firms. First, they are almost invisible, so that only a few people[56] have detailed knowledge of their operations. Within the trade unions, these enterprises, especially if overseas Chinese owned or POEs, are notoriously bad employers. Second, their size and flexibility makes them suited to exploit market niches, *guanxi* relations and local-level anomalies in the market economy and political authoritarian system to make fast money. Whilst it may seem unkind, an accurate analogy would be that the large and high-profile firms form the structure of the economic engine and political stability but the small firms are scavengers. They do not oil the economic machine as government policy and liberal economists would like us believe, but pick over the bits of the economy too inefficient to bother the interests of the larger animals. As scavengers, the smaller firms have no time or patience for the social etiquette of systematic industrial relations regulation or workers' rights in general.

A final distinction is between entrepreneurs and members of the new capitalist class, who see themselves in control of their destiny and have a pragmatic and minimalist view of industrial relations, and the cadre manager, still in the majority, who seeks to balance narrow managerialist interests with broader political concerns. The latter kind of manager retains a somewhat ambiguous position between state and worker, with autonomy to act at the formal level, but keenly aware of the need to maintain a broad constituency of support. This is likely to create a preference for stability, a desire both of state workers (given the alternative – probable unemployment) and of the CCP, whose ultimate aim is self-preservation, which can only be guaranteed through social stability at present. In this way, the manager in many enterprises, where urban workers are employed, whilst wanting to achieve economic targets (growth, market share, profitability or whatever), are still most concerned with political stability. In many respects, it is possible to see the director or chief executive officer not as the employer, but as they are supposed to be in a market economy, the agent of the employer. As most urban workers still work for enterprises whose dominant owner is the state in some form or other, the prevailing form of industrial relations remains that between the state and the worker, not the manager and the worker, even if it is the desire of the state to increase delegation of labour management to enterprise management. In the growing POE and stable FIE sector, this is not so true, the entrepreneur has been (re)born. Moreover, in a large number of TVEs and other forms of quasi-state enterprises the manager has taken on the trappings and mentality of the entrepreneur, using state assets for personal gain.

Whilst size, location, industry and history are important elements shaping industrial relations practices, the dominant context remains ownership for a

---

[56] For example Chan (2001), whilst attempting to explore abuses of labour standards, was unable to do almost any fieldwork in such enterprises, but instead relied on second-hand information and official newspaper articles.

number of reasons. First, whilst there has recently been a strong degree of convergence, laws and regulations apply differently both in provision and application depending on the form of ownership. Second, the social, historical and political functions of different types of enterprise remain important differences shaping the expectations of owners, managers and workers. Third, the early urban reform was initiated with the express aim of developing non-public ownership while maintaining public control of existing enterprises, and allowing each to develop different industrial relations climates.

We need to analyse the management of industrial relations within this context of dualities of size and ownership, tensions within the political economy of governance and in management orientations. It is easy to conclude that the nature of the management and employer side of industrial relations system in China is complex and contradictory. This is true, but at the back of it all, the Party-state feeds this complexity, in both its desire to maintain control over the economy and in its internal inconsistencies, which allow rent-seeking, corruption and other forms of innovative management. At the macro level, however, the state has ensured that big business will prosper, whatever its ownership, and this forms the leading edge of economic and political stability.

# 4. Workers

The foundation of socialism is the primacy of labour as the ideological cornerstone of political economy and labour consciousness. The move away from the rhetoric of socialism towards marketization has seen dramatic changes in the activity and economic position of Chinese workers. Because of changing social, economic and labour relations, the identity and status of workers have also dramatically changed. This chapter will outline the various ways in which the urban working class has been dividing and fragmenting in China, and discuss some of the ways in which this is understood among workers, shaping various forms of experience of work. This fragmentation not only involves divisions in relation to job security, size of employer and ownership, but the changing character of labour itself, with a new post-Mao generation entering the labour force. This chapter will firstly discuss some broad concepts about workers and the working class, and then introduce the development of the labour market, employment conditions in different kinds of enterprises and aspects of the experience and attitudes to work.[57]

## CONCEPTS RELATING TO WORKERS IN CHINA

The word 'worker' carries both a descriptive meaning and an ideological significance. Within the context of socialism, the category of worker also carries great political significance. The worker is the vanguard of revolutionary consciousness for change. However, as previously argued, the vanguard of the Chinese revolution was the peasants. In some ways, this made it undesirable to define the working class clearly in China, although such a categorization still acts as an importance administrative distinction.

---

[57] Whilst this chapter argues that there are growing disparities and divisions among workers, in the concluding chapter, a tentative argument will be made that there is evidence of a 'labour class' developing throughout China, to replace these existing divisions.

## Working Class

Mainland Chinese scholars frequently use the term the 'working class' in research reports, speeches and government documents, but the term is somewhat abused. According to Marx, the working class is a definite social group, whose common identity is their lack of means of production (and thus independent survival), selling their labour power for wages and holding the status of employee (Braverman 1974: 24–5). The Chinese communist government inherited a dual class structure, with extensive feudalism for the majority of the population surrounding a few pockets of industrialized labour in coastal cities. Although the Chinese revolution was essentially a successful revolt against feudalism, and relied heavily on peasant mobilization, the cities were of central significance to control of the country. The power bases of both the republicans and Japanese colonial administration in the first half of the twentieth century relied on the cities, and both needed to be ousted for Mao to unify China under communism. On the eve of the establishment of the PRC, the CCP at its 8th National Congress set out a guideline for transforming the nature of work in China. This formed part of a plan to shift the focus from rural areas to cities where industrial workers, a small minority of the population, were concentrated. Moreover, in the first official version of the Constitution of the PRC, both the working class and peasant class were defined as the basis of the state socialist system (Chapter 1, Article 1).

Before reform, the common conception of the working class in China was that it was a social group comprising urban labourers who did not possess any means of independent production and reproduction of their livelihoods, living primarily from wages based on employment. The main body of the working class was industrial workers, but it also included commercial and agricultural workers who were registered as permanent residents in urban localities (*chengshi hukou*). In this broad sense, the working class included other staff and intellectuals engaged in educational, scientific and health work units (Chang 1988b: 46–55; Kuang 1984: 2). The Chinese economic reform has broadened the concept of 'working class' beyond the limitation of the three kinds of physical workers with urban *hukou*. This led to a new view of the working class, composed of four social divisions: workers who provide their physical labour (*tili laodong*) or blue-collar, workers who provide their mental labour (*naoli laodong*) or white-collar, intellectuals conducting educational or scientific work, and civil servants and managerial cadres in public sectors (Y. Liu 2001).

The CC-CCP and top state authorities have never provided a consistent concept of the working class. The top leaders usually adopt an array of concepts for the 'working class' on different occasions, according their requirements, and then followed by annotations from the official media or scholars. One example is, on the one hand, Jiang Zemin, the General Secretary if the CC-CCP, who summarized 'relying on the working class wholeheartedly', 'Party organs playing the role of the political core' and 'adhering to the system of responsibility of factory directors' as three crucial points to institute a modern enterprise system (Liu and Zhou 1992: 573). Here, the working class can be understood as people who directly provide their physical or mental labour in production, in other words, the concept excludes those in charge of Party and government affairs or management. On the other hand, Jiang (2002) stated that entrepreneurs and technical personnel employed by scientific and technical enterprises in the non-public sector, managerial and technical staff employed by foreign-funded enterprises, the self-employed and private entrepreneurs, if they 'have subscribed to the Party's program and Constitution, worked for the Party's line and program wholeheartedly, and proved to meet the requirements for Party membership through a long period of tests', should be accepted into the CCP. This is because the Party 'has identified itself as a political party of the Chinese working class ever since its founding and has remained the vanguard of the working class, which has laid a solid class foundation for maintaining its advanced nature'. By this second speech, Jiang Zemin implied that, given the appropriate attitude and behaviour, entrepreneurs and capitalists are able to join the working class movement, as represented by the CCP. This is clearly confusing, for a number of reasons. First, and most obviously, is the denial of a division of interests between entrepreneurs and workers. Whilst this has been partially true, and defiantly the Party line for the public sector, there has been little pretence, up until Jiang's comment, that divisions of interest did not exist in the private sector. The early desire to control foreign capital through joint-venture arrangements, unionization drives and so on all reflect the (implicit) official view of division. Second, the first quote excludes the Party leaders from being members of the working class, but the second comment clearly states that the Party is an organ of the working class. This ironically can only be solved by taking Jiang to mean the CCP represents the interests of workers but is not made up of, or controlled by, members of the working class. The problems, in fact, represent the problems of trying to maintain socialist ideology in the context of a market economy.

## Workers and Staff

The second confusion arises from the concept of 'workers and staff' (*zhigong*), which is popularly used in government documents and statistical reports. Statistically, according to the NBS and MoLSS (2001: 572), the term mainly refers to those who work in and receive their income from units with state ownership, urban collective ownership, joint ownership, share-holding stock ownership, limited liability corporations, foreign and 'overseas' Chinese (that is, Hong Kong, Macao and Taiwan) funded enterprises, and their affiliated units. However, we find that the Chinese version provides two different points. First, 'income' is explicitly referred to as 'wages' and, second, some kinds of employment, such as those employed by TVEs, POEs, or *getihu*, retirees, re-employed retirees and teachers employed by the primary schools run by villages are excluded (NBS and MoLSS 2001: 567). The term 'workers and staff' is, therefore, very obscure and broad, covering all labourers who rely on wages and salaries as their main source of income and are registered as permanent residents in cities and towns. This term has also been used in research in recent years. For example, in the ACFTU's survey in 1997, the sample expressly covered 'workers and staff' in urban areas, including those from POEs. However, the title of its final report was 'Chinese working class marching into the 21$^{st}$ century' (Department of Policy Studies, ACFTU 1999: 3).

This ambiguity serves politically to dampen any potential class identity among workers and to some degree reflects a reality that, for urban workers, the main division of interests in socialist China were between superior agencies and the enterprises as a whole. There was a high degree of congruence of interests between managers and workers, set in contrast to the interest of superior agencies, and the peasant class at a more abstract level. At a political level, under the planned period up to the present, it is imperative to officially deny the existence of a class division within the urban areas. To do so, would be to admit a class divide between exploiters and exploited, and undermine the any claims to the principle of socialism. This was not that difficult to do. After all, industrial conflict in the period before the establishment of PRC was highly political, with no institutional frameworks for setting disputes under the late imperial, republican or colonial periods. Workers faced brutal suppression by the authorities and employers, and so conflicts were highly politicized, violent and usually brief. Both early republicans and the CCP swept these conflicts into national unifications and political struggles, so that there were few chances for workers in reality to form a clear class identity in the economic terms Marx considered necessary for evolutionary consciousness. The working class, thus, to a large extent, has been constituted as a politically dependent and ambiguous collection of workers, which was transformed by socialism to a self-conscious class but remained a vague category, albeit an important one, under Chinese socialism.

## Worker

As the economic system has transformed, the composition and characteristics of workers in China has greatly changed. The transformation and structuring of the economy is resulting in the status of Chinese workers changing from being (rhetorically) a component of the leading class to a lower stratum in the social structure. After reform, the study of social stratification has become a popular topic of sociological research in China (Li 1999). The working class has been divided into several strata, based on differences in access to power, income, occupational popularity and social status (Chang 1995b; Feng and Xu 1993; He 1990; Hu 2000; Li and Wang 1992; Li 1995; Li 1993; Liu 2002) leading to the common conclusion that the worker has been separated from the employers, who own the means of production, and from managers who control them. However, the authorities have never given an explicit definition to clarify its position, even in the Labour Law (1994).[58]

According to recent research, entitled 'Research on Changes of Social Structure in Contemporary China', undertaken by the Chinese Academy of Social Science, the former three major components of the working class which were defined to exist under socialist China (workers, intellectuals and managers) have developed into ten strata that separately belong to five rankings within the existing social structure.[59] Within the five social rankings, managers belong to the upper and upper-middle ranks of the working class, and workers belong to the middle-lower and lower ranks.[60] In this research, workers are redefined as 'people who, by their physical strength and skill, directly or indirectly operate the tools of production to produce physical products, provide labour service or provide assistance to such production or service, and are supervised by a manager' (Lu 2002: 127). According to this definition, the strata of commercial and service worker and industrial worker

---

[58] In the Labour Law (1994), it seems the traditional concept of the working class is accepted, in which people who are employed within enterprises and individual economic organizations (employing units) are *labour* (*laodongzhe*) (Article 2).

[59] The five rankings are the upper (including high-ranking leading cadres, managers in larger enterprises, senior professional personnel, owners of larger-sized POEs) upper-middle (including middle-level and lower-level leading cadres, managerial staff at medium level in large-sized enterprises, managers in medium-sized and small enterprises, professional personnel at the medium level and owners of medium-sized POEs), middle-middle (including junior professional personnel, owners of small-sized POEs, office workers, owners of individual economy), middle-lower (including self-employed labourers, original employees of commercial sectors, workers and peasants) and lower (including workers and peasants in poverty and without job security, unemployed, semi-unemployed vagrant) ranking. From the top to the bottom, the ten strata are managerial staff of state and society, managers, owners of POEs, professional personnel, office workers, owners of individual economy, employees of commercial and service sectors, industrial workers, agriculture labourers, unemployed and semi-unemployed in urban and rural areas (Lu 2002: 7-23).

[60] What needs to be pointed out is the above-mentioned changes are not only outcomes of individual researchers, but also the judgment and recognition of the social structure of contemporary China by the government. The research is under the direction of Li Tieying, who is a member of the Political Bureau of the CCP. The publication was also supported by the government (Lu 2002: Preface). Whilst we may see all these strata as a Weberian-style avoidance of Marxist class analysis, it was still seen as highly controversial by members of the CCP.

can be classified in the category of workers. One point that should be noted is that the report of this research states that the workers with rural *hukou*, or *nongmingong*, should be one part of industrial workers, even though they can be taken as a relatively independent group in this stratum because of their *hukou* and their lower treatment in terms of wages, social insurance and benefits compared with urban workers (Lu 2002: 20–1).

Chang (1995a: 16), takes a more abstract definition of workers as 'manual or mental labourers employed by others in modern industrial society and relying on wages and salaries as their main source of living'. This concept focuses on the source of livelihood. Taking both Chang and Lu's definitions together, we may define 'workers' as the people who work for wages as the main source of income and are controlled by others in the process of labour, and whose main function is not to control the work of anyone else. In this definition, three points should be noted. First, the difference with full-time managers is that whilst both work for wages, managers' work is primarily to control the performance of others directly or indirectly. A particular issue revolves around where to place supervisors and team leaders. Supervisors should be considered managers, even though the working background of such persons is usually as workers (and thus they may have a cultural affinity to the working class) but team leaders may be either, depending on whether in the course of their work they mainly direct or actually participate in the production process they lead. If they mainly direct, they are managers. Second, in our discussion, except where specified, we will not make a distinction between workers by urban *hukou* or rural *hukou*, but instead, concentrate on divisions based on the forms of ownership of the places where workers labour. Third, at the present time, more than two-thirds of urban workers are still employed as in traditional manufacturing and heavy industries (NBS-MoLSS 2001: 116–17), and so analysis will focus on these workers. The service sector has developed greatly in recent years in China, and employs an increasing number of workers in small businesses where labour relations are often paternal and institutionally underdeveloped. These workers will be discussed in this chapter and as marginal or vulnerable workers in later chapters. Moreover, the proportion of high-technology industries and incumbent workers is still comparatively small, and whilst their influence is often magnified for political reasons by governments, given the rhetoric of labour, this is less a distortion in China. Therefore, the fundamental nature of industrial relations in China remains based on a quite traditional mass production economy with its contingent skill formation and occupational categories. Moreover, the impact the new high-technology and information technology industries have on industrial relations is still restricted.

# WORK ORGANIZATION IN THE PLANNED PERIOD

Under the planned economy, almost all workers were organized into some form of social, political and economic unit (Lu and Perry 1997b: 8–12), which was administered and experienced as a community in which people were born into, socialized, educated, worked and died in. In the rural areas and in many urban work units, collectives were formed to organize production and the social reproduction of labour. In state-owned enterprises, the work unit or *danwei* was developed as the most sophisticated of the social systems or communities in the planned period. The *danwei* formed in SOEs and were officially treated as the basic administrative unit of urban society, and provided all the social needs of the workforce and mangers, including housing, schools, medical care and recreation. The economic performance of SOEs was strong in the 1950s and 1960s, and the state was able to appropriate a significant surplus from the workers based on this stable employment system.

There are a number of competing explanations as to the origin of the *danwei* system, and Lu and Perry's (1997a) edited volume provides a useful introduction to most of these perspectives. Lu (1997) argues that the *danwei* developed as production units in the rural areas to support the Red Army during the civil and anti-Japanese war, in which workers could not be paid wages but joined revolutionary workshops where they both worked and had access to a free supply of basic needs. Yeh (1997) argues the *danwei* formed during the republican period among some exemplary employers, and although the basis of the argument on the apparent practices of the Bank of China in the 1930s in somewhat tenuous, Yeh links this to an Asian model of capitalism (1997: 65–6). This argument is echoed in various writings of Chan (1995b, 1997), Frazier (2002) and Wang F. (1998: 78–92). Sil (1997), whilst not specifically outlining the Chinese *danwei* system, implies (1997: 132–3) the Chinese adopted the Russian system which originated in a rather romantic view of egalitarian rural society, but which was changed into an authoritarian control system under Stalin (1997: 123–5). Naughton (1997) argues that whilst the *danwei* formed during the early period of Russian influence over Chinese industrialization in the 1950s, the Chinese form emerged during the mid-1960s when the labour market was removed. Naughton (1997: 172) states that 'from the early 1960s, the government began directly or indirectly to allocated almost 95 per cent of first jobs in urban areas'. He goes on to argue that with near zero movement of workers once allocated these jobs, especially within SOEs, the Chinese workplace became very different from either the dual labour market of the Japanese system or the high labour mobility of the soviet workplace. The Chinese workplace thus became a closed, insular system, which facilitated a high degree of corporatism (see

Walder's argument discussed in Chapter 1).

Common to all these explanations is that *danwei* have a utilitarian function, to provide control over the masses in urban areas by the party state, to promote the elitism of the urban worker (through better welfare provisions than other workers) and as a social institution to bind workers to their workplaces under the Marxist principle of the centrality of work to social experience. Some (Hein 2000: 85–6); Sheehan 1998; Sargeson 1999) have argued that the keeping of *hukou* by the *danwei* meant workers were subject to a high degree of control by the employers. Whilst this was undoubtedly one of the aims of the system, the *danwei* also places work within its wider social context, in which mangers could not isolate themselves from the distribution process to concentrate just on accumulation. Workers were allocated to their work units by the state, and dismissal was almost impossible (Naughton 1997: 184). Wages were set by the state, and wage differentials according to jobs were reasonably egalitarian among and between workers and staff. Moreover, as will be discussed in the next chapter, the trade unions took on the functions of allocating welfare, rather than enterprise managers directly, so that managers could not directly employ sticks and carrots. As Bian (1992: 50) indicates in workers seeking to gain membership of the CCP, whilst they must apply through their local *danwei*-based branch, the party committee will examine their 'loyalty to the party and performance (in work-related, political and social activities)' in deciding whether to grant membership. Although there must have been much variation in practice, the *danwei* system provided considerable stability (the so-called 'iron rice bowl') to workers, and a context in which work itself was an important, but not their only, social relation with their employer.

Bian argues that among different *danwei* there was a hierarchy, depending on whether the enterprise belonged to a national or lesser government organ (1992: 52–9), with the difference in status providing material access to funds to support welfare provisions, as well as social status. Perry (2000), Solinger (1997, 2000) and Sargeson (1999) take this further to highlight the importance of differences between those included in the *danwei* system and the masses that were excluded, both (at times) urban residents, and (at all times) the rural peasants. The SOE workers were granted privileged conditions through their *danwei*, and stood as an elite within the working class of China. A good example of this can be seen in that the state allocated funds for housing to SOEs but not to COEs (Bian et al. 1997: 233–4) or other forms of enterprise. The labour allocation system solidified the differences and thus, in effect, status (and material standards) was decided almost entirely by the state. Accusations of nepotism, political favouritism and so on aside, the system tended to create competition among urban schoolchildren as well as encourage students to further their studies, even in the face of the Cultural Revolution's vilification of the intelligentsia. However, with the economic decline caused as a result of the Cultural Revolution, the labour allocation system was strained to find enough places for the growing population. The SOE *danwei* then pressed their employers to provide job succession and institutionalize nepotism which, in turn, further stabilized employment within SOEs. The economic changes of the market economy appears to clash head-on with this stable employment for all urban workers, and particular threaten the status of the SOE 'elite' workers.

## LABOUR MARKET AND EMPLOYMENT PATTERNS

Deng's early phase of urban reform sought to increase productive efficiency, without substantially changing the structure of employment. Increased autonomy given to managers was presumably meant to tighten discipline and improve efficiency of the existing workforce. However, the developments of rural TVEs and urban POEs, as well as the attraction of FIE investment, created the rudiments of a labour market, with a new form of employment mechanism. For many rural migrants and some urban workers, there arose new forms of employment which were not regulated by the government, and ones in which employers were free to set their own demands for numbers and types of employees. It appears certain that this labour market was to grow in parallel, but not interfere with the SOE employment structure.

In December 1994 the MoL (1994b) announced its intention to develop a labour market. First, the system of government allocation of jobs and restrictions on labour migration between different forms of enterprise ownership, different regions and urban or rural areas was abandoned. Second, a set of labour laws and regulations was established to adjust labour relations through labour contracts. Third, the demand and supply of labour in the market was regulated, using economic, legal and, if necessary, administrative measures. Administrative measures, for example, allowed local governments to restrict redundancies or put pressure on enterprises to increase recruitment, on an ad hoc basis. Fourth, a number of institutional arrangements were made to develop systems (institutions and procedures) to cover social insurance, employment services, professional skill training and safety inspection. As discussed later, this combination of changes to the labour system is having a tremendous impact on Chinese workers.

Nevertheless, the government has continued to impose a number of regulations on the labour market, on both the demand and the supply side. These regulations cover much the same restrictions found in corporatist welfare economies of Europe, covering labour supply, through restricting redundancy and the numbers of migrant labourers, and boosting education and training. Demand is influenced through social welfare provisions, minimum wages, and so on. However, the market itself is regulated to a degree higher than in capitalist industrialized countries, with heavy regulation of employment agencies, which remain largely government controlled. The most significant influence is maintained through direct ownership and control of many legal enterprises.

Table 4.1 outlines the change of the employment structure according to form of enterprise ownership.[61] Examining just the urban areas to begin with, employment in state-owned units continued to grow throughout both the communist period and since market liberalization right up to 1995. However, as can be seen in Table 4.1, by the end of the year 2000 employment in state-owned units (SOUs)[62] had declined over 28 per cent from that of 1995. The growth and rapid contraction of collectively owned units is even more dramatic, from a huge expansion in employment during the 1950s (over 42 times from 1952 to 1961), to a marked decline by over 50 per cent from 1994 to 2000. The state sector remains the dominant form of employment, with about 54 per cent of the total workforce. Moreover, collectively owned units have only lost their second place to individual enterprises, which they had gained in 1956, since 1998. Many employees of COEs and, to a lesser extent, stated-owned units in urban areas have been transferred to new forms of enterprises, as well as more recently to unemployment.

The change in the state sector paralleled the growth of the private sector, in which POEs form an important part. POEs include many forms of private businesses, some large, but mostly small in size. Other parts of the private sector are overseas Chinese and foreign investments which accounted for only 4 per cent of urban employment in 2000. Moreover, POE employment increased by over 46 per cent between 1996 and 2000, whereas FIE employment grew less than 24 per cent in the same period. POEs are often neglected in the literature, especially among non-Mainland scholars preferring to examine SOE reform, FIEs and to a lesser extent TVEs. Whilst understandable, given the problems of research access, this remains a major omission. According to official data (NBS-MoLSS 2001: 391) there were over 27 million POEs, employing almost 75 million workers. However, within that figure, over 50 million employees are categorized as self-employed (see Table 4.1) or *getihu*.[63] This means that the average POE actually directly employed only one or two persons, and many employed none at all. Many POEs do not register, which implies that the official figure is an underestimate, and many more do not accurately account for the number

---

[61] Whilst there are problems with the reliability of official data, the sets used are consistent and with the least likelihood of deliberate bias. A good account of the problems of data reliability are demonstrated and explained by Solinger (2001).

[62] SOUs include SOEs and government work units (bureaux and departments).

[63] Choi and Zhou (2001: 112) report that there were 961 000 POEs and another 28.5 million *getihu* (self-employed labourers) in 1997.

Table 4.1 Urban employment (end of year x10 000)

| Year[1] | SOEs | COEs | TVEs | SHUs | JOUs | LLCs | SHCs | Others[2] POEs | HMTs | FIEs | Individual | Others |
|---|---|---|---|---|---|---|---|---|---|---|---|---|
| 1952 | 15.80 | 23 | | | | | | | | | 8.83 | |
| 1955 | 19.08 | 2.54 | | | | | | | | | 6.40 | |
| 1960 | 50.44 | 9.25 | | | | | | | | | 1.50 | |
| 1965 | 37.38 | 12.27 | | | | | | | | | 1.71 | |
| 1970 | 47.92 | 14.24 | | | | | | | | | 96 | |
| 1975 | 64.26 | 17.72 | | | | | | | | | 24 | |
| 1980 | 80.19 | 24.25 | 30.00 | | | | | | | | 81 | |
| 1985 | 89.90 | 33.24 | 69.79 | | 38 | | | | | 6 | 4.50 | |
| 1986 | 93.33 | 34.21 | 79.37 | | 43 | | | | 1 | 12 | 4.83 | 1 |
| 1987 | 96.54 | 34.88 | 88.05 | | 50 | | | | 1 | 20 | 5.69 | |
| 1988 | 99.84 | 35.27 | 95.45 | | 63 | | | | 2 | 29 | 6.59 | 3 |
| 1989 | 101.08 | 35.02 | 93.67 | | 82 | | | | 4 | 43 | 6.48 | 3 |
| 1990 | 103.46 | 35.49 | 92.65 | | 96 | | | 57 | 4 | 62 | 6.14 | 2 |
| 1991 | 106.64 | 36.28 | 96.09 | | 49 | | | 68 | 69 | 96 | 6.92 | 2 |
| 1992 | 108.89 | 36.21 | 106.25 | | 56 | | | 98 | 83 | 1.38 | 7.40 | 5 |
| 1993 | 109.20 | 33.93 | 123.45 | 1.64 | 66 | | | 1.86 | 1.55 | 1.33 | 9.30 | 18 |
| 1994 | 112.14 | 32.85 | 120.17 | 2.92 | 52 | | | 3.32 | 2.11 | 1.95 | 12.25 | 9 |
| 1995 | 112.61 | 31.47 | 128.62 | 3.17 | 53 | | | 4.85 | 2.72 | 2.47 | 15.60 | 11 |
| 1996 | 112.44 | 30.16 | 135.08 | 3.63 | 49 | | | 6.20 | 2.65 | 2.75 | 17.09 | 9 |
| 1997 | 110.44 | 28.83 | 91.58 | 4.68 | 43 | | | 7.50 | 2.81 | 3.00 | 19.19 | 18 |
| 1998 | 90.58 | 19.63 | 125.37 | 1.36 | 48 | 4.84 | 4.10 | 9.73 | 2.94 | 2.93 | 22.59 | 9 |
| 1999 | 85.72 | 17.12 | 127.04 | 1.44 | 46 | 6.03 | 4.20 | 10.53 | 3.06 | 3.06 | 24.14 | 22 |
| 2000 | 81.02 | 14.99 | 128.20 | 1.55 | 42 | 6.87 | 4.57 | 12.68 | 3.10 | 3.32 | 21.36 | 27 |

Note:
From 1952 to 1985 selected years are given only. after that all years are given.
SOUs: state-owned units; COUs: collective-owned units; SHUs: share-holding units; JOUs: joint owned units; SHCs: share-holding corporations

Sources: before 1995 – NBS 1991: 95. 1996: 91. After 1995    NBS and MoLSS 1997: 7. 1998: 7. 1999.. 2001: 3.

87

of workers. This occurs especially in the many smaller private sector employers that employ some of the millions of illegal migrant workers from the countryside, and even neighbouring countries, to be employed as contracted labourers, officially self-employed under *getihu* status, to reduce employer liabilities.

*Table 4.2 Average employment size of enterprises*

| Year | SOEs | COEs | Others |
|------|------|------|--------|
| 1986 | 964  | 19   | 0.11   |
| 1987 | 989  | 19   | 0.13   |
| 1988 | 976  | 20   | 0.16   |
| 1989 | 988  | 21   | 0.22   |
| 1990 | 991  | 21   | 0.27   |
| 1991 | –    | –    | –      |
| 1992 | 1054 | 22   | 0.41   |
| 1993 | 1043 | 19   | 0.67   |
| 1994 | 1066 | 17   | 0.92   |
| 1995 | 928  | 21   | 1.51   |
| 1996 | 962  | 19   | 1.49   |
| 1997 | 1092 | 16   | 1.78   |
| 1998 | 1362 | 11   | 2.63   |
| 1999 | 1360 | 10   | 2.84   |

Source: National Bureau of Statistics and MoLSS (2001: 21) and Table 3.1

Table 4.2 shows the average employment size of the three basic kinds of enterprise in China. The data needs to be treated with some caution, as there are huge variations within each category. This is especially true of the 'other' category, which includes POEs, FIEs and *getihu*. Based on internal ACFTU data from Shanghai, the average size of COEs declined from 102 employees in 1995 to just 62 in 2000, mainly due to shifting workers to corporatized business units or spinning-off surplus workers to private concerns. Thus, there is considerable variation over time and probably between different locations. However, we can conclude that the average size of SOEs is much larger than other forms. Whilst many SOEs are under pressure to shed labour, the figures show that employment downsizing is not as dramatic in SOEs as other forms of enterprise, especially COEs and some FIEs. Moreover, there has been a progressive movement, especially since 1997, to merge SOEs into larger conglomerates. The average size data reinforces the argument of the still strong importance of the state and public sector to current Chinese employment patterns. Among the FIEs, there is a considerable range, with a few very large employers, mimicking the pattern, although not the scale, of SOEs, but most FIEs are medium to small in size. The COEs appear to be declining in size as well as numbers, with an increasing number becoming privatized forms of TVEs of some form or another (see Chapter 3).

## WORKERS' RIGHTS IN POST-SOCIALIST CHINA

As managers change from their role as cadres into capitalist functionaries, managerial concern with workers' interests has also changed to more overtly economic considerations, and in particular to reduce labour costs. The main thrust of government-initiated reform, especially since the start of the 1990s, has concurred with the market economic model, which places emphasis on improving efficiency. In taking this line, the government has allowed social justice and social development to lag behind and be undermined by economic change. This is tantamount to the government sacrificing the interests of workers for the sake of the interests and rights of capital and management. In the process of reform, Chinese workers have endured declining political status and significant weakening of their economic interests. This problem has been made more acute because under the previous (planned) system, the working class in China was not independent of management, nor was it organized as a self-conscious class. Whilst the interests of capital as a defined class were legitimated (through such concerns as property rights, see Chapter 3), albeit within constraints, the interests of workers were not. At the present time, workers cannot strive for and protect their rights as an independent social class or by collective force because, on the one hand, the trade unions are unable to represent their interests and, on the other hand, their class-consciousness is still being shaped by the market economy.

However, the government cannot completely abandon workers' interests, as fear of workers' opposition to further reform will result in social unrest and the moral bankruptcy of the CCP itself. Thus, the government has shown that it is aware of the declining material and ideological status of workers and, at the same time as enforcing reform and advancing the status and rights of capital and management, it has also adopted measures to placate worker opposition, especially among public sector workers (Li 2000). By adopting these measures, the government restrains the authority it had earlier granted employers, especially with regard to authority concerning human resources management, and attempts to compensate workers for their economic losses. The Labour Law of the PRC promulgated in 1994, and subsequent regulations issued, clearly stipulate the rights of workers in industrial relations. The government wished that these laws and regulations would ensure stable industrial relations by promoting a clear definition of the balance of power between employers and workers.

Labour rights can be divided into individual and collective rights. Individuals rights mainly include rights to employment, choice occupations, remuneration for labour, rest and holidays, protection for occupational health and safety, training in vocational skills, receiving social insurance and welfare, submission of individual labour disputes for settlement and other rights relating to labour stipulated by law. Collective labour rights include the right to participate in and organize trade unions, to negotiate and conclude collective contracts with employers on an equal footing, to take part in democratic management, and a limited right to engage in collective disputes.

Compared with international labour standards and international conventions relating to the social and economic rights of labourers, Chinese labour laws are quite comprehensive as regards individuals' rights (see Chapter 2). However, the Chinese labour law system established in the mid-1990s does not provide comprehensive protection to workers in practice, especially on collective issues. The current legal and regulatory provisions do not clearly define legal responsibility for infringing such labour rights and have inadequate measures for legally sanctioned relief in cases where breaches occur. There has been little debate within Mainland China over whether there should be such comprehensive labour laws, but more interest in how to implement them (Wang 2001; Lie and Li 2001; Guan 2001). Furthermore, since the strength and influence of employers and management is much greater than that of workers, even if labour rights become clearly guaranteed by laws, it is not always possible for workers to pursue redress. This is because the legal system itself is not well equipped to sequester employer assets or the like to compensate aggrieved workers.

Besides the drawbacks of the labour laws, the following problems still make difficulties for the realization of workers' rights. First, even though the Chinese government at all levels has placed considerable emphasis on dealing with lay-offs and unemployment in ways which will avoid overt labour conflict, [64] the re-employment of such workers remains the most important problem facing the government in its attempts to push forward the economic reform of the public sector. In 2000, the re-employment rate of laid-off workers (in SOEs) was 35.4 per cent. In the first half of 2001, this rate dropped to 11.1 per cent (MoLSS 2001). After China's entry into the World Trade Organization (W.T.O.), the problem of unemployment is widely

---

[64] In May 1998, the CC-CCP and the State Council held a working conference on guaranteeing the basic living standards of laid-off workers and implementing the re-employment project. Up to August 2001, there were 43 relevant policies published by the central government and its subordinated ministries (Information Office of the State Council 2002).

expected to become more serious (Tang 2001; Chang 2002b).

Second, with regard to the right to remuneration for labour, the current principle of distribution according to productive factors amount to the determination of wages according to supply and demand in the labour market. Moreover, in a labour market where supply greatly exceeds demand, as it does in China, employers and managers can unilaterally decide the wage level, wage form and method of payment. Whilst the wage system generally disadvantages workers, another phenomenon demonstrates the power inequality with managers more starkly. Many employers simply do not pay the agreed amount or pay on time, and in 1999 wages arrears was the foremost cause of labour disputes.[65] Though most cases of delayed payments occurred in POEs, delays or non-payment of wages also occurred in some SOEs, and the rate is increasing due to bankruptcy, operational losses and occasionally also corruption. By the end of 2001, the situation worsened so much that may local governments had issued regulations to help workers demand payment of wages.[66]

Third, the social security system is undergoing a period of transition from enterprise-based labour insurance to a state-managed social security system.[67] The government has made great efforts to establish a comprehensive system, which covers unemployment, old age, illness, maternity and work-related injury insurance. Moreover, a minimum wage system and the minimum living expense assurance system in urban areas have been set up. These systems were designed to play an active role in guaranteeing a basic living standard for workers who could not work for some reason. However, due to the limited coverage of this system, workers with rural residency status are excluded from benefiting from the social security system at present, even if they reside and work in urban areas. At the same time, because of inadequate social security funds and problems with implementation, many urban workers cannot gain access to these funds either.[68]

---

[65] According to incomplete statistics, the wages in arrears in 1999 in China amounted to 363.7 hundred million yuan, owed to 13.82 million workers (ACFTU 2000: 136).

[66] For example, Shanghai, Shenzhen, Zhuhai, Beijing and other local governments have issued local regulations and attempt to manage wage payments and protect workers' right to remuneration for labour through a system of wage in arrears protection (*Gongren ribao*, 6 February 2002).

[67] Under the old system, enterprises had to pay all pension fund contributions for their retirees and all medical expenses for their workers. Through reform of the social security system, the government attempts to transfer the old enterprise-based system to a new one funded by both workers and management, getting rid of the social burdens for SOEs and providing a level of convenience for labour to move between different kinds of enterprises (Du and Zheng 1995).

[68] For example, in 2000 the number of registered unemployed was 5.95 million, but only 55 per cent of them, namely 3.29 million, got unemployment compensation. The unemployed with rural resident status have no right to register and get unemployment compensation (NBS-MoLSS 2001: 67, 443).

Thus, whilst the government has attempted to introduce a comprehensive set of employment laws, particularly with regard to safeguarding individual labour rights and interests, considerable problems remain. The laws mainly specify the content of provisions (see Chapter 2) rather than industrial relations processes. Public sector rather than private sector workers gain more access to these provisions, and there are few penalties or incentives for employers to obey the laws. The differences between enterprise forms warrants further examination, and will be presented in the next section.

## CHANGING EXPERIENCE OF WORK

The change from planned to a mixed economy has increased the types of work units, and consequently the variety of experiences of work. The change from the official unitarist line (Blecher 2002), at least for those working in the SOE *danwei* (Naughton 1997; Lu and Perry 1997b), to a clearer division between owners and employees has necessarily caused the development of different kinds of workplace industrial relations experiences. Although the government officially maintains the unitarist line (Wang 2002: 7), academics usually divide enterprises based on type of ownership in relation to experience of work, such that POEs are the worst employers, followed by FIEs, with SOEs as the best employers (for example Ip 1999, especially p.72). Some acknowledge differences within forms of ownership. Chan (2001) and Chiu and Taylor (2001a) indicate variation among types of FIEs, in which overseas Chinese and some Korean firms are generally despotic employers, whilst Western and some Japanese firms treat their workers much better.[69]

Workers in public enterprises refer to the workers employed in SOEs and the COEs in cities and towns. In the period of the planned economy, workers in these enterprises benefited from the highest degree of job security, better working environments, and higher wages and welfare benefits (Huan and Zhen 1992). Moreover, they had strongly integrated trade union organizations and more participation in management (mainly through the system of WCs, as discussed in Chapter 8). The result was that there was little separation of interests between workers and managers. The party ensured conflicts that did arise were smoothed over, and the system was such that there would be few reasons for substantial conflicts with gold-bricking production operations, and the state production plans were designed to continually expand production, not to reduce it. Finally, in the decade of the

---

[69] However, research by Taylor and Drover (2000) relating to Korean supply chain strategies and labour standards, and by Taylor (1999c; 2001) examining Japanese plants in Chinese, show considerable variation among such FIEs from the same nationality.

Cultural Revolution, managers became extremely vulnerable to political attacks and so those who wanted to keep their jobs were forced to be extremely 'aware' of the working class and to identify themselves with them. Conflicts that might have occurred would be characterized as political. For example, a demand for higher wages would effectively be a demand to change the economic plan. As the plan was constituted under the rhetoric of socialism, such a demand from a relatively small proportion of the working class (such as a few thousand in a large SOE) could easily be labelled as syndicalist or anti-socialist.

However, reform has brought about a declining absolute and relative position of workers in the public sector. To a large extent, urban reform has been mainly concerned with removing the privileged position of workers in these enterprises. Job security (the proverbial 'iron rice-bowl') is broken (Leung 1988) and all workers are faced with the threat of lay-offs and unemployment (Solinger 2002). The basic welfare system, such as public housing and free medical treatment, has been largely cancelled, whilst the new social security system is still in the process of being established and has many problems, resulting in most workers not yet being fully protected by this system (Mok and Cai 1999: 74–5). Furthermore, whilst Mok and Cai, based on a survey in southern China, found state workers' self-evaluation of their status had increased during the 1990s, objectively the economic and political status of workers is continuously declining (Blecher 2002). The income gap between workers and their managers is gradually increasing and the workers' rights to participation are being eroded.

The degree of change needs to be seen in perspective. Bankruptcy and demands for higher economic efficiency in public sector firms is putting pressure on workers in terms of delayed wages and the increasing threat of redundancy. However, research up to the early 1990s indicated that there was little change in the organization of the labour process for those left in employment in the public sector (for example Brown and Branine 1996; Goodall and Warner 1997; Wang 1993; Warner 1995; Zhu and Campbell 1996). Since then, the pace of change has accelerated, but still we see that, while material standards decline for many, research still seems to indicate no great divisions between managers and workers have emerged, at least in SOEs. Li (2000) found that workers lowered their expectations on employment when their enterprise was loss making, so that conflict only arose when management initiated redundancies. Taylor (2002) found that even when SOEs underwent some form of corporatization or privatization, little changed, except a greater emphasis on discipline towards product quality. Moreover, using a detailed survey of 150 workers in seven privatized or corporatized plants, Chiu and Taylor (2001b) found workers were generally compliant with managerial agendas, and saw that corporatization may enhance job security for those transferred to the new enterprise. Even where there are reports of great change, such as Zhao and Nichols (1996), we must be careful about interpreting the data, because the workers they studied were not the usual urban SOE elite, but contracted migrant workers who had never enjoyed such conditions previously (Sargeson 1999).

As a consequence of the government's policy of 'increasing efficiency by downsizing staff' and 'managing large enterprises well while relaxing control over small ones' there is virtually no hope for those made unemployed to return to the public sector once they leave. Now, they can only hope to find jobs in the private sector or seek self-employment either as *getihu* or within the growing informal economy. According to the NBS-MoLSS (2001: 110), there are 106.64 million staff and workers in SOEs and 36.28 million in COEs in 1991. By the end of 2000, the numbers had respectively decreased to 81.02 million and 14.99 million. The public sector has reduced 46.91 million staff and workers within ten years, albeit often simply by changing the name (but not the substance) of the SOEs through such initiatives as corporatization (Taylor 2002). Certainly, the workers can enjoy better job security and welfare in some profit making SOEs or monopoly public sectors, such as post and telecommunication, finance and insurance, real estate trade, government organs and state-owned public institutions. However, these only make up a small proportion of the public workforce.[70] Joining the ranks of the previously excluded groups, made up of urban workers who never had a strong *danwei* organization (such as in smaller COEs – Solinger 1997) and the rising influx of migrant workers (Hein 2000) are growing numbers of former SOE workers (Solinger 2002), who are themselves starting to lead new waves of worker unrest (Cai 2002).

Figure 4.1 shows a typology that may be used to provide a rather simplistic overview of the pattern according to ownership, which we will then examine in relation to different types of enterprise in more detail. The argument underlying Figure 4.1 is that two different pressures shape the treatment of workers, depending on the type of enterprise they work for. For the public sector, economic performance is the main determinant, so that with higher surpluses, more is shared with workers and so their material standard of work improves, and visa versa with increasing losses. However, for the private sector, a completely different context shapes how employers treat workers, one that we may call 'public profile'. This means that a large European or North American firm investing in China, or a famous privatized TVE such as Kelon, is 'encouraged' to offer relatively good employment conditions because it knows it is under public scrutiny either in China mainly

---

[70] For example, by the end of 1999, the on-post staff and workers numbered 1.07 million in the public post and telecommunication industry, 2.05 million in public finance and insurance enterprises and 0.62 million in public real estate trade, accounting for 1.28 per cent and 0.73 per cent of total employment respectively (NBS-MoLSS 2000: 207-8).

from the CCP) or abroad (mainly from labour related non-governmental organizations and home country trade unions). Those less in the public glare, such as overseas Chinese firms and most POEs, are free to exploit up to the level the market can bear. That is, they can exploit workers to the (extent that enough workers are willing to tolerate the working conditions and pay. There are a number of points that flow from this argument. First, organization size is not a real issue. There are huge employers, with over 10 000 workers, which are able to treat their workers as virtual slaves, and there are small firms with conditions comparable to many advanced industrialized countries. Second, although it is likely that employment conditions are a bit better in Shanghai and Beijing than, say, Guangdong this is influenced by the same factors described in Figure 4.1.

| Strategy for IR | Form of ownership | |
|---|---|---|
| | Public | Private |
| Better conditions ↕ Worse Conditions | Large OR Profitable | High public profile OR Strong unions (in China or at home) |
| | Small AND Loss Making | Weak or no union OR Close (personal) relations with local government officials |

*Figure 4.1 Labour conditions*

The CCP is more active in monitoring the private sector in Shanghai than Guangdong and so mistreatment of workers is more likely to be exposed (made public). Moreover, public sector firms in these important cities are likely to be more profitable, both through the market and by state manipulation of the market, than in the decaying industrial areas (such as the north east). Third, implied in this analysis is the fundamental difference in orientation towards employees of the state and the private sectors. Whereas the private sector is based on greed alone (Asia Monitor Resource Centre 1995), the state sector is still required to take account of political considerations as well as economic objectives. Nike and other transnational corporations found that exposure of poor working conditions in factories they control (even if they do not actually own them), if exposed to the consuming public of their major capitalist markets, meant they lost profits, so the company made efforts to publicly demonstrate improvement (Frost 2002: 6–7).

As a rule, there are few private sector employers that even meet, let alone surpass, aspects of current large SOE employment conditions, and the vast majority fall far short in all aspects, except often wages, as can be seen in Table 4.3. Even the appearance of higher wages can be misleading. Although some private enterprises pay high wages to some of their employees, many POEs and overseas Chinese firms pay very low wages, and sometimes pay irregularly, and more significantly, penalties and fines often cut into wages to the point that workers sometimes owe their employers money (Xu 1998).

*Table 4.3: Income structure of Chinese workers and staff by ownership (yuan /%)*

|  | SOU | COU | POE | JOU | SHU | FIE | HTM |
|---|---|---|---|---|---|---|---|
| 100 and less | 0.74 | 1.15 | 0.35 | 0.67 | 0.69 | 0.88 | 0.2 |
| 100–150 | 0.74 | 0.71 | 0.59 | 0.00 | 0.30 | 0.51 | 0.03 |
| 151–200 | 1.45 | 1.88 | 2.96 | 0.77 | 0.98 | 0.23 | 0.28 |
| 201–300 | 6.23 | 10.78 | 5.22 | 5.70 | 4.02 | 4.62 | 4.18 |
| 301–400 | 12.42 | 19.61 | 9.18 | 23.10 | 9.41 | 7.25 | 4.59 |
| 401–500 | 16.32 | 24.22 | 18.27 | 24.81 | 17.74 | 11.00 | 13.75 |
| 501–800 | 40.20 | 32.60 | 38.86 | 34.08 | 32.49 | 23.27 | 46.93 |
| 801–1000 | 12.08 | 5.11 | 15.00 | 6.99 | 16.60 | 16.39 | 12.27 |
| 1000 and more | 9.82 | 3.93 | 9.57 | 3.87 | 17.79 | 35.84 | 17.78 |

Note: Sample: 53,561

Source: Department of Policy, ACFTU (1999: 1329–30).

Moreover, whilst tenure is declining for the public sector, there is still a sense of more security there than in the private sector, and private sector wages need to contain an allowance for the 'risk' to future wages and pensions. Some well-qualified workers choose the opportunities of higher pay in the private economy, but many people have no such choice. Once a public employee loses their job they almost invariably must compete for a job in the private sector and take what they can get. Many younger workers and those from other provinces have few opportunities to get a job in the public sector. Thus, we should not take the development of the private sector as anything positive for the vast majority of workers. Surveys consistently show that given a choice, workers would like to work in SOEs (Li 2000), and an early tradition of married couples experimenting with the potential for higher pay in the private sector continues, so long as one partner maintains their tenure in a public enterprise.

*Table 4.4 Composition of Chinese workers and staff by ownership (1997) %*

|  |  | SOU | COU | POE | JOU | SHU | FIE | HTM |
|---|---|---|---|---|---|---|---|---|
| Education levels | Low | 2.53 | 5.21 | 2.48 | 3.26 | 2.19 | 1.41 | 0.41 |
|  | Middle | 63.87 | 80.99 | 74.59 | 85.35 | 64.02 | 68.95 | 78.79 |
|  | High | 33.59 | 13.79 | 22.94 | 22.8 | 31.14 | 29.63 | 21.25 |
| Age | Below 36 | 45.87 | 44.11 | 62.67 | 42.39 | 52.60 | 54.69 | 59.63 |
|  | 36–50 | 45.90 | 50.02 | 33.60 | 52.95 | 42.73 | 39.15 | 36.79 |
|  | Above 50 | 8.24 | 5.87 | 3.73 | 4.67 | 4.66 | 6.16 | 3.58 |

Notes: Educational levels: Low – illiterate and primary school; middle – junior and senior school, technical school, technical secondary school; high – college, university and above. Sample: 53,561

Source: Department of Policy, ACFTU (1999: 1293–1294, 1272).

The private sector system of industrial relations encourages and emphasizes individual contractual relations between employees and their employers, with little role given officially to unions, and no attempts to involve workers in management decision-making. Except for those transferred from public enterprises, most workers in POEs, and to a lesser extent FIEs (especially overseas Chinese owned), are rural (migrant) labourers, or young workers with lower educational levels and often less technical ability within their age cohort (see Table 4.4). Although the common experience of work would tend to instil collective consciousness among workers, these workers are rarely instilled with the rhetorical eminent position of the working class, which older SOE workers could bargain with. These workers are more likely to choose flight than fight, leaving their employer rather than confronting them and risking being branded a troublemaker. Thus, whilst Table 4.4 shows FIEs to place most emphasis on employing young and highly educated workers, this figure is likely to be slightly inflated. Not only are most highly educated graduates likely to be confined to certain professional and managerial job positions, but the data almost certainly undercounts migrant workers, who tend to work mainly in the private sector (especially FIEs and HTMs indicated in Table 4.4). Moreover, within the private sector generally there is a wide range of types of employment conditions depending on the type and purpose of the enterprise, making averages quite misleading. SOEs and the rest of the public sector have a more consistent employment pattern, employing older workers, but also the bulk of the skilled and educated workforce, even if they employ a decreasing proportion of the educated elite. This implies both the working of the labour market, in terms of the drying-up of demand for workers in the public sector, but still the preference among educated workers to work in the public sector if they can.

Chan (2001) has catalogued the problems, mainly in overseas Chinese-owned firms, but also acknowledges that POEs tend to be the worst employers. Some are little more than 'sweat shops' (Chan 2001), even worse than the textile industry of present-day New York (Ross 2001) or the industrial zones of poor countries bordering rich neighbours (Bowles and Dong 1999). In these enterprises, it is common that the management infringes the rights and interests of workers, and sometimes abuses amount to inhuman treatment and even torture (Chan 2001). The high rate of accidents in general, and a rapidly increasing number of reported industrial accidents (resulting in death of 699 people in the first half of 2000 alone) in POEs and FIEs has reportedly alarmed the CCP leadership (BBC 13 July 2000). In 2000, Wei Jianxing, chair of the ACFTU, commented on the continuing worsening of labour conditions in POEs:

> Currently, the events of infringing workers legitimate interests frequently occurred in POEs. Some employers arbitrarily withheld or delayed paying wages, some arbitrarily beat or insulted workers. In some enterprises, the working conditions were so adverse that some serious industrial accidents and occupational diseases were frequently caused. All these have developed to the extent of being intolerable.
> (Wei 2000)

The major reasons for the situation are as follows. First, the system of labour law in China is inadequate, as discussed in Chapter 2, in not giving either sufficient redress for wrongdoings or supervision by the government to ensure rules are adhered to. Second, workers in POEs have not developed much sense of collective consciousness, and most of them have not been unionized. Even where unions are established, as will be discussed in Chapter 5, employers generally control them. The one exception to this are the widely discussed (Chen 2001) clan or village networks which bind many of the migrant labourers into communities. Anecdotal evidence suggests these communities often act as grapevines for new jobs or occasionally form squads of thugs to beat up particularly disliked supervisors at neighbouring factories for friends working there. Third, officials in local government let matters slide because their personal interests are aligned with those of private entrepreneurs. Fourth, the abundant supply of cheap labour in China provides advantageous conditions for private entrepreneurs to pursue surplus value. For these reasons, most workers in POEs submit to humiliation in order just to keep their job.

*Table 4.5 Workers' evaluation of SOE management*

| Question | Negative view (%) | Positive view (%) |
|---|---|---|
| Management can accept workers' suggestions and requirements | 30.4 | 26.1 |
| Management uses fair standards for deciding promotion | 53.2 | 40.4 |
| The relationship between promotion and achievements | 39.5 | 7.8 |
| Fairness of the wage system | 3.0 | 57.4 |

Source: Qin and Wang (2001)

Song and Ding (1993) argue that workers in SOEs may have grown up with a strong sense of their 'rights' born out of the rhetorical master status they held, and consequently they remain highly conscious that increased management autonomy threatens to undermine those rights. A survey conducted in five large-sized SOEs in Zibo City, Shandong Province showed that in assessing management practices, workers gave more negative evaluation than positive ones of their bosses (Qin and Wang 2001), with the exception of wages (see Table 4.5).

It is thus possible to see two types of workers: those rather passively acquiescing to changes in the work environment, so long as they do not lead to redundancy, and an increasingly agitated employed or highly vulnerable labour group. This compliance is echoed in Sheehan's (1998) study of the history of labour movements in China, which also highlights the importance of vanguard labour movements in stimulating political responses from the state, and even in Chan's (2001) review of labour atrocities mostly in FIEs. Whilst Chan's findings can partly be answered by a genuine fear for personal safety and loss of self-esteem that appears to accompany some of the worst cases of labour abuse that exist in China, compliance in the public sector is more difficult to explain. Bu and Xu (2000) claim to find that Chinese SOE workers have a low expectation that their employers should provide secure employment in cases of poor business performance or for sick or lazy co-workers. Lee (1999), in a more convincing argument, discusses various reactions from resignation to one's fate (see also Blecher 2002), through passive resistance to flight (taking additional jobs or leaving their SOE altogether). However, if labour turnover is used as a measure of worker dissatisfaction,[71] then FIEs provide the most impressive examples, with anywhere from anecdotes of 100 per cent (Taylor 2001) to systematic surveys of 42 per cent in Guangzhou (White et al. 1999: 69) for workers, and as high as 63 per cent for technical and supervisory staff.

As discussed in Chapter 3, from the 1980s onwards new forms of enterprise developed that were initially of mixed ownership, involving public and private interests. However, gradually the emphasis has moved towards private ownership. Even in joint ventures and corporatized TVEs with heavy public ownership, there is an increasing emphasis on profitability. For POEs and among most FIEs, profits are paramount. The establishment and operation of internal governance structures also help to achieve clearer definitions of ownership, power and responsibility for the employers. This process has, with the assistance of increased labour market regulation, led to workers becoming 'employees', selling their labour for wages and various other returns (including some expectation of relative job security or insecurity). Nevertheless, whilst the status of employee has emerged, there are great differences among enterprises, and between different types of labour. Rather than a tendency towards a single unit price under capitalism, there is considerable variation in labour standards and employment conditions between different enterprises, depending on the public profile of the enterprise.

## CONCLUSION

The transition to a 'market economy' has brought back the idea that the price of labour is economically determined. Thus, we can analyse features or 'parties' of employers versus employees, workers versus cadres and labour versus capital in industrial relations terms. To go back to the example of wages – who decides the price of labour? Clearly it is now the employer and the employee, whether the employer is the sate or an FIE. The wage is not simply determined by the state, as there is now considerable autonomy in paying wages. Moreover, employees are implicitly at least also involved, because open labour markets mean disgruntled workers (with the power to do so) can leave to find work elsewhere. Wages are appallingly low, not because of state decree but because labour is weak vis-à-vis employers. This is partly because state policies advantage employers (both directly, limiting worker

---

[71] We should be careful in doing this, as there are other factors affect the level of labour turnover, such as access to labour markets, job choice and so on. However, as a rough comparison it is reasonable to compare the low rates of voluntary labour turnover within SOEs compared to the private sector.

rights in practice, promoting employer rights, but also indirectly, through taxes, economic, social and welfare policies, and so on). Of course, there is a 'grey area', where the state directly determines wages, in terms of defacto minimum wages, overtime pay calculations and so on, but there are supposed to be social policy measures, which restrict abuses at the margins. The fact that they have become benchmarks for maximum as well as minimum wages reflects the realities of power distribution in the labour market.

The development of new divisions of labour is complex and is still unfolding. At one level the privileged position of the urban SOE worker has been undermined by the market (Leung 1988) but the evidence that workers are still willing to fight to cling onto their position in their *danwei* is proof that the *danwei* remains important (Naughton 1997). COE and peasant workers of the planned period had at one level been freed from their interior position within the status system, with opportunities to move jobs, but in practice their sense of insecurity has seldom been compensated for by increased earnings. For this reason, a skilled or white-collar job in an FIE, or any job in an SOE, is still the main goal of the Chinese worker, for pragmatic reasons.

# 5. Trade unions

The major focus of industrial relations has been the role and capacity of trade (or labour) unions[72] to collectivize workers to pursue common or sectional membership interest. However, arguments over business unionism, seeming fragmentation of the working class in many industrialized countries and concerns over minimum labour standards has created much discussion over the role of unions in promoting both the individual and collective interests of workers and members. The official unions in China face similar dilemmas and problems in trying to establish a position for themselves in the emerging market economy. Moreover, as the previous three chapters have demonstrated, there is rapidly increasing fragmentation and divergence of interests between the various parties involved in industrial relations, which creates tremendous difficulties for the official unions to define a position for themselves.

The official trade union in China, the All China Federation of Trade Unions (ACFTU), is a single organizational federation that is being pulled in several directions at once and appears ill-suited to adapt to the changes around it. Many critics have argued that the ACFTU cannot be considered a trade union by democratic standards because it lacks the voluntarist and participatory principles of unions. Members may elect their union leader at the enterprise level, though this is a largely ineffectual procedure, but they certainly have no control over who is appointed at more senior levels in the union hierarchy. Moreover, participation is highly circumscribed because there are no effective channels for members to raise policy issues or influence decision-making, which is almost wholly a top-down process. The ACFTU is an integral part of the state apparatus, with direct links to the Party and an obligation to carry out state policy. As such, the interests of the ACFTU and the interests of trade union cadres personally are linked to the interests of the Party and the government, not workers and members. Nevertheless, the argument of this chapter is that unions play a necessary and crucial part of the emerging industrial relations scene in China.

---

[72] We usually use the term 'trade union', rather than 'labour union' as this is the official translation in China.

There are no viable alternatives to the ACFTU, however, it has some positive advantages in seeking to articulate workers' interests compared to other organs, existing or imaginary, and so there are a number of reasons why we should take it seriously. First, the ACFTU's constitutional obligation, reinforced in Trade Union Law (2001) is to represent workers' interests through peaceful means. It is thus a state-appointed agent of the workers, and is supposed to represent their interests. Second, the ACFTU has a tremendous political significance in a country that claims to be socialist, with its chairperson being among the top seven most powerful political leaders in China. Whilst the power of the ACFTU chairperson.does not derive from being head of the organisation the fact that a leading political figure was put into that position indicates that it is considered an important political instrument of Party rule, and the position is an important state position. Finally, the ACFTU faces many of the same problems and concerns of democratic and voluntarist unions of advanced industrialized economies as it tries to transform itself to be effectual in representing its members in the emerging market economy of China, which is itself an improvement on many unions in other countries of the world.

The chapter will first outline the changing role and function of the ACFTU in China. This will lead to a discussion of the different types of problems confronting the ACFTU as it seeks to find relevance in the present market economy. The chapter will return to assess the importance of the ACFTU and the significance of its crisis of identity in the conclusion.

## THE ACFTU IN THE PLANNED ECONOMY

The legally sanctioned monopolistic status of the ACFTU is a result of the particular history in which Chinese trade unions developed. The Chinese labour movement dates back to 1920, when the Shanghai Machinery Trade Union and Shanghai Textile Trade Union were established under the leadership of the 'Shanghai Communist Group'. These unions were the foundation of the present ACFTU, which was established by the CCP in 1925, at a time when China was still controlled by the Kuomintang government. Since the time that the trade unions of the Kuomintang withdrew to Taiwan and the People's Republic of China was established, there has been only one national trade union federation in Mainland China, under the control of the CCP.

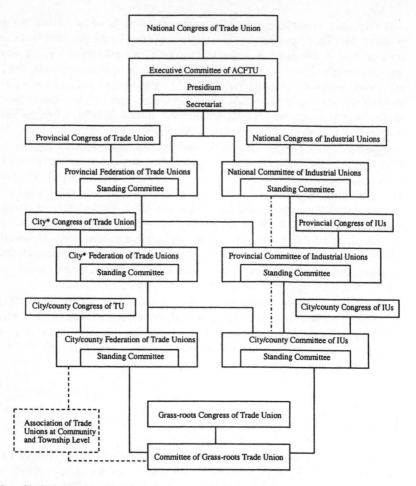

Note: City*: the municipality directly under the provincial government.
      The dotted lines and box refers to a new form of union organization being developed in a
      few cities at present. The Trade Union Law (2001), Article 10 officially recognized them.

Source: adapted and translated based on Chang and Zhang 1993: 227.

*Figure 5.1  Structure of the ACFTU*

## Structure and Organization of the ACFTU

As shown in Figure 5.1, under the organizational principle of democratic
centralism, the ACFTU utilizes a structure of combining organizations

formed along industrial lines with those formed within geographic boundaries. The highest leading bodies of the ACFTU are the National Congress of Trade Unions and the Executive Committee elected by the national congress. When the Executive Committee is in recess, the Presidium, consisting of a chairperson and a number of vice-chairpersons and members, exercise the powers of the Executive Committee. The Secretariat is set up under the Presidium and takes responsibility for the daily work of the ACFTU.

The local organs of the ACFTU include three levels: province (including autonomous regions and municipalities directly under the central government, such as Shanghai), city and county. According to the needs and structures of industries, the headquarters of the ACFTU and local unions, several industrial trade unions have also been established. These industrial trade unions adopt a similar system to those of the geographically organized unions, though with concentration in only some provinces, depending on the industry. The grass-roots unions include the trade unions in enterprises, undertakings and state organs. The grass-roots unions are set up according to an administrative system by which there can be only one grass-roots union in each administrative unit (enterprise, state organs and so on). The larger unions also set up branch trade unions and trade union groups for different work-sites of a single enterprise or unit. To the end of 2000, the number of grass-roots trade unions in the country totalled 850 000 with a total membership of 103 million (ACFTU 2001: 36). In Figure 5.1, the 'Association of Trade Unions' refers to a new form of union organization within the ACFTU structure (Fu et al. 2001). In some cities, these associations act as local trade unions with grass-roots unions reporting to them. In other places, these are a form of grass-roots union that directly organizes workers working in small POEs and FIEs, and can represent workers in collective consultation, negotiating directly with employers and employers' associations.

## *Characteristics of Chinese Trade Unions in a Planned Economy*

It is impossible to evaluate the Chinese trade unions without taking the historical background into account. Whilst some argue that the origins of industrial relations date back to the pre-Mao period (Frazier 2002) the present system and structure of Chinese trade unions was founded under the conditions of the planned economy. In the planned economy the government administered work units on the basis of public or collective ownership and the principle of distribution according to work. As the rhetorical representative of the interests of the whole society, the government superintended the process of economic operation through various administrative instruments and organs. In terms of labour relations in the urban economy,[73] the state was the employer of 'workers and staff' (*zhigong*), including workers, technicians and managerial staff. Enterprises were just 'workshops' of the 'state-factory'. The characteristic of labour relations was a vertical structure containing relations from state, through enterprises, to workers and staff. The intention was that the state represented the interests of enterprises while the enterprises represented the interests of workers and staff, and as such the interests of the state became the sovereign interests of the whole society. Trade unions, thus, had no need to be involved in labour relations since workers were not supposed to be a special interest group, and the trade unions were not supposed to represent workers either (that was the job of the enterprise directors). The trade unions were nothing more than assistants or subsidiary departments of government organs to support enterprise management. Their basic function was to assist government or enterprises' management to mobilize and organize workers and staff to fulfil production assignments of the planned economy. There was no intention that trade unions were meant to be independent organizations.

There are two main reasons for Chinese trade unions being given this subsidiary role. On the one hand, the experience of the Soviet Union provided an early role model for China. For example, in the early days of the Cadre School of the ACFTU (predecessor of the China Labour College, founded in 1949 before the establishment of the People's Republic of China), major courses were taught by experts from the Soviet Union. In a textbook entitled 'Tutorial of Trade Union Work of the Soviet Union' written by a professor from the former Soviet Union, Li Lisan, chair of the ACFTU at that time, wrote the prologue and highly praised the experiences of trade union work of the Soviet Union. On the other hand, the unions continued, the tradition of trade unions formed in the early revolutionary bases during the civil and anti-colonial wars. As a part of the 'mass work' of the Party, the trade unions mobilized and organized the masses in order to fulfil the central tasks of the Party (China Labour College 1993: 4–7). In the middle of the 1950s, combining the experiences of the Soviet Union and practices in China, the ACFTU put forward a 'three-in-one' work guideline called 'taking production as the central task, and paying attention to workers' living and education'.

As the Party had selective membership, during the period of the planned economy it sponsored a number of mass organizations, such as the Youth League, Women's Association and the trade unions. The unions met the

---

[73] Chinese society may be characterized as having a dual structure, divided by urban and rural areas. Before reform, the economy in rural areas was dominated by an autarkic economy without modern industrial relations.

objectives designed by the CCP through organizing labour contests, technical innovations and increased production drives and propagandizing workers' political and ideological thinking. Moreover, the unions took on direct management of such activities as organizing sports and entertainment events for workers, supervising the implementation of occupational health and safety and providing sanatoriums, rest homes and public welfare services for workers (Wang 1992: 325–91). Thus, the Chinese trade union organization should be seen as administration-oriented (as opposed to collectivist or representative) organizations that were controlled by the Party and government through a top-down bureaucratic system of responsibility to superiors. This organization had a highly centralized internal structure that emphasized that the unions should assist management in production and improve the welfare of staff and workers where this was possible.

Generally, in the planned economy period, the trade unions had not been truly an organization of the workers, but served as a 'transmission belt' between the Party and workers and staff, with the aim of realizing political and economic goals. However, the trade unions still played an active role in promoting economic development and social stability, improving the welfare of workers and staff, caring for workers' spare time and so on (Chen 1999; Fang and Lin 1990). This meant that the unions were useful to managers, workers and the government, and undertook activities which would be difficult for any of the other parties to have undertaken as easily.

## CONTRADICTIONS IN ACFTU'S REFORM

The present role of the ACFTU has been analysed by many scholars, and these may be categorized into three basic approaches: corporatist (for example Chan 1993), Party organ (for example White 1996) and intermediary (for example Zhang 1997). Each approach will be briefly outlined in turn.

Chan (1993) examined the role of the official Chinese trade union movement in the 1950s and 1980s and concluded that the unions' role was 'functional corporatist representation', operating within a context of a corporatist-oriented social development. Chan (1993: 35) attributes this orientation to two elements: institutional demands from above, and workers' independent spontaneous protection of their interests from below. Chan notes that before 1989 the ACFTU underwent a series of changes, including more active participation in national policy-making and pursuing initiatives for the legal protection of workers' interests. At the same time, using various opportunities and in different ways, cadres of the trade unions begun to see their primary roles as protecting workers' interests and wished to separate themselves from the state's administrative structure (Chan 1993: 36–38).

Chan also finds that the economic reform in the 1980s had brought about two important impacts on workers. First, the income differentials between workers and other social groups were felt by workers to be unfair. Second, the introduction of Taylorist management practices, such as tightening labour discipline and raising production norms, had become one of the main causes of worsening management-labour relations and labour unrest (1993: 41–2). After 1989, the Party-state made some concession to the ACFTU, in allowing it to continue to expand and consolidate its power and in seeking to match the interests of the workers. When this process of liberalization reaches a certain point, Chan suggests the state corporatist system will be changed (1993: 59). Then workers will be able effectively to change the existing state corporatist structure by using the protective legal structure that now only exists on paper. In case a democratized process of state corporatism does not materialize in China, in Chan's view, more social unrest may occur. One of the possibilities is that the conservatives will become weaker and may give up their will to dominate, preferring to form an alliance with the workers for their survival. In this case, the autonomous trade unions would be recognized and a genuine form of societal corporatism might emerge (1993: 59).

White (1996), on the basis of fieldwork examining Chinese trade unions, denies the existence of state or societal corporatism or civil society. White was much more concerned with the dominance of the CCP in China, and outlined a context in which the trade unions play the role of policy-makers and their position in a triadic structure of power in enterprises, involving the CCP, management and the unions. In his opinion, even though the trade unions gained some role in decision-making at all levels, and take part in the formulation of state policies, the element of increased union autonomy that developed before 1989 had been extinguished after June 1989 (1996: 443). At the same time, the officials of local Party and government organs usually held simultaneous positions in trade unions. The trade unions, therefore, achieve some limited influence over reform policies at the cost of a high level of dependence on the Party (1996: 445). Therefore, it would be difficult to describe this post-Tiananmen arrangement as a corporatist relationship (1996: 445), but one in which the CCP has re-established its former dominant position over industrial relations in general and the unions in particular. Based on previous research, White finds the progress towards democratizing enterprise unions very limited. Within the triadic structure of power in enterprises, management has taken a dominant position. Because of the reform measures, unions are often ignored by workers when they try to deal with a disagreement with their supervisors, most chairpersons of unions are not directly elected by the membership, and the new reforms, such as 'modern enterprise system', puts them in danger of being further marginalized (1996: 449). In considering the development of unofficial workers' organizations and the reappearance of a small band of labour activists in the mid-1990s, White (1996: 450–1) argues that these trends increase the Party's concerns about social and political stability and push it towards a greater reliance on the official trade unions to maintain labour peace. In this context, there will be the possibility of a new deal between the Party and the ACFTU. This would be a type of 'tripartite corporatism' involving the state, business and unions, and would operate at micro, meso and macro levels. The trade unions would keep their close relationship with the Party and retain their monopoly position in representing workers' interests while realizing a degree of autonomy within strict legal limitation (1996: 451).

Zhang (1997) defined the Chinese trade unions as an intermediary organ between the state and workers. Moreover, Zhang (1997: 139) argues that within the process of reform the official unions developed dual roles: to link workers and the state bureaucracy by playing the role of a transmission belt, and to link workers and the management by acting as a mediator. In this way the unions act to restore social cohesion by counteracting the growing divisions between the state and society, and the general segmentation of society. Zhang (1997: 140) argues that, with the government retreating from direct administration of enterprises, a gap between workers and the state appeared. Moreover, as mangers separated from workers as an organizational category, there was a rising division of interest. These gaps need to be compensated for if they are not to threaten social stability. The role of the trade unions as a transmission belt, according to Zhang, stresses bottom-up transmission, communicating workers' complaints and requirements to the state bureaucracy. This role can be seen in some of the speeches of top leaders and the fact that trade unions actually get involved in drafting some regulations concerning the interests of worker. Within the enterprise, the grass-roots unions either play a role of mediator or serve as a bridge between the management and workers, negotiating within the former in the capacity as workers' representatives, and explaining management policies to the latter (Zhang 1997: 145). In Zhang's view, the intermediary role of trade unions makes it hard for them to fit the framework of 'corporatism' or civil society'. In contrast to the organizations under state corporatism, intermediary organizations symbolize an expansion of the societal power into some places that were either previously occupied by the state or newly emerged in the reform (1997: 151). Without voluntarism and a high degree of autonomy, the intermediary role of trade unions also does not represent the characteristic features of civil society (1997: 151). This role, in Zhang's opinion, is just a result of the Chinese way of doing things – gradualism and orderliness (1997: 152).

These three views are very different, not only in their understanding of the present situation of the official unions in China and their incumbent roles, but also in their predictions for the likely trajectory of industrial relations in to the future. Chan and White provide opposing interpretations of the trajectory of China, with Chan emphasizing the opportunities for liberal democratic development (albeit with a Japanese corporatist branding) whilst White argues the CCP will seek to maintain hegemonic control. Zhang, however, whilst appearing to regress the argument into clichéd Chinese state rhetoric, allows for a more dialectical view of the problems facing the ACFTU both in defining its role within the authoritarian political context and as an organization, which provides its cadres with personal jobs, careers and motivational dynamics.

## Reform of the ACFTU

In the process of the transformation of the economic system, the former functions and role of the Chinese trade union system have encountered a number of severe challenges. These problems may be grouped into four main issues. First, the trade unions can no longer maintain their former status of 'assistants' or 'subsidiary departments' due to the development of different types of enterprises. There is no longer a single production plan to support or type of enterprise to assist. Second the trade unions have lost their original reason for existence, as their status and role is no longer assured by state or management. This is because the function of production has become the 'professional' concern of management, as opposed to a political concern of all. Third, the traditional corporatist mode of conflict suppression and resolution, in which the trade unions played a minor role, has gone. Wide and easily identifiable conflicts of interest have arisen between capital and labour, between managers and workers and between employers and employed. The unions, having reduced their function of assisting production, are faced with the need to cling onto the other function of helping the Party to maintain social stability as a mass organization. This would appear to force the ACFTU to take a position in relation to emerging overt conflict and to seek to define a role for itself in conflict resolution. Fourth, the trade unions are faced with organizational problems, in which the administrative style of disseminating policies and action plans from the top of the union hierarchy to the bottom, which itself takes directives from the Party, cannot adequately cope with the much more complex industrial relations of the market economy. It is quite evident that Chinese trade unions cannot survive and develop if they still stick to the old model. Chang (1993a, 1993b) argues that the unions have to reform their methods of working and define their own role so that they can join the system of industrial relations in a market economy.

The reform of Chinese trade unions was first considered in 1978, when the CC-CCP put forward the goals of 'achieving the four modernizations (of agriculture, industry, national defence, and science and technology) (CC-

CCP 1987). This set out to extend managerial power and establish the system of 'overall responsibility by factory managers led by the Party Committee' in SOEs. At the 9th National Congress of the ACFTU, on behalf of the CC-CCP, Deng Xiaoping stressed that:

> In order to accomplish the four modernizations, all our enterprises, without exception, must adopt democratic forms of management, combining them with centralized leadership [and therefore] the trade unions of each enterprise will function as the executive organs [and thus the trade unions] will not be superfluous as some people think they are. (1983: 125)

Deng also required that the trade unions:

> Must get the workers to regard them as truly their own organizations, which they can trust and which speak for them and work in their interests... [they] must maintain close ties with the workers, [and] must be models of democracy. (1983: 126)

It is clear that the central government expected that the trade unions could shoulder the responsibility of mobilizing workers and staff and somewhat restrain the management who had just gained some autonomy in decision-making powers. Meanwhile, the central government worried about the trade unions' organizational character of being only responsible to management, while being divorced from the workers. Deng Xiaoping criticized this working style more severely than ever. He even pointed out that the trade unions 'must not be the organizations whose leaders lie to workers, lord it over workers or work for their own private interests while living off the members' dues' (1983: 128).

Deng's idea of 'speaking for and serving workers', 'setting up close ties with the workers' and 'implementing democracy' became the goals of reform for the official Chinese trade unions. According to these goals, as its' 11th National Congress in October 1988, the ACFTU established four functions of 'protecting' the legitimate rights and interests of workers and staff, 'constructing' the socialist economy by mobilizing workers and staff, 'participating' in the management of state and social affairs as well as the management of enterprises, and 'educating' workers and staff to raise their ideological, political, cultural and technical levels. The 'Tentative Plans of Trade Unions Reform' was also put forward at this congress (Department of Trade Unions Science 1993: 215–6). The significance of this congress is that it took protecting workers' interests as the primary and basic function of trade unions and changed the former three-in-one work guideline. It also defined the mass-oriented and democracy-oriented goals for trade union reform.

Moreover, it instituted democratic ideals of union organizational forms, particularly by instituting an association system, whereby lower unions form associations of higher unions, and a delegate system, whereby lower unions send delegates to higher-level forums, as the organizational principle of trade unions. The purpose of these organizational changes was supposed to lead to greater control from the bottom of the union structure, and from members, and replace the previously existing top-down hierarchical structure.

After the Tiananmen protests in 1989, there appears to have been considerably less support for this line of reform from among the top leadership. Along with the slowing down of reform in the period from 1989 to 1992, the 'Tentative Plan of Trade Unions Reform' was not implemented. In general, the trade unions' reform in this period was still restricted to renewed political subordination of the ACFTU to the Party, leaving little change in the unions' involvement in industrial relations.

From the beginning of the 1990s, along with the deepening reform of the economic and labour system, the ACFTU has renewed its efforts to participate in the transforming process of China's political economy, especially in industrial relations, in order to both influence the development of the market economy and to avoid its own obsolescence. At the 12$^{th}$ National Congress of the ACFTU in 1993, Wei Jianxing, a member of the Standing Committee of the Political Bureau of the CC-CCP, was elected to chair the ACFTU. He has been enhancing trade unions' reform through promoting laws, such as the Labour Law (1995), involvement in the implementation of the modern corporate system, and putting forward the 'General Thinking of Trade Unions' Work' (*gonghui zongti silu*) in December 1994 (Wei 1995: 14–20). The 'General Thinking' required the trade unions to take part in and coordinate industrial relations activities as the representative of labourers, primarily by promoting the development of protecting labourers' interests though the system of collective contracts. In this way Wei established that trade union reform would clearly follow the principles of market orientation and provide the unions with a degree of autonomy to act in workers' interests.

In the process of implementing the 'General Thinking of Trade Unions' Work', the ACFTU has been changing its style and system of work. Whilst there are no tangible changes at the national level, the organizational structure and activities of local and enterprise-based (grass-roots) unions have started to change, especially in local and industrial trade unions at the city level. These unions have increased their efforts to set up trade union networks in their localities, and to establish that the role of the unions is to represent workers and to give priority to protecting labourers' rights and interests in work. Moreover, there are even attempts to experiment with elections of union chairpersons directly by union members.[74]

With the rise in the number of enterprises and employment in the non-public sectors of the economy, the ACFTU responded by setting out a principle called 'where there are workers, there must be trade unions' (ACFTU 1999: 448–9), which kicked off a nationwide organizing drive. At the same time, the ACFTU also started to set up grass-roots unions in communities in urban areas and in villages and towns in rural areas to organize workers in newly built smaller POEs and FIEs (Fu et al. 2001).

## Chinese Trade Unions in Contradiction

The Chinese trade unions' function of protecting the interests of workers is stipulated in the amended Trade Union Law of the People's Republic of China (2001). The law defines that 'the basic function of trade unions is to protect the legitimate rights and interests of workers' and staff (Article 2), and the ACFTU and its subordinate unions represent and protect legitimate rights and interests of workers and staff in accordance with law (Article 6). Compared with the Trade Union Law of 1992, which emphasizes 'two protections' (of representing and protecting both the specific interests of the workers and the general interests of the people), the amended law is much more comprehensive and specific. However, although trade unions' status in labour relations has been provided in law clearly, it is still different in the actual situation. In terms of adjustment of industrial relations, it is difficult to implement the legal provisions relating to trade unions because there have been no reforms to the Chinese political system; despite economic reform, a strong degree of state planning remains within the overall market system. The actual situation means that the trade unions must continue to play multiple roles beside that of representing the interests of workers.

Chinese trade unions exist in two modes of industrial relations, based in the two dominant types of economic system (public and private economic sectors). On the one hand, Chinese industrial relations have become more and more market oriented, with clearer identities and divisions of interests between the two parties (employers and employees). The former vertical

---

[74] These reform experiments were carried out in Shekou Development Zone and Baoan District of Shenzhen, in Lishu County of Jilin Province and Huludao City of Liaoning Province. Although these local reforms appear to have been successful in promoting interest among union members, it is difficult to extend the experiences nationwide for many reasons. There are problems of employer interference, reluctance by union cadres, differences among potential voters and so on. Nevertheless, a precedent has been set and, given political will, national elections may follow, once the bugs in the system are ironed out. One 'bug', however, is how the CCP can ensure its control over the system within the context of open elections. Lessons may be learned from these experiments and from recent village elections, but widespread elections are unlikely in the near future.

administrative labour relations have changed into sets of supposedly horizontal economic relations between 'voluntaristic' parties to economic exchanges. The economic and social conditions in which trade unions continue to be subordinated to government and management have changed, providing a background for the transformation of status and functions of trade unions. On the other hand, a number of factors in the present situation in China make it impossible for the ACFTU to act as a singularly focused organization to represent and protect the interests and demands of workers. The reasons for this are discussed below.

First, China has not accomplished the transformation into a market economy. Although market rules have been introduced into SOEs and state-holding corporations, the government, to a great extent, still intervenes in enterprise-level industrial relations. For example, no matter whether these enterprises make profits or not, they are required to reduce the number of employees according to specific instructions from superior government agencies. In this case, the enterprise unions are unable to oppose this policy on behalf of laid-off workers.

Second, the Chinese political system has not changed, while the economic reform is deepening. Since the Tiananmen event in 1989, the CCP has strengthened its control over trade unions and has not relaxed this control even when it started to return to its policy of stimulating economic reform from around 1992. This can easily be seen in the Trade Union Law of 1992, in which union subordination to the leadership of the Party was reflected indirectly through 'trade unions must abide by the constitution, and take the constitution as essential rules of action' (Article 2). The amended Trade Union Law of 2001 supplements this with provisions concerning the leadership of the Party over the trade unions. It provides:

> Trade unions shall obey and defend the Constitution and follow the Constitution as the basic guide for their activities. They shall take economic construction as the centre, adhere to the socialist road, uphold people's democratic dictatorship, abide by the leadership of the Chinese Communist Party, adhere to Marxism-Leninism, Mao Zedong Thought, and Deng Xiaoping theory, persevere in reform and opening [the economy], and conduct trade union work independently and voluntarily in accordance with the Trade Union Charter (Article 4).

In SOEs that have established a 'modern' corporate structure, the Party organs have placed themselves as the leaders, with management and unions in subordinate power positions. Nevertheless, the CC-CCP stressed that the Party organs in SOEs shall strengthen the leadership and instruction of mass organizations such as the trade unions (CC-CCP 1997). In this way, the position of the trade unions is not only an issue relevant to micro-level industrial relations, but also to macro-level politics. This centralized system gives Chinese trade unions a rich political colour. Trade union cadres at all levels must be responsible to the Party organs since their role is designated by the Party organs.

Third, although the Trade Union Law of 2001 makes headway in the aspect of trade unions' functions, the law does not abandon the 'two protections' that the traditional system required trade unions to perform. It still stipulates that 'protecting the interests of workers as well as the general interests of the people' is the basic task of trade unions (Article 6, Trade Union Law 2001). In fact, this is self-contradictory, reflecting the features of transition. This self-contradiction prevents the trade unions from performing their function of representing workers' interests.

We can conclude that the aim of trade union reform was to transform the unions from 'transmission belts' to representatives of workers. Whilst the ACFTU has made some headway in this direction over the last decade, the trade union system and its situation have not changed greatly thus far. The reason for this relates to the relationship between the ACFTU and the CCP at senior levels as well as the relationships between the trade unions and employers (management) at the enterprise level. We still now examine this in more detail.

## TRADE UNIONS' EXTERNAL RELATIONS

Much has been discussed already in the chapter about the way the CCP defines the power and authority of the ACFTU and the general context of trade unionism in China. This section will address more specific structures of relations between the CCP and the unions and go on to discuss relations between lower-level unions and enterprise management.

### *Relations between the ACFTU and the CCP*

As the Chinese trade unions confront role-conflicts (Ng and Warner 1998), scholars pay particular interest to the relationship between trade unions and the Party (for instance, Biddulph and Cooney 1993; Chan 1993; Coll 1993; Fewsmith 1994; K. Jiang 1996; Tang et al. 1993; Walder 1989, 1991; Warner 1995, 1996a; White 1996; Zhu 1995). They identify two contradictory tendencies that have developed as a result of economic reform. On the one hand, the SOEs have had their ties with the government greatly reduced and their independence enhanced. On the other hand, the trade unions have continued to be subordinated to the authority of the Party (Child 1994,

O'Leary 1998). In other words, the autonomy of trade unions does not mean that the CCP-State favours polarization or confrontation between trade unions and itself (Zhang 1997). Even as the ACFTU tried to reform itself in the past few years, the state and Party placed several limits on how far this could go (K. Jiang 1996). This control extends to the appointment of the heads of trade unions, in which such persons should in practice be approved by the local Party organs, in an attempt to ensure such persons are not troublemakers (Coll 1993). Still under this control, the trade unions continue to be required to undertake a number of functions, such as motivating workers and providing material and ideological support for their welfare, training workers in production techniques, and least of all, protecting the interests of workers to some degree (Zhu and Campbell 1996). In Chinese official thinking, autonomy is only a means rather than the end (Zhang 1997) of reform. Leung (1993) summarizes that 'without critical political transformation, it is difficult to find the basis for fundamental change in the nature of the union, from that of a Party administrative agency, to that of a bargaining representative'.

The basic political principle of Chinese trade unions is to accept the leadership of the CCP's organs at all levels (Article 4, Trade Union Law 2001). The CCP's basic requirement for trade unions' work is that the ACFTU should keep its own policies and activities consistent with those of the CC-CCP, while the subordinate trade unions (for example at provincial and city levels) should be consistent with the Party organs at their respective levels. Some overseas scholars argued that Chinese trade unions 'had several times challenged the Party-state in order to strive for independence and autonomy since the 1980s' (K. Jiang 1996; also Sheehan 1998). This conclusion is somewhat subjective. In history, some top leaders of the ACFTU, such as Li Lisan and Lai Ruoyu (the former chairpersons criticized for allegedly wishing to 'contend for powers with the Party' in 1950s) had put forward opinions different from the CC-CCP. However, their starting point is not to oppose or challenge the Party, but to implement the workers' movement guidelines of the CCP, but with a different interpretation than the mainstream views at the time.[75] Since the 1980s, there have been no union leaders who can put forward a systematic theory or line of argument for the appropriate role of the ACFTU in the way Li Lisan and Lai Ruoyu were able to do. We can indicate that Chinese trade unions have not conflicted with the Party-state because the ACFTU has never (up to now) opposed the Party's discipline or ideological line. The only conflicts that do occur are over methods of achieving CCP objectives, not the objectives themselves, and such conflicts since the 1980s have been very minor.

In fact, trade unions at all levels have very close relationships with the

---

[75] In the 1980s, the CC-CCP announced the rehabilitation of Li Lisan and Lai Ruoyu.

Party organs. In general, the Party organs decide upon who will be nominated to be trade union leaders before election takes place at the trade union congresses.[76] The chairpersons of trade unions at all levels can always become members of the Party committees, even of the standing committees, and become the backbone of the leadership of the Party. The relations between trade unions and administrative organs at all levels are very close too. The post and treatment of major leaders of the trade unions is decided according to their administrative level. In accordance with such regulations, chairpersons of trade unions in enterprises should hold the same rank as the deputy-director of the enterprise or deputy-secretary of the Party organ. Quite a number of senior local unionists have become the deputy leaders of the People's Congress or Political Consultative Conference at the same level.

With the deepening of reform and the resultant rise of sensitive social conflicts, the trade unions have been redefined by the state as an intermediary (Zhang 1997) or as 'anti-shock valves' (Warner 1995). This role reflects the state's necessity to allow some intermediary organizations to share their pressures from society and in order to carry economic reform without destabilizing society (Zhang 1997), which would in turn threaten the position of the CCP. These two roles led to a vague status of trade unions because they are expected to function for both workers and management within enterprises, and for workers and the Party in society in general (Biddulph and Cooney 1993; Warner 1995; Wu and Chang 1995).

However, within the trade union, the internal mechanism of mutual restraint between the cadres and the members is quite weak. The major reason for the weakness is that the cadres of trade unions must be responsible to the Party and the administration. The promotion and career tracks of trade union cadres are not decided by union members, but by the Party and administrative organs. This means that the members have little or no relation with the union in their enterprise or locality and, consequently, the unions have a weak organizational basis in enterprises. The ACFTU is a huge organization with numerous grass-roots unions and members, but it is not intrinsically powerful; it is just a huge organization.

---

[76] The trade union leader nominee recommended by the Party organs usually wins the election in trade union congresses, but there are exceptions. For example, in the 9th National Congress of the ACFTU in 1988, Wan Shaofen, the former deputy secretary of the Party Committee of Jianxi Province as well as the nominee for vice-chairperson of the ACFTU, presided over the opening ceremony but lost the election as a member of the Executive Committee and had to be transferred to another post. However, in the reform of trade unions, a type of direct election of chairperson has been emerging in some small-sized grass-roots trade unions. Namely, the chairperson of the trade union is elected by union members directly, without any recommended candidate.

## *Relations between the Trade Unions and Employers*

Compared with the Trade Union Law of 1992, the amended law of 2001 provides more rights to trade unions. In this law, there are 16 provisions concerning the rights of trade unions, including rights to participate in democratic management on behalf of workers and staff, to collective consultation and signing collective contracts with employers, to protect workers' right of employment, remuneration for labour, occupational health and safety and labour disputes settlements, and so on (Articles 19–34). However, in practice, the status, functions, rights and the activities of trade unions vary significantly between types of enterprises.

In SOEs, the status of trade unions has not changed from the subordinate position as a department of the management of enterprises. As such, the union must assist the management to fulfil reform tasks required by the superior administration. In recent years, SOEs have laid off large numbers of workers due to pressures from the central government's policy of 'increasing efficiency by downsizing staff', and from the need to reduce loss-making activities. Therefore, the unions in such public sector organizations take on the role of supervising and helping laid-off workers at enterprise level. They are in charge of the 're-employment centres' in SOEs, delivering living expenses and offering training to laid-off workers. Besides this, they are responsible for organizing some new activities relating to democratic management, such as 'opening corporate affairs', appraising managers and reporting the expenses used in entertaining business guests and so on, as internal financial auditors. At the same time, they are also responsible for caring for workers' welfare, organizing sports and entertainment activities and other work they traditionally have always done. In recent years, according to the Trade Union Law, the system of collective contracts has been carried out in most SOEs (see Chapter 8), and this involves the union in a good deal of administration of the system.

In corporations with mixed public and private ownership, the identities of the actors in labour relations are more clearly defined and separated. In these corporate enterprises, property rights and managerial rights are guaranteed by a governance structure composed of the councils of shareholders, the board of directors, the board of supervisors and managerial ranks. Consequently, a mixture of market rules and managerial demands govern labour relations, but the public element also encourages labour and collective contracts and internal regulations of these enterprises are still controlled to some extent according to public sector criteria. Labour rights, however, are usually neglected, while the status and function of trade unions is often left unclear. In comparison, in the state-owned and state-holding corporations, most grass-roots unions can maintain their position if they existed before restructuring.

In newly founded enterprises with significant private ownership or ambiguous public ownership rights, the trade unions are invariably weak or non-existent. Since the governance structure of corporations is not consistent with that of SOEs, there have been contradictions between the new structure formed (the councils of shareholders, board of directors, board of supervisors) and the old structure (of the Party committee, WCs and trade unions). As a result, the trade unions cannot find a secure and meaningful position between these two countermanding structures. In order to adapt to theses pressures, the ACFTU put forward the idea that it should reflect and protect workers' interests through establishing the systems of employee directors and supervisors, the council of employee shareholders, collective contracts and so on. However, the regular work tasks of grass-roots unions in these corporations remains relegated to assisting management in organizing production, building a corporate enterprise culture, and organizing sports and entertainment activities.

Except for a few larger-sized European and North American companies, employers dominate labour relations in the private sector (Chang et al. 2001). The decision-making processes related to employment conditions and other labour issues are exclusively managerial concerns, excluding participation from either workers or the trade unions. Moreover, the employers usually control the grass-roots unions, if such unions exist at all, and if independent from management, their survival is precarious. In recent years, the ACFTU gave priority to the activity named 'loving each other and appraising each other' (*shuangai shuangping*), which is a colourful slogan to mean unions should appraise excellence in workers defined in terms of their 'loving' (loyalty) to their enterprise and appraising excellence in bosses 'loving' (looking after the interests of) workers. Within the ACFTU, there are different views about whether this activity should be given much emphasis in the work of trade unions in POEs.

Since 1996, the ACFTU has focused its attention on implementing collective contracts (see Chapter 8). Due mainly to resistance or opposition from FIEs and POEs, trade unions are still hindered in their implementation of their bargaining rights. Management in these forms of enterprises usually utilize one of two strategies to achieve their aims: rejection or domination. Both FIE and POE management generally simply reject requests to bargain collectively. Thus far, the ACFTU has not found an effective method to deal with this problem, and the labour law provides little support or guidance. In cases where management permitted negotiation, few have been willing to bargain in good faith. In reality, many of the collective contracts negotiated in these enterprises result from a process that is heavily controlled by employers. This strategy of employer domination unfortunately is often overlooked by the ACFTU, which is concerned primarily with the number of contracts that are negotiated, rather than the quality of those contracts.

## Status of Chinese Trade Unions

The legal and administrative means available to trade unions to protect workers' interests are inadequate (Coll 1993; Zhu 1995). Whilst the trade unions have been permitted to participate in the policy-making process on different levels, trade unions do not have enough power to bring action against managers or employers who abuse their workers. Workers, and thus the unions, lack not only the right to strike, but also the right to almost any form of overt collective displays of power (Ng and Warner 1998, and also Chapter 7). Biddulph and Cooney (1993) examined the regulations concerning unions' activities and came to the same conclusion. They found that, even though the trade unions have the status to supervise the health and safety of firms, this status usually only involves the right to make criticisms and suggestions according to government regulations. In terms of dismissal, Granick (1990) found that the enterprise trade union presented no obstacle to such managerial action.

On the one side, under the political and legal controls discussed above, Chinese trade unions are responsible not only to the workers, but also to the Party, the government and enterprises (entrepreneurs).[77] On the other side, they have no intrinsic power to serve any of these stakeholders. Their multiple status and functions make it difficult for them to play the role of protecting workers' interests. In reality, they serve at best as a coordinator between employers and labourers. Therefore, Chinese trade unions' status in industrial relations is neither that of the purposeful subordination to enterprise management of the planned economy era, nor the representative of labourers within the general logic of market economics.

In Chinese enterprises, the grass-roots unions are supposed to take up a position which places them between employers and workers as go-betweens.[78] At the macro level, the structure of actors can be shown in Figure

---

[77] In reality, the trade unions are responsible to the government and to the Party at the same time. In theory, there are somewhat different relationships between the trade unions and both organizations. In theory, the relationship between the trade unions and the Party organ may be thought of as the union *subordinating* itself to the Party. The relationship between the trade unions and the government may be considered as the unions *cooperating* with the government. Through their cooperation, both trade unions and government are responsible to the Party.

[78] Legal provisions and the fact that the grass-roots unions do not often take a neutral position between the workers and management mean that the workers rarely trust them. 'The Regulations of the Worker' Congress in State-Owned Industrial Enterprise' (issued by the State Council in 1986) provides that the chairpersons of trade unions in publicly owned enterprises should join the leading group of their enterprises and enjoy the treatment of a 'deputy post' at the same level. This provision, apart from its effect in advancing grass-roots unions' status, can also make them more administrative and more dependent on the management. In fact, it is not uncommon that the chairpersons of trade unions attend hearing meetings for labour arbitration on behalf of management, and seek to oppose worker demands.

5.2 to represent the position of trade unions in industrial relations in China. The power structure within the enterprises forms a triangle between the government, the employers and workers (represented by trade unions) to adjust the relations between parties, but one in which the government is the most powerful actor. However, in contemporary China, the structure of the actors is like a 'cross' formed by the four parties, in which the trade unions are responsible to the government, enterprises and workers at the same time, thus reflecting their multiple status and roles.

Compared with the theoretical structure of actors in a market economy, the major difference in the structure of China is that the trade unions have not sided with the workers. Therefore, currently within Chinese enterprises, industrial relations are composed of three parties: employers, trade unions and workers. The basic function of the trade unions is to coordinate the relations between workers and employers.[79] The 'structure of three actors' in a market economy is changing into a 'structure of four actors' in China. Although the tripartite mechanism is being set up in China,[80] the workers are excluded from this mechanism because the trade unions are not representative of the workers.

At both the micro and macro levels, the system of industrial relations in China places on the official trade union multiple functions and responsibilities to meet the interests of multiple parties, including workers, enterprise management and the Party-state. Certainly, in the hypothetical event that there were no conflicts of interest between these parties, the contradiction of this multiple status would not be important. Indeed, this is the view rhetorically maintained as a continuance from the planned economy, when such conflicts were more narrowly defined. However, as in reality there are conflicts between the employers (entrepreneurs and/ or the government) and workers, the multiple status of trade unions cannot meet with the requirements of each party. As a result, the trade unions often uphold the stand of employers or the government, as economic reform is the dominant overall objective of the Party-state in China.

The confusion in the structure of Chinese industrial relations reflects a period of transition. In general, within the context of advanced industrialized market economies, the significance of trade unions' existence is, as a collective force, to balance the power of capital and protect the interests of

---

[79] The function and status of trade unions at the enterprise level can be seen in the composition of Labour Dispute Mediation Committees in enterprises. This committee consists of the representatives of management, the trade union and workers, and is chaired by the chairperson of the trade union (see Chapter 7).

[80] In 'The Ninth Five-Year Plan of labour undertaking development and long-term goals in the 201s' (21 May 1996), the MoL stated its intention to establish a tripartite mechanism composed of the labour administrative departments, the associations of employers and the trade unions at all levels to coordinate labour relations.

members. Rather than being the representative of workers, the role of Chinese trade unions is more like that of a neutral organization, such as the neutral 'commonweal party'[81] in the Japanese industrial relations adjustment mechanism. The problem is that if workers have no representatives, they will find their own leaders and establish informal organizations of their own. However, it is impossible for Chinese workers to receive protection under the law if they create another organization outside the authority of the ACFTU, due to the existing legal provisions restricting membership to ACFTU affiliated unions. Therefore, they have to protect own interests through informal networks and spontaneous actions. The situation is unfavourable to both workers and the state. In order to avoid this situation, one of the alternatives the ACFTU must face up to is how to become the real representative of workers.

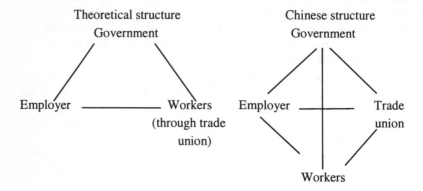

*Figure 5.2 Structure of actors: a macro system of industrial relations*

The trend of industrial relations development in China is not what is called the 'structure of industrial relations with Chinese characteristics', but instead, the existing structure of actors is one with a high degree of ambiguity, uncertainty and latent pressures for rapid change. Some scholars have argued that Chinese trade unions are functional organizations rather than representative organizations (Feng 2001). This view may reflect the present situations of Chinese trade unions, but this pattern cannot remain the organizational basis of unions for much longer. Theoretically, the market

---

[81] In general, the commonweal members in the Japanese Labour Committee consist of government officials, experts, scholars and other worthies (Shouda 1979). However, claims of neutrality invariable imply either that there is a balance of power already, and the other parties do not wish to upset that balance, or that they accept (and implicitly support) the prevailing dominant power structure.

economy needs unions that operate much more in the economic sphere, such as in pressing for a higher wage, which the ACFTU is unable or unwilling to do at present. The official trade unions will lose their capacity to survive if they cannot be the representatives of labourers in the market (Chang 1993b), even if this continues to be characterized, within the Party-state context, as promoting social stability. The governments of capitalist industrial countries, especially in Europe, have promoted union representation of members in the past, specifically because such institutionalized management of conflict helps dissipate pressures towards social upheaval, and the promotion of trade unionism was a central component of the anti-Communist stabilization of Western Europe and Japan immediately after the war. In fact, some unofficial workers' organizations have emerged sporadically nationwide [82] and are feared by the Party-state to constitute a serious threat to social order and to the existing trade union system. Although the provisions in the Chinese Labour Law and Trade Union Law on trade unions' status in a market economy are not thorough, the basic legal principle is clear, namely, the trade unions must represent and protect the interests of labourers. The basis of trade union reform is also moving in that direction, but there remains much distance between the reality and the law.

## RECOGNITION AND THE RIGHT OF ASSOCIATION

Trade union activities, from a legal perspective, include exercising rights and implementing obligations required by law. The legal provisions of Chinese trade union rights, especially the 'right of association', are very significant in shaping the characteristics of industrial relations. Chinese workers have the right to organize trade unions which is guaranteed within the Constitution of the PRC. The constitution states that 'citizens enjoy freedom of speech, of the press, of assembly, of association, of procession and of demonstration' (Article 35). According to the Trade Union Law (2001) 'all workers doing physical and mental work in enterprises, institutions, and government organs within Chinese territory, who rely on wages and salaries as their main source on income, have the right to participate in and form trade union organizations' (Article 3).

There are two significant points of difference between the ILO standard and the Chinese trade union law. First, the Trade Union Law defines the

---

[82] Despite usually being illegal, in recent years there have been more and more spontaneous workers' organizations that have characteristics of trade unions, namely, to strive to protect workers' labour rights. Due to legal restrictions, most of these organizations are unable to take on the full functions of unions. Bai (2001: 211-26).

ACFTU as the country's sole unified national workers' organization (Article 10), and therefore confirms the monopolist statue of the ACFTU. Second, although Chinese trade unions can enjoy guaranteed funding and access to facilities and state protection,[83] Article 9 of the Trade Union Law heavily qualifies freedom of association. In states that trade unions at various levels shall be established according to the principle of democratic centralism, and a trade union organization at a higher level shall exercise leadership over a trade union organization at a lower level. Furthermore, Article 11 stipulates that 'the establishment of grass-roots union organizations, local trade union federations, and national or local industrial trade union organizations shall be submitted to a higher-level trade union organization for approval'. Where workers have sought to establish their own independent unions officially or affiliate with independent international unions, they have been suppressed. The ILO has rejected such actions as violations of the fundamental right of association, and the ILO has issued detailed recommendations on the Chinese trade union laws (for example ILO 1993).

The development of private enterprises within China and the country's expanded trade ties with other nations has fundamentally altered the needs of workers and employers with regard to representation (Chang 1998). The emergence of new types of employers in China has led to pluralism in the area of employers' associations. These national or local associations include bodies to represent foreign investors, private enterprises and national enterprises. The fact that workers and employers enjoy unequal rights of association points to a need for legal reform in this area (Chang et al. 2001).[84]

However, despite the existence of a number of international conventions,[85]

---

[83] The Trade Union Law (2001) provides that the enterprise, institution and government organ, where a trade union is established, shall pay a contribution equivalent to 2 per cent of workers' monthly payroll (Article 42). The People's government at all levels as well as enterprises, institutions and government organs shall provide trade unions with the facilities, venues and other material requirements necessary for performing their job and conducting union activities (Article 45). No organization or individual may seize, misappropriate or arbitrary transfer a trade union's assets, funds or immovable property allocated by the state for use of the trade union (Article 46).

[84] For example, although CEC, originally the association of SOE directors, is mandated by the government as the official employers' association in China, there are similar associations for each form of enterprise, including, for example such organizations as the Association of FIEs, the Association of JVs and the Association of POEs.

[85] The ICESCR provides for the right to form and join trade unions. Article 8 of this Covenant provides:

The right of everyone to form trade unions and join the trade union of his choice... for the promotion and protection of his economic and social interests. No restrictions may be placed on the exercise of his right other than those prescribed by law and which are necessary in a democratic society in the interests of national security or public order or for the protection of the rights and freedoms of others.

in the current legal and political circumstances, China's government finds it unacceptable to allow 'freedom of association.' Some overseas activists have encouraged Chinese workers to establish independent trade unions. Although these gestures are often done for the sake of improving workers' freedom of association, at the same time, they are encouraging the workers to violate the law. Some Chinese officials have reacted by calling on the government 'to keep away the infiltration and sabotage from domestic and overseas hostile forces in order to maintain the solidarity of workers and staff, to maintain social and political stability' (Zhang 2001: 17–18). Whilst breaking a bad law is not wrong, it is unwise if more harm than benefit flows from the act of breaking a law. Those who set up independent unions or even promote workers' rights outside the official political or union structures face imprisonment and persecution, whilst their achievements are generally very short-lived. Therefore, a more realistic approach is to organize workers into the existing trade unions, and to change the situation of unions being controlled by employers at the local level.

Table 5.1 shows the change in union density over the last decade. Whilst union density has been increasing in the public sector, the organization rates in the private sector seem to have peaked and are now declining again. Moreover, the unionization rates outside SOEs are very low, despite the ACFTU figures. The ACFTU uses extremely selective criteria in calculating potential membership in each sector, and so, when available, Table 5.1 uses more accurate employment data collected by the NBS.

By the end of 1998, membership in FIEs and POEs was only 31.1 percent and 9.6 per cent respectively (Zhang 1999: 30–5). In many non-publicly owned enterprises without trade unions, the workers' status is very disadvantaged. The ACFTU has taken the unionization of non-publicly owned enterprises as a major task for the past few years. It had planned that by the end of 2002 it would increase the number of grass-roots unions in POEs, FIEs and TVEs to one million (from 250 000 at the end of 1999) and union membership to 36 million members (from 13 million at the end of 1999) (Wei 2001: 8–12). Fu et al. (2001) examined ACFTU-initiated unionization drives in three coastal cities of China – Shanghai, Dongguan and Zhuhai – and found city-level unions are experimenting with various forms of new union organizations in an attempt to boost union, membership, particularly among POEs and smaller FIEs.

The main advantage of increasing union membership for the ACFTU is that it increases the number of workers covered by a conflict minimizing,

The Standing Committee of the National People's Congress of PRC ratified this covenant in March 2001. However, the Committee announced at the same time: to Article 8 of the ICESCR, the PRC will apply the Covenant according to the Constitution of PRC, the Trade Union Law of the PRC and the Labour Law of the PRC (*Renmin ribao*, 1 March 2001).

*Table 5.1 Union membership rate by ownership*

| | | 1990 | % | 1996 | % | 1999 | % | 2001 (Sept.)* | % |
|---|---|---|---|---|---|---|---|---|---|
| SOUs | No. of Employees | 90 119 322 | 92.16 | 89 995 225 | 92.66 | 70 794 562 | 92.38 | 70 593 213 | 94.23 |
| | Union Membership | 83 055 849 | | 83 393 894 | | 65 400 050 | | 66 516 707 | |
| COUs | No. of Employees | 20 847 777 | 85.52 | 16 525 873 | 86.14 | 8 107 953 | 88.46 | 8 251 838 | 88.83 |
| | Union Membership | 17 829 343 | | 14 236 932 | | 7 172 392 | | 7 330 233 | |
| POEs | No. of Employees | 6 783 | 69.52 | 160 490 | 70.62 | 892 577 / 16 991 660 | 4.07/ 77.64 | 5 764 379 | 75.87 |
| | Union Membership | 4 716 | | 113352 | | 693 004 | | 4 373 516 | |
| FIEs | No. of Employees | 595 575 | 78.32 | 2 237 931 | 80.21 | 2 521 399 / 6 120 000 | 32.82/ 79.65 | 6 003 791 | 40.22 |
| | Union Membership | 466 500 | | 1 795 039 | | 2 008 367 | | 2 414 705 | |
| TVEs | No. of Employees | | | | | 3 541 383 / 127 040 900 | 1.96/ 70.39 | 6 306 751 | 82.97 |
| | Union Membership | | | | | 2 492 820 | | 5 232 662 | |

Sources:
(1) Absolute numbers are sorted from ACFTU (*1991, 1997 and 2000c*);
(2) Italic absolute numbers are collected from NBS and MoLSS (*2000*);
(3) All union membership rate are calculated by the authors.
* (4) All numbers for 2001 are from ACFTU (2001) only.

avoiding and managing apparatus, and thus ensures the unions' continued relevance to the CCP as a facilitator of social stability, even if in practice, this means simply ensuring workers do not organize independent (illegal) unions. Moreover, the search for new enterprises in which to set up unions provides the hope of other sources of funds for union coffers in the face of the growing financial crisis within the ACFTU. This crisis is brought about partly through the declining ability of public sector units to pay their union dues (deducted at the rate of 2.5 per cent of the units total payroll) resulting from units becoming loss making, bankrupt or needing to suspend production, and partly through poor investments made by many provincial and city unions.[86] However, the strategy of increasing recognition in the private sector has not been very successful because, first, local governments see it as potentially disrupting their goals of economic expansion based on attracting foreign and private investment and, second, because of opposition and resistance from non-state sector employers. To deal with the first problem, the trade unions have sought to gain what assistance they can from local governments and Party organs. To resolve the second problem, the trade unions adopted a package of compromising or concessional strategies, such as guaranteeing no collective action, allowing the employer to effectively appoint the chairperson of the union, and reducing union dues owed to the union by the employer, in exchange for allowing a union to be formed. The result of these strategies has been to undermine the grass-roots unions' ability to represent the interests of workers and operate independently once formed. Most trade unions in non-public enterprises are still controlled by employers. What is more, the employers or their stooges set up some unions. Some chairpersons of unions are even the relatives of the employer or the second owner of the plant.[87] There are a number of reasons for this problem, but one needs highlighting here. The recognition process is a top-down administrative procedure, not a bottom-up conscious action of workers. The ILO

---

[86] Some city and provisional unions have been able to use their property and other assets to greatly increase union wealth, with Shanghai providing one of the best success stories, but most unions appear to make bad investments. A couple of unions in Guangdong Province for example appear to be subsiding their business from union dues, which are themselves meager, given the small number of public sector enterprises in their jurisdiction and the great efforts needed to establish unions in the private sector. Making things worse, the only way to gain recognition is often to discount or postpone the requirement for employers to pay union dues. This issue is sensitive and so we cannot provide more details, but a general discussion in given in Fu et al. (2001).

[87] These cases were discovered by authors from their fieldwork in some POEs and FIEs, but not shown in documents delivered by the ACFTU and local trade unions. In recent years, recognition in POEs and FIEs has been introduced under a guiding principle called 'establishing grass-roots union firstly and improving it secondly (*xianjianzhi houwanshan*). Therefore, the ACFTU and local unions ignore the problems of 'boss's trade unions and yellow dog unions' at present. Some domestic scholars and cadres of trade unions have shown concern over these problems (see *Gongren ribao*, 1March 2000, 10 March 2000 and 10 April 2000).

Convention No. 98 elaborated that laws should be enacted to forbid employers from discriminating against unions or union members, as well as prohibiting the creation of company unions or company-dominated trade unions, but these legal provisions are absent in China (Chang 2002a). The amended Trade Union Law provides the restriction of employer-dominated trade unions.[88] However, because the workers in POEs are weak in the labour market, the ACFTU still has a long way to go to remove the effects of strong employers on trade unions.

## CONCLUSION

The labour movement in a market economy is a mass movement in essence. Currently, the Chinese trade unions are caught between the impacts of two pressures. On the one hand, the CCP government requires the trade unions to reform in order to attract more workers and stabilize the workforce in the process or reform. On the other hand, the workers need the trade unions to represent their interests, or 'voice' their requirements.

In terms of the attitudes toward union reform, there are three main streams inside the ACFTU system. Some trade union cadres expect to keep the existing system and their own personal interests; some work towards the idea that there will be a reform to make the trade unions effective representatives of workers; the third kind of cadres have no personal opinions and are content to take orders from the superior leaders and the Party. Among these three streams, the last on is still most common. Moreover, any mass or democracy-oriented reform movement within the trade unions will damage the interests of union cadres to a certain extent, as it creates uncertainty for career paths and disrupts bureaucratic stability. Therefore, there is quite strong internal resistance to trade union reform. In general, the process of trade union reform falls behind other aspects of social and economic reform in China. Nevertheless, where the party organization is stronger, such as in Beijing and Shanghai, the union cadres also tend to be more assertive in making calls to define a new role for the unions. Younger cadres, on the other hand, appear to be discontent with the weak and subordinate position of the unions to the party, and a few even see advantages to unofficial conflicts such as strikes and demonstrations and rival (illegal) unions in stimulating further changes within the official trade union movement.

The most important point to note is that the ACFTU has to introduce any

---

[88] Article 9 of the Trade Union Law (2001) state that 'the close relatives of the major managerial staff of an enterprise shall no be candidates for election as members of the grass-roots union in their own enterprise'.

reforms to its organizations, policies and methods within the current political and legal circumstances, in which there is no chance for ACFTU to be independent from the CCP. Under these restrictions, the main goal set by the ACFTU is to reform its organizing structure to focus more on members and to experiment with democratically-oriented working arrangements, such as through setting-up the association system and delegate system. An optimistic view is that once this goal is achieved, the trade unions will be responsible to the members through an internal democratic system while becoming workers' representatives, independent of employers. This is a goal not only provided by the amended Trade Union Law (2001), but is also approved by the CC-CCP. Since the ACFTU's reform cannot go beyond the framework of the existing political system, it is hard to expect a remarkable achievement without a breakthrough in political system reform.

There is considerable unevenness in the development of trade unions within China. In some regions, the status and role of trade unions have been steadily improving because of opportunities brought about by economic development or a good historical foundation to the local union movement. The most outstanding example is the Shanghai Federation of Trade Unions, but the provincial federations of Liaoning, Shandong and Jiangsu are also rich with experiences (ACFTU 2001: 135–70). In terms of the internal system of trade unions, compared with the headquarters of the ACFTU in Beijing, the status and role of local trade unions are becoming more important while their level of autonomy is in general increasing. In local trade unions, due to the regional characteristics of the economy and its reform, the role of trade unions at city level (subordinated to the province) is becoming much more important. From a long-term point of view, the development of local unions at city level would be the energy and hope of trade union reform in China. The emergence of trade unions at village and township level is positive and inspiring to the trade union movement in a market economy, but the critical mass of size, contacts with local state organs and resources lies with the city-level unions. Within the ACFTU, the trade unions at county level seem not to have kept pace with changes around them, and are falling behind other sectors in the process of reform.

Chinese trade unions occupy a space in Chinese society that is at an intersection point between the economic and political systems. The progressive pace of Chinese economic reform and the stagnation of political reform place trade unions in a very contradictory and awkward position. At the same time, rapid political change, as in the case or Russia, is no guarantee that the trade unions will change in consequence (Ashwin and Clarke 2002). Thus, the future direction of the trade unions is very uncertain, and there is no clear normative pattern to follow.

# PART II

Industrial relations processes

# 6. Participation

The amended Constitution of the PRC (1982) states that labourers are entitled to the right to participate in 'democratic management' (Article 16). In a broad sense, this right means that labourers can participate in the political, social and economic affairs of their places of employment as well as their residential communities. In a narrow sense, participation rights in China refer to labourers having rights as employees, to participate in the operation and management of their work units (enterprises or government organs) or be involved in the affairs that concern their material interests. This chapter will confine examination of the changes to industrial participation in China to the narrow definition of 'democratic management'.

Theoretically, the right to participation stems from the social and political principles of the socialist system of China, in which workers and staff are the 'masters of these enterprises as well as the country'. Therefore, workers are entitled to participate in managing the affairs of enterprises and the country as 'masters'. This right appears to extend control far beyond the purposes of protecting the interests of workers and staff (Shi and Wang 1999: 38), but in practice has much in common with classical management participation in much of Western Europe. Participation and democratic management are also supposed to have the motivational function of simulating workers' enthusiasm to engage in production, to encourage them to cooperate with management in fulfilling the economic targets specified by the owners. The only difference is that under the ownership of the state, workers were expected to comply with political targets as well.

This chapter will trace the development of participation in enterprises and then go on to discuss three specific policies aimed at increasing 'democratic management'. These polices include workers' congresses (WCs), employee director and supervisors (EDS) and 'opening corporate affairs' (OCA).

## CHANGING FORMS OF PARTICIPATION IN CHINA

Management participation is a long-standing topic. However, no matter what forms of participation are adopted, employees' motivation is quite simple and logical – their desire for participation, to a great extent, is determined by the benefits they can gain from this process (Tang 1996: 29). For their part, those employers and managers who support some form of participation hope to enhance employee job satisfaction, or even contribute to productivity, and thus increase productivity and profits (Rose 1988). As one of the actors with a direct interest in industrial relations, the government is concerned with spreading participation more widely, embracing macro economic development and social fairness (Hyman and Mason 1995: 7) and perhaps even enhancing social capital (Carroll and Bebbington 2001).

The Chinese path to 'democratic management' began in the revolutionary bases controlled by the CCP in the 1930s and 1940s and developed on into the period of planned economy. In this economic system, besides its role in the administration of national affairs, the government was also a major employer of SOE workers. The government was thus of crucial importance in deciding the way and extent that 'democratic management' would be carried out in China. COEs, being collectively owned, could also have developed truly socialist forms of participation, with the owners and the workers combined as single entities, but in practice, as in everything else, it was the SOEs that took the lead, because of their importance to government's social, political and economic planning.

The 'democratic management' that developed during the planned system can be categorized as a pattern of 'political mobilization', which emphasized mass mobilization and was closely connected with the political and social contexts of the planned economy (Chang et al. 1999). This 'political mobilization' pattern is characterized as having four main attributes.

First, it was given a strong political character to meet the requirements of the political system and reflect the political ideology that the CCP wished to be propagated in a socialist society. In order to make some genuine attempt to develop socialism, within the constraints of centralist power, the government took 'democratic management' as an appropriate measure to boost workers' status and to provide some meaningful basis to the claim that workers were the masters of their enterprises, as well as leaders in society. Accompanying a series of political movements, the central government constantly launched various campaigns to boost production. The authorities regarded these campaigns as political tasks, and allocated participation campaigns through a top-down chain of command to the industrial enterprises to be fulfilled by workers and managers. In the early post-liberation days, the strength of these campaigns lay in their effectiveness to mobilize workers, launching democratic reform, abolishing the old management systems and rapidly carrying out socialist education programmes (ACFTU 1995a). Through these campaigns, the CCP government could establish a new regime in enterprises and urban communities within a short period of time that resembled aspects of socialism.

Second, political mobilization was developed as a means to promote production. In the early days of the PRC, 'democratic management' was adopted to motivate workers to contribute to the recovery of the national economy, which was largely destroyed during the Liberation War (1947–49). For example, the government often called for 'labour emulation', which was created in the 1950s, in nationwide production campaigns, such as 'increasing production and practice economy', 'technological innovation' and 'rationalization proposal' (ACFTU 1995a). Moreover, managers sometimes used emulation campaigns to mobilize workers into fulfilling or over-fulfilling the state plan quota at the end of the year or in busy periods.

Third, in organizing these campaigns, the central government and the ACFTU paid particular attention to creating opportunities for political mobilization and agitation. Campaigns were usually initiated through mass education. Adopting a method referred to as 'demonstrating with a typical example', the central government and the ACFTU would mobilize and inspire workers by selecting and publicizing some 'labour models' who were identified as undertaking the ideals of the campaign to heart (whether this be output targets or whatever). After such 'education', most workers gradually changed their attitudes toward production campaigns from passive acceptance to involvement, and often then to fanaticism. In this case, the achievement of these campaigns often far exceeded the hope and expectation of the exponents.

Fourth, there was little attempt to maintain a continuity of goals or contents between different campaigns. The duration of each campaign was determined by the goal the organizers wanted achieved, which also determined their contents. Thus, for a long time there was no systematic approach to developing democratic management in China. Even the most popular labour emulation scheme, which was favoured by the top leaders of central government and the ACFTU, kept on changing the contents and targets each time a new campaign was initiated. Undoubtedly, such constant change in campaigns led to fatigue among participants and their effectiveness began to wear off after a few years.

'Political mobilization' was both practical and effective in the 1950s, at a time when the CCP was eager to strengthen the national economy. Workers were mobilized to throw themselves into improving productivity and management of enterprises, and to show commitment to the construction of a 'socialist economy'. The prerequisites implied in this form of mass mobilization were that the workers were the masters of their enterprise and they had rights to participate in the operation and management of their enterprises. At the same time, workers had certain obligations as 'masters', to fulfil the production tasks assigned by the state. The existence and implementation of this mass mobilization pattern essentially characterized the social relations of production in the urban enterprises, and particularly the SOEs, during the early period of the planned economy.

The initial success of the system was based on the social and political situation of the early stages of the planned economy. There were two main social divisions with potential for serious conflicts of interest. These were the divisions between the urban and rural populations, and divisions between controllers (senior political leaders) and the controlled. Following the strict separation of rural and urban citizens, and the rigidity of state economic planning within urban communities and workplaces, there was no space for conflicts of interest, even between plant directors and workers. Instead, what was referred to in Chapter 1 as 'magnified' or enlarged unitarism in labour relations existed, in which both managers and workers were masters and had rights to participate in the operation and management of enterprises. The interests of senior managers were similar to those of workers, because in the planned economy managers took little personal risk or responsibility, and their only economic objective was the need to fulfil the planned quota assigned by the senior administrative agencies. This essentially meant mobilizing and organizing their workers to achieve the planned quota, and the main goal of 'democratic management' was often directed towards this same end. Moreover, the government ensured a strong connection between the economic goals and political targets in most 'democratic management' campaigns. This meant that managers would not simply pressure workers to reach production targets, because the managers themselves were appraised by both output achievements and some kind of criteria that might be characterized as 'socialist' political leadership. If the work unit was identified by the superior agencies as a 'model' in such campaigns, both the workers and managers benefited, through prestige, career opportunities and occasionally access to additional benefits.

Detailed information on the motivations of workers to participate in these campaigns is not available.[89] The very nature of the 'political mobilization' pattern meant there was political pressure on workers to join these campaigns. However, we suspect most workers were driven by a sense of responsibility of being 'masters' of society and to a greater extent, masters of their

---

[89] By the end of 1952, three years after the foundation of the PRC, more than 220 000 'labour models' were elected at the city, provincial and higher levels (ACFTU 1995: 301). It was claimed that by 1954, the fourth year of the 'Five-year Plan', 1.83 million 'rationalization proposals' were put forward by workers to resolve the crucial problems in production and 750 000 were adopted (ACFTU 1995: 331).

enterprise. These were the heady days of socialist construction and many people had family who had sacrificed lives and security for the new country. Moreover, the politically appointed or secured managers were just as keen on the political construction of socialism as on economic development. Nevertheless, these campaigns focused on the work units and were experienced by both workers and management at this level. It was difficult for the government to mobilize workers on a nationwide basis to join some production campaigns, and the implementation was often patchy.

The 'political mobilization' pattern was replaced by a 'selective participation' pattern in the 1960s, after the government ended the Great Leap Forward movement in 1958. The 'selective participation' pattern can be categorized as 'employee involvement', by which management provides employees with the opportunity to influence decision-making on matters that affect their interests (Hyman and Mason 1995: 21). Such participation mainly focuses on employees' direct participation in which they can discuss work matters with their supervisors and managers directly through various formal and informal forums, such as consultative meetings. These meetings and forums are often organized by managers in order to test the feasibility of management decisions or ensure their implementation.

This shifting course resulted from the central government adjusting its economic and enterprise policies to deal with the serious problems brought about by the Great Leap Forward. The CC-CCP formulated the 'Draft Regulation on the Management of State Industrial Enterprises', popularly called 'Seventy Articles on Industrial Work' (*gongye qishi tiao*). In this document, the CC-CCP defined the nature of the state industrial enterprises and their fundamental tasks, and reaffirmed the system of factory directors assuming overall responsibility under the leadership of the Party committees. In September 1962, the CC-CCP issued the 'Directive on Discussing and Trying out the Regulation on State-owned Industrial Enterprises' requiring that 'the workers' congress meeting or workers' meeting must be regularly held by the grass-roots unions... the grass-roots union shall oversee the day-to-day work of workers' congresses when the congress is not in session' (quoted in General Office, Centre for Economic Law, State Council 1982: 440–72).

There are major differences between the two forms of political participation. First, the selective participation schemes initiated and managed by the central government and the ACFTU were far more limited and selective in coverage. Campaigns were no longer launched on a national scale, but within selected enterprises, and a small number of workers' representatives participating in management replaced the mass mobilization of workers. Second, the targets of 'democratic management' were switched from politics and ideology to production, operation and workers' welfare. So participation became limited to areas related to work (for example, methods of working, allocation of tasks, maintenance of quality, and so on). Its purpose was to increase job satisfaction and encourage a sense of identification with the aims, objectives and decisions of management, as well as to reduce the potential for unexpected conflicts. Whilst there was some political significance to conflict avoidance, the main focus was on economic improvements, with greater emphasis on the need for workers to participate based on a sense of responsibility to economic development rather than a political right stemming from being masters. Third, government domination of these participation drives markedly decreased. Even though the central government still mobilized workers by issuing documents, the detailed administration was undertaken by the ACFTU. This shift resulted in reinforcing the image among workers that the unions were managerial organs rather than political or welfare agents. This helped to undermine the status of the unions and strain the sense of unitarism between managers and workers. Fourth, the form of 'democratic management' had changed from a national political movement to a management institution. The legal regulations explicitly defined the rights and duties of workers' representatives as well as specifying the procedure for participation. As a result, the new scheme was highly formalized and could continue over the long term, as compared to the erratic and sporadic nature of the original participation movements.

The structures and formalism of the second form of participation continues to influence work units today. We will now examine the workings of three particular formal institutions that were developed out of the selective involvement round of political participation, which serve to encourage employee commitment (to the Party) and stimulate improvements in production and productivity in enterprises, starting with the role of WCs.

## WORKERS' CONGRESS IN ENTERPRISES

The beginning of 'selective involvement' was marked by the implementation of the WCs system in SOEs in 1962, although the system was suspended, along with the ACFTU, during the Cultural Revolution (1966–76). It was restored by the central government in the 1980s, when SOE managers were growing in power in many aspects and the Party organs' status and power was in decline. By restoring the system of WCs, the CCP government intended to set up a power structure in SOEs, which can be referred to as 'factory director responsibility and WCs under Party committee leadership' (General Office, Centre for Economic Law, State Council 1982). While reaffirming the leading status of the Party organ, the government hoped the WCs would serve as a restraining mechanism against management domination over SOEs. The CCP saw the need for particular urgency to defuse rising worker unrest in state enterprises following the rise of Solidarity in Poland (Sheehan 1998: 170–78), which was associated with a general improvement in welfare provisions for state workers in urban areas (Naughton 1997: 182–83).

In contrast to the pattern of 'political mobilization', the WCs system was explicitly defined by a set of systematic regulations. After the 9th National Congress was held in 1978, the ACFTU placed more weight on implementing WCs system and set about drafting relevant legislation. In May 1981, the Organization Department of the CCP, the State Commission of Economy and Business and the ACFTU jointly held a seminar on 'democratic management'. At this meeting, the document drafted by the ACFTU was adopted with the title of the 'Interim Regulations on the Workers' Congress in State-owned Industrial Enterprises'. In July of the same year, the CC-CCP and the State Council approved and required implementation of the document. In accordance with the Interim Regulations, they required that every enterprise must establish the system of WCs in an effective way. Moreover, the Party organ shall play an active role in leading and supporting workers to realize their master status in enterprises, and to achieve this they would make sure that the WCs could exercise their power given by the Interim Regulations. In September 1986, the State Council issued the 'Regulations on the Workers' Congresses in State-owned Industrial Enterprises', in which it states that the WCs are the basic organs for the practice of democratic management, and are for workers to exercise their rights to democratic management (Article 3).

The Interim Regulation also sets out detailed provisions in five areas that empower WCs, as follows. First, WCs are to receive the work reports of the factory director at regular intervals; to discuss business policies, long-term and yearly plans, plans on major technological transformation and technology importation, staff training programmes, financial budgets and final accounts, and the proposed distribution of capital and assets owned by the enterprise. Moreover, WCs should comment and make suggestions on the previously mentioned plans and proposals, and decide whether they shall be implemented. Second, WCs are to discuss the proposals on economic responsibility system, wage adjustment plans, bonus distribution schemes, labour protection schemes, reward and punishment measures, and other important rules and regulations, and to make decisions on their adoption. Third, WCs are to discuss and decide on schemes proposed that draw on the enterprise's welfare funds, schemes for the allocation of workers' residences, and other important matters relating to the lives and welfare of workers. Fourth, WCs are to appraise and supervise the leading cadres at all levels in the enterprise, and propose measures for their rewards, punishment, appointment and dismissal. Fifth, WCs are to recommend a candidate to be the factory director (or elect a factory director by democratic means) for examination and approval by the relevant (government) authority. These provisions appear to give wide-ranging powers to workers, and three of these areas are beyond what are often thought of as workers' narrow or individual interests, showing the governments' purpose of restraining management power after reform.

The WCs were revived in an environment in which the managers had been granted more autonomy, and implementation depended on managers' active support. However, given the close alignment between senior managers and local Party cadres in increasing the economic performance of the public sector, and particularly SOEs, the political empowerment of workers was largely ignored in the process of implementation. WCs inevitably became characterized by a top-down process of participation, in which the draft of a managerial decision will be submitted to the workers' representatives for review or approval, but in turn, they are always approved unopposed and unaltered. Meanwhile, problems raised for discussion and suggestion are usually ones the management finds hard to resolve without workers' extra efforts or acceptance (such as redundancies). Therefore, the functions of the WCs are restricted to supplement, complete, approve and explain the decisions already made by the management. This pattern may be thought of as sharing the burdens of management but not sharing the power of management. Moreover, whilst the Party wanted to curb the power of managers, it did not want to inflame or inflate the expectations of workers either. Thus, the ACFTU colludes with management to ensure 'responsible' workers sit on the WCs, ones that will not threaten industrial 'harmony'.

WCs show clearly the shift from 'political mobilization' to 'selective involvement', with its emphasis on economics (rather than politics), and have gradually become regarded by managers as a means to motivate workers towards the principles of human resource management. For example, the Regulations on the Workers' Congress in State-owned Industrial Enterprises states that the aim of establishing the system of WCs is 'to guarantee workers' rights of democratic management, to give scope to the workers' initiative, wisdom and creativeness, to run perfectly the enterprise owned by the whole people, and to develop the socialist economy' (Article 1). In the 'Opinions about Strengthening the Work of Democratic Management during Establishing a Socialist Market System', issued in July 1994, the ACFTU also states that the:

> Labourer is the most active one of the productive factors. In the new environment of reform, development and stability, a variety of initiatives must be adopted to encourage workers to participate in management, decision-making and supervision, so as to give full play to workers' wisdom and creativity, to refuel the running of their enterprise. This is a requirement of social production and modern

> management, of the development path of management in the world as
> well the advantage of management in socialist enterprises ... [Thus, the
> function of WCs is for] motivating workers, increasing workers'
> satisfaction in their jobs and raising the economic efficiency of the
> enterprise. (Department of Trade Unions Science 1999: 103–12)

As the government introduced schemes to promote decentralization of decision-making to enterprises and remove public sector dependence on the state, initially managers were required to answer to the WCs. In the 'economic responsibility system' and 'contract management responsibility system' in the first stage of reform, WCs were already ineffectual restraints on managerial power. Nevertheless, managers were required by State Council regulations to work with the WCs, which amounted to little more than a duty to complete the paperwork to show superior regulatory agencies, rather than a responsibility to be accountable to WCs. In this first stage of urban economic reform, it was officially reported that effective WCs had been established in most publicly owned enterprises. However, workers' evaluation was consistently low. In a nationwide survey conducted by the ACFTU, out of a sample of 10 000 workers and staff, few people gave a positive assessment of WCs, whilst 45.19 per cent viewed them merely as managerial requirements to satisfy senior agencies (ACFTU 1987: 151–55). Five years later, an ACFTU (1993: 322) survey of 50 000 workers and staff still showed a higher rate of negative evaluation than positive views in assessing five functions of WCs. Some respondents in this later survey described the behaviour of their representatives during meetings as 'what they could do was use their hands three times shaking hands with leaders, raising hands for approving the decisions made by the director and clapping hands at the end of meeting' (ACFTU 1993: 319–28). A 'model entrepreneur' from an SOE also recognized that only directors could make WCs effective because meetings could only be held with their permission. He also thought that because 'workers had become accustomed to pursuing their interests through competition, it was unnecessary to encourage them to join activities which would not bring about any benefits for them', implying WCs fell into the category of having 'no benefit to workers' (ACFTU 1993: 92–110) and the basic function was to improve production.

In the second round of reform, with its establishment of the modern enterprise system and the change of governance structure, WCs seemed to have lost much of their logical basis (that is, they were now formally irrelevant, as well as irrelevant in practice). Under the requirement of the modern enterprise system, boards of shareholders, boards of supervisors and boards of directors form the corporate governing structures. The new structure contradicts the old governance principles enshrined (at least nominally) in the tripartism of the Party committee, WCs and trade union.

The debates range on how to deal with the contradiction between the so-called 'three old organs' (*lao san hui*) and 'three new organs' (*xin san hui*). Some people view the *xin san hui* as a corporate governing structure based on the relationship of principal-agent, and whose purpose is to achieve economic efficiency and profit maximization for the investor. In contrast, the *lao san hui*, with their stronger political orientation, rests upon the political leadership of the CCP in enterprises and the rights based on the 'master status' of workers (Guo and Li 2001; Jin 1997). To deal with this contradiction, the CC-CCP issued the 'Decision on Major Issues Concerning the Reform and Development of State-owned Enterprises' in September 1999, which states that Party committee leaders in wholly state-financed companies and in state share-holding companies can be included in the boards of directors and supervisors in accordance with legal procedures. Moreover, workers representatives should be included in the boards of directors and supervisors. Finally, the regulation also permits the Party secretary and chairman of the board of directors to be the same person (*Renmin ribao* 23 September 1999 [1]). In this way the government was trying inject a political role into the director system, as well as provide an avenue for the WCs to draw on the access to information the director and supervisor system appears to allow.

Data from the Shanghai Federation of Trade Unions shows that there were rank and file worker representatives serving on WCs, and claimed this was one of the major reasons for the low effectiveness of WCs. Among 100 enterprises surveyed, representatives from the rank-and-file workers only accounted for 42.5 per cent, while in 13.8 per cent of enterprises more than three in four representatives were managers and 'the meeting of workers' representative has became a one of managerial cadres' (Shanghai Federation of Trade Unions 1999: 328–52). However, according to Article 12 of the 'Regulations on the Workers' Congresses in State-owned Industries', the number of managerial personnel drawn from all levels should not exceed one-fifth of the total membership of the WC. It thus appears that employers and management can flout the legal provisions relating to WCs, even in localities where CCP control remains strong and pervasive, such as Shanghai.

The Corporation Law (1999) further erodes the status and functions of WCs. In the 'Industrial Law on State-owned Enterprises' (1988), there was a special chapter concerning workers' rights to 'democratic management' and the function of WCs. The law explicitly provides that the 'workers' congress is the basic [organizational] venue for the practice of democratic management, also the organ for the workers to exercise their power of democratic management' (Article 15). In the Corporation Law there is one article that stipulates that the state-owned corporations shall exercise democratic management in accordance with the provisions of the Constitution of the PRC and relevant laws through the workers' congress or otherwise (Article

16). However, besides this, there are no special chapters or articles giving regulations that detail the power or role of WCs within the context of dramatically changing governance structures. According to the 'Regulations on the Workers' Congress in State-owned Industrial Enterprise' (1986), WCs have five kinds of rights in terms of reviewing business policies and long-term and yearly plans of enterprises, as discussed previously. These rights were systematically detailed in the 1986 legislation, but were greatly simplified in the Corporation Law, diluting and obscuring them in two abstract concepts: 'democratic management' and 'democratic supervision'. All rights in this law are transferred to the board of directors or the general manager,[90] leaving only a few issues concerning workers' rights for the WCs to give their opinions on.[91] In the new law, it seems that the concept of workers as 'masters of the enterprise' and the ways of realizing this status have been considered no longer relevant. Tang and Zhu (2000) argue that the Corporation Law stresses that the 'share holder' is the master of the enterprise rather than the workers.

## EMPLOYEE DIRECTORS AND SUPERVISOR SYSTEM

There has been a significant movement to change the ownership structure of state enterprises. Many SOEs, before and after the publication of the Corporation Law, changed to become limited liability companies or joint stock companies. As mentioned above, this conversion has brought about a great impact on governance structures in public sector enterprises, as well as a conflict between *lao san hui* and *xin san hui*. While the role of WCs is undermined, if not completely forgotten, a new system called 'Employees' Director and Supervisor' (EDS) has been established under the Corporation Law. According to this law, the EDS system should only be implemented in solely state-owned companies and limited liability companies established by more than two state-owned investment entities (hereafter state-owned corporations). According to the Corporation Law, a state-owned corporation must establish a board of directors that must include representatives of

---

[90] Two important powers of workers' congresses (namely appraising and supervising the leading cadres at all levels in the enterprise, and electing the director by democratic procedure), have been deleted and replaced by the supervisory committee and the board of directors in the governing structure of the corporation. According to the 'Corporation Law' the general manager should be appointed by the board of directors and supervised by the supervisory committee.

[91] Such as whenever considering and deciding on wages, welfare, production safety of the staff and workers' and labour protection and labour insurance and other issues concerning the personal interests of the staff and workers. Opinions of the trade union and the workers of the company should first be solicited, and representatives of the trade union or workers should be invited as observers to meetings concerned (Article 55, Corporation Law).

workers (Article 45). Larger limited liability companies must establish a supervisory committee that includes a certain proportion of workers' representatives (Article 52). The workers, through democratic processes, should elect the workers' representatives in both boards.

The Corporation Law establishes a legal basis for the EDS system, promoting the importance of democratic management again, and raising it from 'employee involvement' to 'employee participation'. 'Employee participation', according to Hyman and Mason (1995: 21), refers to initiatives that promote the collective rights of employees to be represented in organizational decision-making, or because of the efforts of employees themselves to establish collective representation in corporate decisions. The representatives in EDS, on behalf of employees, can directly access the governance structure of corporations, to voice employees' opinions and demands. This system, at least in conception, compensates for the defects of WCs that arose from corporatization of state enterprises. Moreover, at least in law, the status of employees as being the 'master of state-owned enterprises', even if only in name, is re-established to a limited degree.

Most accounts publicized in the Chinese media, and reflecting the official line, give very positive evaluations of the effectiveness of the EDS system. According to several reports, in some state-owned corporations the employee directors and supervisors played very active roles in decision-making and supervision. Some employee directors, especially the ones who take the position as chairperson of the enterprise union, are said to be able to voice workers' opinions and requirements at the meetings of boards of directors. They were able to raise and eventually help resolve several complex and longstanding problems related to workers' interests. For example, in Taishan Iron and Steel Corporation there might have been a dispute because the management had delayed paying wages and implemented some draconian workplace policies. However, the employee directors and supervisors, as 'middlemen', stepped in to give some explanations to workers to seek their understanding and pacify their anger (Anonymous 2001). A few employee directors could even mobilize workers to boycott decisions passed by the meeting of the board of directors, forcing the board to change these decisions concerning the development of such enterprises (*Shenzhen fazhibao* 16 August 1999). Some employee supervisors played active roles in inspecting the operation and accounting practices of their corporation, and in the process warning of and policing illegal activities, whether inadvertent or not. It appears at least one employee director could even suggest that the general manager withdraw his decision to promote some senior managers (Economic and Business News 2000).

However, some accounts indicate that these may be atypical cases, and that the EDS system is far more restrictive. For the employee director or supervisor, one of the prerequisites of taking this position is to be an employee of the corporation, which in practice means the candidate will hold a subordinate employment position to that of the senior managers, no matter how they are elected or who take these positions. This relationship restrains the supervisors and directors who stand in a subordinate workplace position to exercise their power of supervision or their influence on decision-making in cases where this contravenes the interests of their bosses (Lei 1997; P. Luo 2000). In a survey to 200 stock market listed corporations, Li and Deng (1999) found that few supervisors could play their role because of the subordinate positions they held in their in enterprises. 'This position has brought about so many inconveniences to supervisors that the board of supervisors in some corporations exist in name only, they have not met for more than one time in a year' (Li and Deng 1999: 10).

In fact, the concept of 'employee' is too broadly defined in China, especially in the public sector (see Chapter 4). From the general manager to the rank-and-file workers, they all can be referred to as employees. After public sector reform, the director or the general manager have distinguished themselves from other employees in terms of income, power, responsibilities and status. However, so far, for some other senior managers, such as the deputy general manager, no standard has been agreed upon to define whether they are still in the category of 'employee' or 'manager'. Therefore, in some corporations it is perfectly justifiable to appoint such senior managers to be an employee director or supervisor (Wu 2001; He 2001). Whilst there are some advantages to having experienced mangers taking this role because they know how to analyse the data in directors' meetings, it has the potential, if abused (through gerrymandering the election process) to further divorce workers from participation.

To strengthen the status of trade unions, some local governments required that, when SOEs introduced their corporate system, the chairperson of the grass-roots union should be the first candidate for the position of employee supervisor or director.[92] This requirement, to a certain extent, helps to increase the status of employee directors and supervisors because, according to the CC-CCP and the State Council, the chairperson of the grass-roots union holds the same rank as the deputy director or deputy secretary of the Party committee in SOEs (Anonymous 1983: 2). However, another problem brought about by this requirement is that the election procedure becomes less significant because the chairpersons of unions have in fact been appointed by the local government to take these positions, gerrymandering the whole

---

[92] For example, the 'Opinions about Establishing and Perfecting the System of Employee Director and Supervisor', issued by the Organization Department of CCP, Commission of Trade and Business and Federation of Trade Union, Henan province in February 2001 (see *Henan ribao* 27 February 2001). Also, the 'Opinions on further Support the Work of Trade Unions', issued by the Xian People's Government, Shanxii Province in May 2001(Xian Government 2002).

procedure. Significantly, the Corporation Law neither provides the legal qualification and duties of candidates nor details the procedure for proper elections. A questionnaire survey, conducted by a deputy to the National People's Congress, showed that in Tianjin City, within a sample of 120 employee directors and supervisors, only 38.2 per cent were elected through the meeting of WCs (Pan 2001). Even within this low figure of elected directors and supervisors, how many of them came from the rank-and-file workers still remains in question. In reality, the importance of the position of chairperson of a trade union may still not be enough to guarantee their seat in the board of directors, because of the limited number of such posts.[93] A survey in Hubei Province indicated that, whether the chairpersons of the grass-roots unions could enter the board of directors would be determined by many factors. These factors include such matters as the union's support from the local government and Party committee, the degree of support from and coordination with the senior trade unions and even the personal relationship between the union chairpersons and the chairperson of the board of directors. In such circumstances, only a few chairpersons of unions could be appointed as employee directors, most were elected or appointed to the more junior level of employee supervisors (Anonymous 2002).

Some commentators conclude that a lower 'quality' (skills, education or/and experience) of employee directors and supervisors is another problem in implementing the EDS system. A survey conducted in Shanghai indicated that, compared with that of other directors and supervisors, the general managerial skills of employee directors and supervisors are much lower. Some respondents from among the rank-and-file workers revealed that, at the meeting of their board of directors, when discussing issues such as wages and benefits, the employee directors could put forward suggestions; however, when making decisions relating to a proposed stock issue and listing, investment or engaging in international operations, that also have an impact on the long-term interests of workers, they found it difficult to be able to put forward their opinions. The survey also showed that most employee supervisors, including the chairpersons of the unions, were unable to read the accounting materials, such as balance sheets, and did not have an overall understanding of the operational procedures of their corporations. These respondents felt worried about their representatives' capabilities to be effective supervisors (Anonymous 2002). Lower capabilities of employees' representatives have long been a hot topic, even from the period of re-establishing WCs. In the 'selective involvement' pattern, this was a common problem, but not a crucial one, because it was almost impossible for the representatives of workers to join the process of substantive decision-making

---

[93] According to the 'Corporation Law', the board of director shall be made up of three to nine persons (Article 68).

anyway. The EDS is different, and competency in market economics and management is important. According to the Corporation Law, the board the employee director joins is the highest organ of decision-making in the company, and the employee supervisor is also required to attend the meeting held by the board of supervision. When the EDS system allows democratic management (a collective right to share responsibility among several people), the managerial knowledge of these people becomes an important factor in determining their ability to function in both boards as well as to act in the interests of workers. This provides a much less positive picture than that presented by the domestic media. However, the problems mentioned above cannot be resolved quickly.

Whilst WCs were never supposed to be very effectual in shaping management decision-making, their influence within the governance structure is being further weakened. It is important to note, however, that the government continues to try to stress its own relevance and function at the enterprise level as and when it feels the need. In the name of being responsible for, and the representative of, state assets, the government tries to establish a supervision system outside the governance structure of state-owned corporations, under the pretext of protecting state assets, assuring adequate access to information (Lin et al. 1997), and to prevent corruption. On 3 March 1997, the Organization Department of the CC-CCP, the SETC, the Ministry of Personnel and the ACFTU jointly issued the 'Notice on Strengthening Evaluation and Building of a Leading Body in SOEs', reaffirming the importance of evaluating the work of management in state-owned enterprises. According to this document, a range of criteria are used to assess the performance of directors, which draws on their political duties, as well as their economic objectives. The evaluation is comprehensive, covering issues from management capabilities to 'keeping the hands clean' (General Office 1997: 13–19).[94] In turn, this new regulation reinforced the significance of WCs within the state sector, and established the idea of 'democratic supervision'. The senior managers should undergo regular appraisal, consisting of providing a regular report of their work, which is then appraised by the workers' representatives of the WCs. Even though the notice could not reinstate the participative function WCs were once supposed to hold, 'democratic appraisal' may provide a more systematic and effective role for WCs, although one which moves from that of 'democratic management' to one of 'democratic supervision'. Supervision in this sense means post-hoc evaluation. The question is whether in practice this amounts to little more than 'closing the stable door after the horse has bolted' or a real policing role.

---

[94] 'Keeping the hands clean' means not being involved in corruption.

# THE SYSTEM OF 'OPENING CORPORATE AFFAIRS'

Further steps are being taken to control managers, through a phased introduction of a system called 'opening corporate affairs' (OCA), currently popularized in SOEs, COEs and state-owned corporations, which was initiated in three loss making SOEs in northern China in the middle of the 1990s. It is said that within a period of between six months to three years after starting their OCA schemes they had all turned their deficits into growing surpluses (Wang Chidong 1999). These miraculous experiences and achievements were reported to Beijing and raised the attention of the ACFTU. The ACFTU sent three investigation teams, one to each of these enterprises, with the purpose of finding out the reasons for their apparent success. In October 1998, the ACFTU, in association with the Central Commission for Discipline Inspection of the CCP and the Organization Department of the CC-CCP, held a conference on the topic of OCA. After this conference, the ACFTU put forward the 'Opinions about Implementing OCA, Strengthening the System of Democratic Supervision and Democratic Management' to the CC-CCP. Under the coordination of the General Office of the CC-CCP, a task force was set up, composed of the top leaders from the Central Commission for Discipline Inspection, the Organization Department, the State Commission for Trade and Economics and the ACFTU. In February 1999, the Central Commission for Discipline Inspection, the State Commission for Trade and Economics and the ACFTU jointly issued the 'Notice about Implementing OCA', requiring the spread of this system to all SOEs and to state and collective stock-holding corporations.

The initiative to implement OCA, according to the document issued by the central government, is to give the 'right to know' to workers. Knowing the situation of their enterprises is the prerequisite for the workers to exercise their rights of democratic management and democratic supervision, the document claims. They cannot 'exercise their rights of participating in management without the right to know' (Wei 1999). The document and speeches of the top leaders revealed another goal of the central government, which was to revise and improve the WCs because of a number of shortcomings they identified. First, the former system did not provide the right to know to workers and it was impossible for the workers' representatives to participate in and supervise the management of enterprises without sufficient information. Second, under the former system, the workers' representatives should hold one or two meetings annually. Whilst the congress is not in session, workers' representatives have no chance to exercise their right to participate in the process of decision-making as and when emergencies occur. Third, the former system was established in 1988 when a mandatory planning component coexisted with the developing market sector. Some of the WCs could not cope well with the emerging market (Wang Chidong 1999). However, given our criticism of the effectiveness of WCs as a whole, and with the increased drive towards marketization since the end of the 1990s, there is no indication that the right to know will make much, if any, difference. The Party and the government understand well these deeper and more systemic problems, so why do the central government and the ACFTU continue to try to improve the WC system?

In contrast to the system of WCs and EDSs, established by government planning and edict, it appears enterprise managers initiated OCA. In the three pioneer SOEs, the managers realized that it was necessary to set up a channel through which they could directly communicate with their employees, raising some questions concerning decision-making and business operations in the process. Through such 'mutual' and direct communication, the managers expected to vindicate their managerial practices and personal integrity by offering workers selected 'correct' information, in the hope that they could prove their honesty in performing their official duties in business and management (and no doubt avoid criticism which may endanger their own job tenure).[95] Whilst this account may seem a little out of place in the context of strong state regulation, and managerial desire for autonomy, there are two reasons to explain this. First, as explained, some mangers fear being accused of corruption, and as explained in Chapter 3, some managers, particularly in the public sector, maintain a political as well as economic interest in their careers. The second explanation is the straightforward desire to motivate staff, just as occurs in some capitalist enterprises.

However, after OCA was approved and introduced by the CC-CCP and the ACFTU, its functions became more complex. First, in enterprises where there are few restraints on the power of management, either through inadequate institutions or through incompetent worker representatives, the central government needed a new system to monitor the behaviour of managers. The OCA required managers to open some information and justify aspects of their decision-making, so that 'public' scrutiny has become possible, which at least circumscribes managerial autonomy to some degree. Second, in the course of public sector reform, several new forms of enterprise governance structures have been encouraged (such as reorganization, association, merger, joint stock partnership, leasing, sell-offs and bankruptcy of enterprise), which have all been used in part as managerial strategies to reduce workers' job security and benefits (whilst often enhancing their own interests). In this atmosphere of increased insecurity, suspicion and distrust, the government thought that encouraging managers to make performance-related documents open to workers' scrutiny would enable the latter to understand their employers'

---

[95] In their reports of summarising experiences, the management in both enterprises initiated OCA respectively mentioned this intention (Wang Chidong 1999: 93–130).

situation, in the hope that this will decrease conflicts between the two parties and maintain overall social stability. In enterprises where managers intend to violate workers' interests, OCA can share 'understanding' of the needs for changes. In enterprises where management might otherwise use workers' vulnerability in the market economy to extract concessions, OCA is supposed to make this less likely to happen because the right to know would expose this. Thirdly, from the government's point of view, the implementation of OCA was initially driven by the top leaders' worry about increased corruption as directors gain more power. Given a lack of sufficient supervisory institutions to monitor managers, OCA was thought to provide sufficient deterrent to reduce the extent and opportunities for 'abusing power for private gain' (*yiquanmousi*). A senior official from the Ministry of Monitoring believed that the Party's Department of Discipline Inspection and the government's Department of Monitoring at all levels would be the first beneficiaries from the system (H. Zhao 1999: 168–78). Here, the political target of implementing OCA has been extended well beyond the scope of management participation (Lu 2001). The government attempts to establish a new system to restrain the power of managers, maintaining social stability and reducing corruption. It appears that the WCs provide a ready-made platform for this new system.

In the process of implementing OCA, the ACFTU issued a document called 'Opinions about Implementing OCA, Democratic Management and Development Supervision' to define three areas that should be opened to workers. These were, first, affairs regarding production, operation, management and internal reform. These covered such matters as yearly development goals, medium and long-term development plans, important proposals for production and operation, product sales, proposals concerning change of property rights (for example, merger, bankruptcy, and so on), proposals about lay-off and resettlement of employees. Second, matters affecting workers' material interests, such as policies and plans about selling and allotting public housing, conditions for promotion, proposals relating to the distribution of bonuses and other benefits, plans for improving working conditions and payments for social security funds. Third, matters that, in the government's view, may easy become the vehicle for creating corruption, such as subcontracting construction projects, purchasing production materials and equipment, entertaining travelling merchants, annual wage bill and living space of senior managers (Wang Chidong 1999: 157–61). The meeting of workers' representatives is stipulated as the main channel for opening affairs. According to the ACFTU, at this meeting the matters mentioned above shall be reported by the senior managers concerned, then reviewed and passed by the workers' representatives and, finally, announced to all workers. An information feedback system must also be established to collect workers' suggestions.

All told, the OCA system appears to be a fairly comprehensive system for holding management accountable to workers, and goes some way to compensate for the ineffectiveness of WCs and the defects of the 'employee director and supervisor' systems. Through this direct communication, workers can learn more about the operation of their enterprise so as to strengthen their supervision of the management. Theoretically, this system can promote cooperation between the two parties, avoiding the conflict brought about by irrational or individualist behaviour of either party. Because this system has only started recently we cannot give a reasonable evaluation. However, some data indicates that OCA, if really carried out, could result in a positive effect in reducing the tension between workers and managers, at least in the public sector. The practice in some enterprises where OCA has been employed by the management in the process of bankruptcy and reorganization seems 'positive'. It is said that in a few cases where managers informed workers as to the reasons for bankruptcy or reorganization and released draft plans for settling laid-off workers, most workers understood the situation their enterprises faced, and followed the arrangements of management.[96]

However, the practical effectiveness of the OCA system should not be overestimated. From the legal perspective, some affairs, such as subcontracting construction projects, and purchasing production materials and equipment, are not provided in the Corporation Law as the information that should be made public. In the amended version of this law (1999), OCA is also not stipulated as an approach of 'democratic management'. From the perspective of management, managers have been in a strong position to control all information that is made available to workers, and some surveys indicate that this is a crucial problem in implementing OCA. In most cases, managers determine what information should be made available to workers and the timing of its release. Sometimes they made available some less important information to satisfy the requirements of inspections by supervising agencies (Lu 2001). Sometimes managers release information only when they meet some problems they are unable to cope with alone, such as lay-offs (Zou et al. 2001).

The government, on the one hand, obviously intends to establish an extra supervisory mechanism within SOEs, but on other hand, it provides little power for this mechanism to interfere with the autonomy of management in practice. Either in the document or the speeches of top leaders, the stress is on propagating the function of OCA in realizing 'democratic supervision',

---

[96] The Central Party Committee of Beijing Timber Mill. *Yikao qunzhong wancheng jianyuan he qiye gaizhi* (Relying on masses to fulfil lay-off and ownership reform). The CCP Committee of Beijing Jingmei Limited Corporation. 2001. *Quanmian shishi changwu gongkai tuidong pochan chengxu* (Comprehensively implementing OCA, promoting the procedure of bankruptcy). For both of these see Beijing Federation of Trade Unions (2001).

with no emphasis given on how to respond to complaints from workers when they are unsatisfied with the information. Therefore, whether the workers, once they have gained information, can actually participate in decision-making and realize their rights to democratic management is still very doubtful. From the perspective of trade unions, OCA seems not to provide them with an opportunity to develop a meaningful role in the new enterprise culture. If OCA is effective, it represents a human resource management approach to worker communication, whereby the managers can directly communicate with workers. In this context grass-roots unions will lose one of their most important roles, that of being a 'middleman' between workers and managers (Han and Morishima 1992; Lu 1996: 120; Zhang 1997). Thus, in the unlikely event that OCA proves to be effective in stimulating worker participation, it will undermine the position of the trade union further, and if OCA fails, it will further demonstrate the political weakness of labour in the face of state-initiated economic reforms.

## CONCLUSION

The dominant status of government in the labour relations of SOEs determines the patterns and approaches that 'democratic management' in China has taken. In the planned economy, employee participation was given a strong political colour that led to WCs being vanguards of what the CCP meant by a socialist political economy. It was employed by the Party and the government to mobilize workers politically and economically, to be propagated as a means to demonstrate to workers their master status in the new China and to be adopted by management to help them achieve the assigned production quotas. Whilst there was, however, no real attempt to make these democratic management forums or to lift the 'master' status of workers above a rhetorical and symbolic level, they did act as a check on managerial autonomy. After this pattern was replaced by 'selective involvement', the WCs and worker participation were all but abandoned, as managerial autonomy increased. Although the central government continues to try to breathe some life into the WCs by providing then with new functions and roles, the congresses are at odds with the 'modern enterprise system', but not because they are anti-capitalist, because they are not so different from German works councils or other managerial incorporation schemes. Their problem lies in their providing workers with a political rallying point to counter the realities of economism within the market, and their declining status generally under reforms. Approaches such as employee directors, supervisory boards and OCA have so far failed to change the operational logic of governance structure, but reinforce the new 'economism' of production. Therefore, participation in practice has often become a human resource management tool that managers can use to suit their own increasingly separate interests.

All the approaches to participation discussed in this chapter (and in relation to collective contracts discussed in Chapter 8) have been initiated and implemented by the government, usually through management. So far workers, who are supposed to enjoy the benefits of these schemes, have had their voices almost completely absent. It is true that potential civil unrest resulting from widespread worker discontent over corruption forced the government to initiate OCA to a large extent, but no one has been interested to ask what workers themselves think of these particular forms of participation. It is as if the workers have been forgotten, or worse, cannot be trusted to participate without guidance from higher authorities. Even the original success of involving workers in production drives has lost its appeal, as technology, 'modern management' and professional training are seen as more valuable ways to boost profits than relying on the intellectually impoverished proletariat. For their part, workers have difficulty in pressing any demands for participation they may have. First, they lack sufficient power to contend with management at the workplace, and perceived segmentation of labour is worsening this tendency. Second, workers have accepted and become used to the authority of management and it has only been relatively recently that managers' interests diverged significantly from workers in public sector enterprises. Third, the grass-roots unions are unable to organize their members, because they lack autonomy from the government in the case of publicly owned enterprises, and management in privately owned enterprises, and alternative unions are prohibited in China.

In the early years of the Chinese communist state, urban workers did enjoy something of a boom in worker participation that must have given many the feeling that they were important in (perhaps rather than masters of) the enterprise and a leading class in society in general. This withered on the vine of the Cultural Revolution, and a shadow of the former WCs was reborn in the push for marketization. By all accounts, worker participation since then has been almost completely a failure. This is not to say workers have no influence over management, because they can have some influence through the Party, and through the media to a lesser extent. However, the institutional arrangements the government has brought in to inject worker participation to balance managerial power are unsuccessful. The question, then, is given the government's resounding success in economic reform of the political economy of China, why has worker participation been such a failure?

The failure of current approaches to democratic management demonstrates that there is a contradiction between the economic and political systems in China. In the process of reform, the government has, on the one hand, to push forward the restructuring and development of SOEs and resolve the problems of numerous loss-making enterprises, which resulted directly from government economic policy in the first place. To realize this target, the government has established the 'modern enterprise system' and delegated significant autonomy to management. On other hand, the government has to keep one eye on managers to prevent them from abusing their power, and another eye on the material interests of workers to stop widespread overt conflicts disrupting social stability, and thus potentially threaten CCP hegemony. This contradiction contributes to the difficulty for the government and the CC-CCP to find suitable ways to realize the socialist principle of democratic management by workers.

# 7. Labour conflict and settlement

In the traditional planning system, labour conflict between management and workers was restrained (or concealed) by the state ensuring interests between managers and workers were aligned, forming a kind of state corporatist unitarism. The tight network of political control in enterprises (Walder 1986) also generally meant conflicts that did occur were resolved quickly. During the process of economic reform, industrial relations have become more complex within a context of changing economic, social and political environments. As a result, labour conflict is not only intensifying at the enterprise level, but also developing to become the early stages of broader class-based conflict.

In the second half of the 1980s, when the labour contract system was established, the central government also established a legal system for handling labour conflict, which includes three procedures for dispute settlement, mediation, arbitration and law suits. However, the development of labour conflict in the 1990s has demonstrated that this system has serious shortcomings. The rapid spread of collective labour disputes in recent years also demonstrates the failure of such forms of dispute settlement.

This chapter will track the rise and fall of government attempts to regulate conflict as well as explain the causes and patterns of conflict in China. A distinction will be made between formal procedures and informal means for handling labour conflicts. The analysis of conflict in China is incomplete because there is no reliable data of either the scope or extent of individual or collective forms of conflict. Nevertheless, using partial data sets and other indicators we will show that escalation of conflict is occurring.

## MEANING AND CAUSES OF LABOUR CONFLICT

Salamon (1992: 567–9) distinguishes between 'grievances' and labour 'disputes'. He states that when one or a group of employees' complaints have been ignored or unfairly handled by their bosses, their dissatisfaction may be expressed as a 'grievance'. This is a formal expression of individual or collective employee dissatisfaction and is usually associated with dissatisfaction over the application or non-application of collective agreements, managerial policies and actions or custom and practice. He defines a labour 'dispute' as a formal expression of collective employee dissatisfaction at the organizational level resulting from either a prior failure to resolve a grievance or a failure to agree on a matter of interest within the negotiating process.

Chinese scholars have no clear concepts of such differences. It is common to see dissatisfaction expressed by either party as a 'labour dispute' in a number of ways. Fan (1998: 13) refers to the dispute relating to labour rights and obligations between an employment unit (*yongren danwei*) and a labourer. Zhang Zaiping (1996: 12) sees a labour dispute as concerning the matters of labour relations between employment unit and labourer. Shi (1990: 343) sees a dispute that occurs due to the different demands about rights and obligations of each other between the parties of labour relations. Among these definitions, there is little difference in reality, but two points have been identified. First, the labour dispute is one that occurs between people who are employing labour and people who are supplying their own labour. Second, labour disputes are related to issues over the rights and obligations of the parties joined in an employment relationship. Current legal regulations for handling labour disputes also define labour disputes based on these definitions, to identify the scope and jurisdiction of the agencies handling such disputes.[97] Therefore, Salamon's (1992) definition of 'grievance' and 'labour dispute' are both included in the Chinese concept of labour disputes, once work related issues are raised by one party against another party or presented to a third party for mediation, arbitration or judgement.

Chinese legal regulations covering the handling of labour disputes mirror the Chinese characteristics of labour law that have been outlined in Chapter 2. First, this system has changed from a vague general collective legal framework towards a more specific and 'individualist' approach. The labour dispute handling system gives priority to settling individual labour disputes and disputes related to individual rights. The Labour Law of the PRC

---

[97] According to the 'Rules on Handling Enterprise Labour Disputes', promulgated by the State Council on 6 July 1993, the following items are labour disputes that should come under the jurisdiction of legal procedures:

> (1) a dispute which occurs due to an enterprise discharging an employee, removing an employee's name from its books or dismissing an employee, or due to an employee resigning or voluntarily leaving his/her position; (2) a dispute which occurs due to implementation of regulations of the State concerning wages and salaries, insurance, welfare, training or labour protection; (3) a dispute arising out of performance of a labour contract; and (4) other labour disputes which should be handled pursuant to the provisions of these Rules as stipulated by laws and statutory regulations.

provides that 'if a labour dispute between the employing unit and a labourer arises, the parties may apply for mediation or arbitration or take legal proceedings according to law, or may seek for a settlement through consultation' (Article 77). The 'Rules on the Handling of Enterprise Labour Disputes' also provide that 'an enterprise and its employee(s) who are involved in a labour dispute shall be the parties to that dispute' (Article 3). Second, the regulations covering labour disputes stress matters of rights, referring to the differences over the use, interpretation and application of existing rules (ILO 1977: 7). Those enterprises regulated by the Rules on Handling Enterprise Labour Disputes cover disputes that arise over disagreements in applying legal regulations, and do not specifically cover differences regarding the terms and conditions of employment.[98] Third, according to the law, a dispute involving more than three labourers should be defined as a collective dispute. However, in the labour dispute handling system in force up to the end of 2001, trade unions, in most cases, were not allowed to be involved in labour disputes. In other words, collective disputes represented by the trade unions were not recognized in this legal system. The amended Trade Union Law (2001) has entitled the trade unions to be a party involved in labour disputes specifically concerning collective contracts. Article 20 of the Law provides that:

> Where an enterprise infringes upon the workers' labour rights in violation of the collective contract, the trade union may demand that the enterprise be held liable under the law. Where a dispute occurs over the performance of a collective contract and where consultation has failed to produce a solution, the trade union may ask for arbitration from the labour dispute arbitration organ. Where the arbitration organ refuses to hear the case or if the party is not satisfied with the arbitration decision, it may initiate legal proceedings with a People's Court.

Further, in the newly added chapter (Article 49) on 'legal responsibility', it provides that:

> Where its legitimate rights and interests provided for in this Law are infringed upon, trade unions shall have the right to ask the people's government or its departments concerned to handle the matter, or to initiate legal proceedings with a People's Court.

---

[98] The labour administrative departments are also given the responsibility to handle the labour disputes that occur during the process of collective consultation. According to the 'Provisions of Collective Contract', where the two parties concerned are unable to settle a dispute arising from collective consultation, either party or both parties may file a written application for coordination and settlement to the departments, who shall normally conclude the settlement within 30 days from the date of deciding to accept the cases (Article 32, 35).

These provisions marked a great change in labour legislation through confirming the right of trade unions to bring a lawsuit in labour disputes against an employer. However, the Trade Union Law, following the 'Provisions on Collective Contract' (1994) does not take account of the possibility that an 'employing unit' might refuse to undertake collective consultation, or recognize that a collective dispute exists or allow the trade union to initiate a labour dispute handling process with itself. Therefore, once a labour dispute occurs, the Chinese trade union's function in protecting their members' interests still remains very limited and subject to employer compliance.

Along with the deepening reform of SOEs and the rapidly increasing employment in POEs, labour conflict is becoming more and more severe in China. Conflicts range from everyday workplace resistance, petitions, work stoppages and strikes to public protests, violence, independent unionism and political movements (Lee 2000: 41). It is not possible to gain accurate data for all or even some of these types of conflicts, although we will discuss what data is reliably available. Figure 7.1 shows the number of labour disputes referred to arbitration committees at all levels nationwide from 1986 to 2000 increased dramatically over the period. Considering the fact that many labour disputes do not apply for arbitration, the number of labour disputes is much higher than the statistics show.

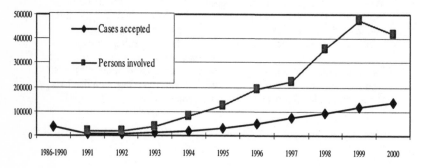

Source: NBS and MoLSS (various years 1990–2001).

*Figure 7.1  Labour dispute cases accepted by arbitration committees nationwide*

Figure 7.1 also shows that the number of labourers involved in labour disputes increased sharply, from 221 115 in 1997 to 422 617 in 1999, a rise of 91 per cent in two years. One of the explanations for this growth is that the forceful implementation of the 'staff downsizing' policy from 1997 resulted in many large scale lay-offs and led to collective disputes between laid-off workers and their management.[99] In 1999, the number of collective disputes accepted by the labour arbitration organs was 9043, amounting to 7.5 per cent of the total 120 191 cases submitted for arbitration. However, the number of

*Table 7.1 Scale of labour involvement in collective disputes (1999)*

| Scale (persons involved) | No. of collective disputes |
|---|---|
| 101 – 200 | 4 256 |
| 201 – 300 | 1 821 |
| 301 – 500 | 2 123 |
| 501 – 800 | 1 356 |
| 801 – 3000 | 2 963 |
| more than 3000 | 1 653 |
| total | 14 163 |

Source: Department of Policy Studies, ACFTU (2000: 157)

labourers involved in these collective disputes was 319 241, making up 67.3 per cent of the total number of workers in disputes (473 957). This indicates that more than two-thirds of labourers were involved in collective disputes. Another notable point is the increasing scale of collective disputes. Table 7.1 shows the scale of labour involved in 14 163 collective disputes in 1999.

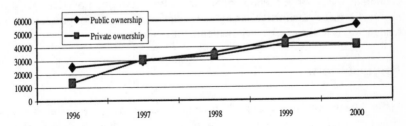

Source: NBS and MoLSS (various years 1997–2001).

*Figure 7.2 Labour disputes accepted by arbitration committees by ownership*

The number of labour disputes in non-public enterprises exceeds that in SOEs. Figure 7.2 shows that the increase in the number of labour disputes in non-public ownership enterprises was higher than that in the public sector.

---

[99] The drop in the numbers of workers involved in such disputes in 2000 seems not to indicate an overall or lasting decrease of collective disputes. One possible explanation, as we will discuss later, is people turn to public protests to express their demands. For example, in 34 'labour chaos' events reported by Jiang (2000), no one applied for arbitration before the event took place.

During the five years from 1996 to 2000, the number of labour disputes that occurred in the private sector increased by about 200 per cent, while that in the public sector rose by 120 per cent.

As shown in Table 7.2, of the disputes accepted by the arbitration committees nationwide, the first three categories accounted for 80.2 per cent of the total. Apart from disputes over labour contracts, according to P. Wang (2000) the main causes of labour conflicts were related to wages and social insurance, especially where labourers asked for remedy to solve delayed wages, payment or amount of social insurance fees, funds collected by employers, medical expenses, basic wages and severance pay.

*Table 7.2 Issues of labour disputes in 2000*

| Wages | Labour contract | Social insurance & benefits | Remedy for injury suffered on the job | Training | Others |
|-------|-----------------|-----------------------------|---------------------------------------|----------|--------|
| 41 671 | 35 794 | 31 350 | 13 008 | 12 549 | 834 |
| 30.8% | 26.3% | 23.1% | 9.6% | 9.2% | 0.6% |

Source: NBS and MoLSS (2001: 429).

There are three types of causes that lead to labour disputes: political, economic and infringed labour rights. In reality these often overlap, but it is useful to make distinctive analytical categories so as to present broad tendencies as to the causes and escalation of conflicts.

## Political Causes

Many labour disputes occurred directly because of government policies aimed at extending economic reform. SOEs (both in their original form and in new corporatized versions) in China have not become truly independent corporations that can be operated under market rules. The government directly intervenes in enterprise management and enterprise managements' decisions, over such matters as divestment, transforming from state ownership to shareholder ownership, contracting out, merging, downsizing, closing units, bankruptcy, lay-offs and so on. These decisions are usually made as a direct result of government policy or are instituted by government agencies themselves. In carrying out these policies, workers often resist privatizing their enterprises or oppose being laid off. The process of implementing these government policies is creating a strong sense of grievance among public sector workers (P. Wang 2000), which often puts managers in an awkward position of conflicting pressures.

Examining disputes related to one important issue, redundancy, a survey conducted by the MoLSS in 1998–99 summarized a number of causes that led to labour disputes among laid-off workers (Institute of Labour Science, MoLSS 2001). One cause was that the workers were reluctant to terminate their employment relationship with SOEs because they were worried about their future. Another was that neither the central government nor the local governments have promulgated a unified set of standards to compensate the laid-off workers. On this latter point, in different cities, even in different enterprises within the same cities, SOE managers follow different standards to provide compensation to laid-off workers. There are three standards promulgated by the central government. The first one is giving a living allowance under the 'Temporary Provisions on Implementing Labour Contract System in SOEs' (issued by the State Council in July 1987); the second is paying economic compensation to laid-off workers according to the 'Measures of Economic Compensations for Violating and Revocation of Labour Contracts' (issued by the MoL December 1994); and the third one is, according to the 'Notice of Some Issues about Experiment of Bankruptcy in SOEs in Some Cities' (promulgated by the State Council, in October 1994), paying a lump-sum severance payment to the workers dismissed because of their enterprise's bankruptcy. However, these are interpreted differently in different situations, and the enterprise's supervising agencies and local governments often make their own additional regulations.

Other problems include how to settle retirees and how to pay their pensions, in which managers of publicly owned enterprises have no discretion to develop their own measures, but instead must rely on policies from government. The pensions are paid out of the cumulative deferred wages of workers and vary considerably between enterprises, but government policies on disbursement are often inappropriate for particular enterprises, especially within the context of competing demands placed upon them by government. Therefore, the nature of labour disputes in the public sector is not only one between workers and their managers, but also includes tripartite disputes concerning workers, enterprises and the government. The foundation of these disputes is conflicts between the workers' interests and the government's policies (which reflect CCP interests).

## Economic Causes

Economic competition is often used as a weapon to force concessions from workers, especially in the private sector. However, the political economic reality of market-based resource allocation is the desire of capital to organize their power to disadvantage workers in the market place. This can be seen most clearly in the private sector in China, which has large income disparities between managers and workers but also among workers themselves. In the public sector, the whole function of the market economy was to drive up their efficiency. Accusations of poor management, corruption, loss of product markets and inability to secure appropriate resources are common criticisms of the public sector in China and overseas. Whilst this smells of self-righteous liberalism, the fact is that a large number of public enterprises (as well as good number of private ones) are now defined as 'loss making'. As the government has increasingly taken the policy of not 'bailing out' public enterprises, managers often choose to delay wage payments, deny medical reimbursements or go into arrears over pension and living allowances. According to the ACFTU, wage arrears among SOEs and COEs in 1999 reached 249 and 40 billions yuan, and involving 8.64 and 1.88 million workers respectively (Department of Policy Studies, ACFTU 2000: 136). At the same time, in many cases the directors may well be 'selling off the family silver' and lining their own pockets in the process (often self-justified, based on fear of non-payment devaluing their own pensions in the future). A survey conducted by MoLSS indicated that about 70 per cent of laid-off workers were creditors of their former enterprises (Mo 2002: 165–74). Delayed wage payments have become a major nationwide problem in recent years (*Gongren ribao* 7 February 2002). Some enterprises' inability to pay labour insurance premiums has led to protests by laid-off and retired workers who cannot be paid out of these depleted funds.[100] According to information from Jiang (2000), the widespread escalation in overt labour conflict in Mainland China between 1997 and July 2000 was mainly due to delayed wage payments, involving 50 000 to 100 000 workers. The labour chaos which occurred in Daqing City, Heilongjiang Province and Liaoyang City, Liaoning Province in March 2002 were also caused by the decisions of management to tear-up an agreement concerning severance pay and refusal to continue payments of an 'arming fee' (BBC 13 March 2001).

## Infringing Labour Rights

Another reason behind increasing labour conflict is illegal employer behaviour that infringes workers' legally enshrined labour rights. Figure 7.3

---

[100] Some accounts have reported that failure to pay insurance fees for workers has been the main cause of collective labour disputes. For example, on 6 July 2001 when over 1000 workers from a sugar factory in Linhe City, Inner Mongolia, gathered outside the offices of the Lake Bayan district Central Party Committee offices. They were protesting against the company's failure to pay labour insurance premiums and demanding that the government fulfil its duty to provide workers with livelihood guarantees (see Pringle 2001).

shows the outcome of labour dispute arbitration, and indicates that the rate by which labourers win their cases continually increased from 31.7 per cent in 1992 to 51.9 per cent in 2000, while that of employers decreased from 32.8 per cent to 10.4 per cent. This shows not only that the arbitration system does appear to be upholding justice and protecting the disadvantaged, but also that there are more and more severe illegal infringements of workers' rights and interests by employers.

In the private sector, the major cause of labour disputes is the exploitation in a pattern resembling Marx's early stage of 'primitive capital accumulation', and such despotic capitalism is experienced especially by workers from rural and inland provinces who go to work in coastal and industrialized cities. Most labour disputes occur in medium to small-sized FIEs invested by Asian and overseas Chinese capital and in POEs. The infringement of labour rights covers several areas, such as working time, wages, working conditions and physical freedom. It is common in many POEs and FIEs that forced overtime working can stretch the working day to 14 hours or longer (Ouyang 2000; Huo 2000). In some processing enterprises, overtime with little pay is also common. In most POEs and FIEs, migrant workers can only gain low wages, sometimes even lower than the locally mandated minimum wages. The result of a survey of migrant workers showed that about 52 per cent of them were dissatisfied with their wages (Huo 2000). Wage arrears and deductions are also serious problems in these enterprises. In some enterprises there are draconian work rules that involve a set of fines that are deducted from wages.

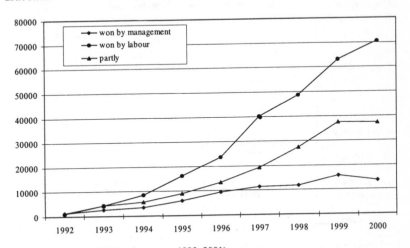

Source: NBS and MoLSS (various years 1993–2001).

*Figure 7.3 Labour dispute cases arbitrated by the labour dispute arbitration committee*

There are cases where workers end up owing their employers money at the end of the month. In some enterprises, workers have between three months to half a year's wages held back by management to prevent workers leaving (Qu 2000; Huo 2000). There are also cases where workers could not gain their withheld wages at the end of their contract because the employers absconded with the funds (Qu 2000). Disputes caused over who bears responsibility for workers' (and occasionally managers') injuries are some of the most distressing conflicts. Often poor working conditions in these enterprises and some collective disputes over personal infringement of migrant workers are the usual causes of sudden outbursts of overt conflict, as well as a growing underlying tension within private sector labour relations. These infringements cover numerous problems, from personal insults to physical punishment and restrictions on personal freedom (Yin 1999; Qu 2000; Song and Ding 1993; Huo 2000).

The course of economic reform saw a marked increase in labour disputes. While the individual disputes are increasing sharply, collective disputes are spreading significantly, both geographically and in different types of enterprises. Besides the causes of infringing labour rights, the political and economic causes also lead to these disputes and combine to make settlement more difficult.

## HANDLING LABOUR DISPUTES

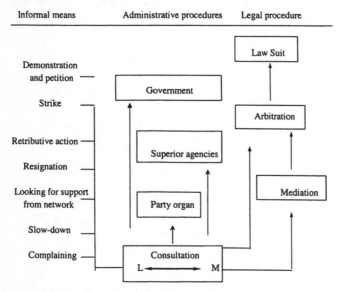

*Figure 7.4 The procedures and means of handling labour conflict*

Along with the market-oriented development of China's labour relations, the increase in labour disputes has caught the government's attention again. The increase in labour disputes both contributes to and reflects a general growing unrest in Chinese society. From the beginning of reform, the central government has realised this problem and initiated a legal system to settle labour disputes. Figure 7.4 lays out the formal procedures for dispute settlement. In addition to the forms discussed in Figure 4.1, workers often use various informal means to express their conflict with management.

## Legal Proceedings: Mediation, Arbitration and Lawsuit

After the PRC was established, the MoL issued the 'Provisions on the Proceedings of Labour Dispute Settlement' in 1950, which stipulated four methods to settle disputes: consultation, mediation, arbitration and judicial decision. In 1956, after the socialist transformation of ownership occurred, the labour dispute-settling organs at all levels were repealed and replaced by the process known as 'letters and calls of complaint from the people' (*renmin laixin laifang* or *xinfang*). After 30 years, in 1987, the State Council renewed the labour dispute settlement system by issuing the 'Temporary Regulation of Labour Dispute Settlement in SOEs'. In 1993, the State Council promulgated the 'Rules on Handling Enterprise Labour Disputes', initially making up the framework of the labour disputes handling system that it thought was suitable for a market economy in China, and supposedly closely following practices in industrialized countries. This system includes proceedings for mediation, arbitration and judicial settlement.

As the lowest level in labour dispute handling, mediation is exercised mainly within enterprises. The regulations lay down clear guidelines for mediation, as follows. When both parties fail to settle their dispute through consultation, either party may apply to a mediation committee. An enterprise may establish a labour dispute mediation committee consisting of representative(s), each for employees, the enterprise and the trade union. An employee representative shall be elected by the workers' congress; an enterprise representative shall be appointed by the factory director (manager); and the trade union committee shall appoint a trade union representative. The chairperson of a mediation committee shall be the representative of the trade union. The office of the conciliation committee of an enterprise shall be established in the trade union of that enterprise. In mediating a labour dispute, the mediation committee shall observe the principles of voluntary participation by the parties concerned. If an agreement is reached through mediation, a mediation agreement shall be produced and shall be conscientiously implemented by the parties concerned. If mediation fails to resolve the matter, the parties concerned may, within a stipulated period of time, apply to the labour dispute arbitration committee for arbitration. However, mediation is not the only way available to an aggrieved party to proceed in handling a labour dispute. When a labour dispute occurs, the parties concerned may choose mediation, or choose to go directly to arbitration.

Arbitration is a procedure led by the labour administrative organs of the government within the MoLSS. It has become the major method to process enterprise-based labour disputes in recent years. A labour dispute arbitration committee shall be established at either of two levels: county or municipality. In recent years some labour dispute arbitration committees have been established at the provincial level as well. An arbitration committee consists of representatives of the competent labour administration organs (labour bureaux), representatives of the trade union and enterprise representatives. The number of members of an arbitration committee shall be odd, and the chairperson shall be the person drawn from the labour bureau (the competent labour administration department). The organizational structure of the arbitration committee reflects the tripartite principle of industrial relations handling in a market economy that the government wishes to develop. Any party to a labour dispute may apply in writing to the labour arbitration committee for arbitration. The labour dispute arbitration makes a finite decision that provides for a one-off settlement or award. If a party disagrees with an arbitration award, that party may file a suit in the People's Court. In 1999, there were 26 000 enterprise-based labour dispute mediation committees, more than 3000 arbitration committees, more than 1.5 million enterprise mediators and 17 000 full-time and part-time labour arbitrators (Department of Policy Studies, ACFTU 2000: 157–59).

A lawsuit is a legal proceeding of labour dispute handling to hear and settle labour disputes in court. There are no special labour courts or labour tribunals in China. In the past either administrative courts or economic courts accepted most labour dispute cases. In recent years, civil courts accept all labour dispute cases. In accordance with the proceedings of a civil suit, the labour dispute suit adopts the system of final judgment by court of second instance. The precondition for a labour dispute suit to be accepted by the court is that the dispute has been given an award by a labour arbitration committee. This means an attempt at labour arbitration must precede a lawsuit. Along with the growth in the number of labour disputes and an increasing legal consciousness among labourers, the number of labour dispute lawsuits has been rapidly increasing. During a five-year period from 1995 to 1999, the number of labour dispute lawsuits accepted by courts nationwide increased by 26.9 per cent every year (Supreme People's Court of the PRC 2001).

## *Inadequacy of Legal Proceedings*

Since being re-established in 1987, the system of labour dispute settlement has played an active role in handling labour disputes and protecting workers' rights and interests to some degree. However, the labour dispute handling system in China has a number of problems, some of which are discussed below.

First, in the mediation system established within enterprises, the grass-roots unions' role as mediator contradicts its legal role as representative of workers. This contradiction results from the provisions of the current Trade Union Law (2001). According to the Trade Union Law, where an enterprise infringes upon workers' labour rights, the grass-roots union shall make representations to the enterprise on behalf of the workers and demand that the enterprise take corrective measures (Article 22). At the same time, the law states that the trade union shall participate in the enterprise's labour dispute mediation (Article 28). Both provisions place the grass-roots union in an embarrassing position when it is involved in labour disputes where the employer is in the wrong. On the one hand, it has to represent workers to fight for their interests; on the other hand, as the chairperson of the mediation committee, it is required to keep a neutral status as the third party. The trade unions' contradictory roles in mediation procedures reflect the tripartite structure of labour relations in Chinese enterprise, but in so doing highlight the ambiguous role of the trade unions as to where they stand in tripartism.[101]

In reality, the grass-roots trade unions play the role of coordinating labour conflict. The significance of legal regulations in setting up mediation committees and appointing the trade union as the mediator is in defining this role for trade unions. Guan and Cao (2000) found that in the mediation committee (consisting of three representatives from workers, management and trade union) only the last-named is the real or active player. No matter how effective the union is in playing its role as mediator, its position between both parties can at least relax the tension that results from labour disputes. Therefore, in a survey conducted by the ACFTU in 1997, workers gave higher evaluation to the role of grass-roots unions in mediating labour disputes than other union functions (Department of Policy Studies, ACFTU 1999: 1249). However, when collective disputes occur resulting in overt

---

[101] Such a 'tripartite' structure, consisting of workers, trade unions and employers, is a special case in transition period of China. It is not only different from the tripartite structure consisting of the government, employers and workers in a market economy, but also different from the administrative structure consisting of state, enterprises (trade unions) and workers of the planned economy. Since the 1990s, the ACFTU gave priority to 'adjusting labour relations as workers' representative' in its work (D. Zhang 1994) However, the problem of how to represent workers as well as adjusting labour relations remains unsolved both in theory and in practice.

conflict, trade unions usually fail to respond. These collective disputes may have indicated the failure of mediation, but the organizers in most cases ignore or by pass the official union, and in these disputes (including strikes, slow-down and demonstration) the scope for settlement has developed beyond the control or capacity of trade unions. For example, a survey conducted in 47 shoe-making factories showed that, among the 11 in which collective disputes had occurred, none of the disputes were settled by the trade unions (Lu 1999).

Second, in the Chinese system of labour dispute settlement, the arbitration procedure must precede the lawsuit. This means that neither party to a labour dispute can bring a lawsuit if the case has not be accepted or given an award by arbitration organs. While this encourages the parties to seek settlement before escalation to a formal legal setting, it also denies either parties rights to legal recourse or to gain legal protection through lawsuit, which is supposed to be the right every Chinese citizen enjoys under the constitution. It also makes the proceedings to handle labour disputes longer and more complex, and raises the cost for both parties (Luo and Chen, 2001). The arbitration award has no legal effect at the time it is made if a party disagrees with the award. The dissenting party may file a suit in the People's Court within 15 days of receiving that award. Therefore, having arbitration and lawsuit proceedings sequentially delays settlement, which can seriously disadvantage workers. At present, both domestic and overseas labour law academics and practitioners have a common understanding that arbitration is not absolutely necessary in handling labour rights disputes. There is no theoretical problem in allowing parties to a labour dispute to directly file a civil suit, and the present system in China goes against the interests of labourers. Huang (1994: 353) argues that whether or not the parties to a labour dispute decide to apply for mediation and arbitration should be left to them. Referring to the experiences of liberal industrialized countries, there is a growing preference to allow the parties to choose labour arbitration or alternatively choose a lawsuit, and arbitration or court judgement would give a final award in each system (Xia 1999: 18).

Third, the Chinese government has not set up a system of labour courts to settle labour disputes. Once the civil court accepts the labour dispute, it will apply the principles of civil and commercial laws to make its judgements, dealing with labour disputes as original civil cases. In reality, the civil court is puzzled by the principles of both kinds of law. Theoretically, civil laws are based on the equal rights of parties while the labour law is based on the reality of labour relations, recognizing inequality of power between employers and employed (Nishitani 1992: 45). In cases where there are gaps or ambiguities in the provisions of labour laws, the provisions and principles of civil laws are used instead. However, the provisions and principles of labour laws are used as the basis for filing a civil labour suit. The judge is faced with a dilemma in this, because it is quite difficult to decide such cases since one judicial organ cannot refer to two distinct sets of legal systems and legal principles. Without a specialized labour court or tribunal system, it is difficult to overcome these problems.[102]

Fourth, apart from labour disputes relating to collective contracts, trade unions have not tried to develop a system for dealing with collective labour disputes. The concept of 'collective labour dispute' referred to in the current system is a labour dispute that 'involves more than three employees with common reasons'.[103] This is naturally a kind of individual labour dispute with more employees involved but without the intervention of the trade union. The exception that allows the trade union to be involved is when a labour dispute concerns performance of a collective contract. However, few if any such cases have ever been sent for arbitration. In ACFTU's statistical data collection system, this kind of labour dispute is not categorized. To a great extent, the Chinese government's policy may contribute to this situation. For a long time, the government has taken an avoiding attitude towards collective labour relations, and avoided the official unions being involved in such activities, in case they are seen to encourage and legitimize the precursor to class-based struggle. As will be discussed latter, the lack of a clear right to strike serves as an example. Although the collective contract system has been implemented in Chinese enterprises, the government does not regard it as the major mode for adjusting labour relations in practice. In addition, once arbitration is introduced as a method to deal with collective labour disputes, it will bring about many new legal problems, such as the right to strike. Because there are no definite provisions within China's laws yet, collective contract dispute handling is simply evaded.

## *Administrative Procedures*

In spite of the discussion above, in practice most labour disputes are settled through administrative procedures. When there is a labour dispute the aggrieved party will complain to their superiors and mangers first, but often quickly seek to involve the Party organ of their work unit or to the local government offices to demand settlement. This amounts to an informal use of the administrative system to settle disputes. Through these activities, people usually believe their supervisors can act as mediators and believe their 'superiors' can handle these disputes fairly. Due to the traditional paternalism rooted in the state sector, workers 'looking for assistance from the Party

---

[102] It is reported that a 'labour arbitration court' with the nature of 'quasi-court' has already been set up in Shenzhen City, Guangdong Province (*Gongren ribao* 25 Janaury 2002 [2]).

[103] Article 5 of the 'Rules of the PRC on the Handling of Enterprise Labour Dispute'.

organ' is still taken by many workers as the way to resolve their conflict with management, at least initially. In a survey conducted by the ACFTU in 1997, the most common response (28.4 per cent) among SOE workers and staff was to ask assistance from Party organs or senior supervisors as their first choice when they have a problem (Department of Policy Studies, ACFTU 1999: 1641). Liu's survey (2002) in a large-sized SOE in Beijing also indicated this point. Among six formal means for settling labour disputes Liu found respondents favoured 'looking for leadership's assistance and requiring fair treatment' the most, and this was especially the case for rank-and-file workers. When this trust is betrayed, as appears increasingly to be happening, Western press and media often report the subsequent struggles. This can be misleading because the fact is many workers still look to the administration (management, party and government) to act fairly, and/or in their interests.

In situations where a labour conflict could not be resolved within the organization, the parties can enter the second step, which involves 'letters and calls of complaint from the people' (*xinfang*). *Xinfang* is a system of administrative appeal set up in the initial stage of the establishment of the PRC and is still effective in settling labour disputes. Some parties to labour disputes appeal for settlement through this system. In the 'Regulations on *Xinfang*', issued by the State Council in 1995, this system is defined as the one through which 'citizens, artificial persons and other organizations reflect information to the governments above the county level, offering their opinions, suggestions and demands, and asking for administrative settlement'. This system embodies the government's direct intervention into labour relations in enterprises, and has had some effectiveness in dealing with large-scale collective labour disputes in recent years. However, this is an administrative procedure rather than a legal redress system, and is rather special for handling labour disputes. It adopts the principles of:

> Taking charge according to grade, settling matters according to sector ... persons who are in charge of [or] responsible for settlement [and] coming in time and on the spot with persuading and instruction.[104]

Except for very large-scale collective appeals that are clearly related to government policy, which will be settled by the central and provincial governments directly, individual and small-scale collective appeals are transferred to local industrial bureaux, government offices and the like for settlement. Therefore, few individual or collective disputes joined by a few labourers can be resolved through *xinfang* because it has no legal basis to do so, and the department of *xinfang* could not intervene directly in labour

---

[104] Article 4 of 'Regulations on *Xinfang*'.

disputes, being able only to give some advice and without compulsion (Seung 2000).

In recent years, to resolve the difficulties caused by policies and loss making, more and more labourers employed *xinfang* to communicate their demands and dissatisfaction to the government. According to statistics, compared with 1997, the collective-visits-time and person-time accepted by the Departments of *xinfang* at different levels respectively increased 50.3 per cent and 60 per cent in 1998, and 18.7 per cent and 9.9 per cent in 1999 (Li 2001). Some intellectuals think that this tendency to use *xinfang* has been growing for at least ten years, sparked off by the second round of reform in the early 1990s. Li (2001) and Shao (2001) argue that people select *xinfang* as a channel to resolve collective disputes because it is cheap and effective.

## Informal Means Adopted by Workers

The informal means adopted by workers can usually be divided into three kinds of practices: passive resistance, social network support and collective protest. The last will be left to the following section, and the first two dealt with below.

As shown in Figure 7.4, workers' passive responses to conflict include individual tolerance, grievance, slacking off, resignation, stealing raw materials and products, retributive action and so on. It is notable that, through these methods, workers usually sporadically vent their anger rather than seeking to resolve the conflict or gain a remedy from management. Due to the pressures from the labour market, increasing numbers of workers appear to be tolerant of their lost interests and resigned to such inequities as illegal management behaviour. There appears to be a kind of tolerance threshold set by workers, above which they resign themselves to a sinking class status. For public sector workers, the minimum is job security, which does not necessarily mean work or pay, just that the enterprise keeps their employment cards. For the private sector, perhaps the threshold is that pay should be higher than before. Li (2000) studied a declining factory in northern China and found high levels of acquiescence. A printing worker described his attitude in this SOE factory:

> The labour relations in SOEs are so simple that you couldn't believe it. We would follow whatever the managers order us, we are fearful of them breaking our 'rice bowl'. In this case, there are not any labour disputes. If you don't want to be dismissed, OK, you had better shut up, even though you are dissatisfied with something.

Y. Liu's study (2002) also indicated that, among eight informal means for dealing with labour conflicts, 'complaint' and 'tolerating and accepting reality' were the first two choices indicated by workers. Some studies show that migrant workers in POEs and FIEs appear to have similar responses when their rights are ignored or suppressed by employers. For example, in most POEs and FIEs in the Pearl River Delta, migrant workers seem to have become accustomed to the unlimited requirement to do overtime (Luo and Chen 2001; Yu 1999). In addition, in a survey conducted in Hongshan District, Wuhan City, about 45 per cent of migrant workers interviewed expressed that they would be tolerant even though they had realised their rights and interests were infringed by management (Hu and Luo 2001).

When labour conflict cannot be resolved within enterprises, some workers choose to resign. Migrant workers employed in POEs and FIEs use resignation to a great extent, reflected in high rates of labour turnover in the private sector (Song and Ding 1993).[105] The result from a survey involving 1543 workers showed that 32.4 per cent of respondents thought they would resign if they had a conflict within their enterprise that could not be resolved internally (Lu 1999). This action has been referred to as 'recessive gambling' (Zhang 2001), where workers try their luck at different enterprises to see if they can strike it lucky and find a 'good' employer. Taylor (2000) found that labour turnover rates varied significantly between Japanese enterprises in China but also that some FIEs use labour turnover as a strategic management tool to cut labour costs where there is seasonal production. Thus, whilst labour turnover may reflect conflict on the part of workers, for employers it is not certain they feel the same.

A few workers, either in the public or private sectors, vent their anger by destroying machines and raw materials, slacking off or disclosing commercial secrets (Song and Ding 1993). Steeling raw materials, equipment and products from enterprises was also taken as a way to remedy problems (Yu 1999), either taking items to sell to make up for lost earnings or simply to retaliate. In addition, workers' extreme actions to employers, such as inflicting personal injury, have increased. These 'non-rational' actions occurred mainly in POEs before, but injuries to SOE managers may also be on the rise in recent years.[106]

## Local Gangs

The shortage of institutionalized social support for migrant workers in urban

---

[105] Workers changing jobs and employers changing their workers is very common. According to a survey by Feng (1995), 52 per cent of migrant workers have experience of changing jobs.
[106] It is reported that, within half a year, three directors of SOEs in Hubei Province have been killed (Tian 2002).

areas has forced them to look for representation and protection through other informal means. Some unofficial migrant worker groups began to be formed, usually based on regions (that is, hometowns) where member migrant workers come from (*tongxiang* in Chinese), and some bear the features of local gangs. These informal organizations often protect their members' interests in very spontaneous manners, such as random strikes, case-by-case petitions and militant protests (Bai 2001: 211–26; Lau 1997: 64–5). Such informal loosely arranged organizations share some common characteristics, such as focusing on economic issues in a spontaneous fashion and with voluntary participation. They often represent workers' very preliminary effort to organize themselves concerning practical problems and mostly these gangs are non-political (Bai 2001: 211–26).

These gangs form an important social network for the passing of information among members concerning many aspects of their lives, from schooling opportunities to noting notorious employers. A survey of 1504 migrant workers in Jinan City, Shangdong Province showed that about 80 per cent of migrant workers found their first jobs through the assistance of their relatives and fellow villagers (Li et al. 2000: 196). In this way, people usually work in the same sites and for some time, developing their own social network, the so-called 'local gang'. J. Sun (2001), through participant observation on racial groups at an FIE in Shenzhen, Guangdong Province, found that the connection between fellow villagers was a very important, popular and effective relationship. She also found that through these networks certain racial groups grew in numbers, which in turn came to dominate social relations at the workplace in this factory. However, at the same time, the so-called 'local gang' was a kind of informal group whose purpose was to deal with sensitive competition with other social groups in the labour market and provide support to workers to survive when they are far away from their homes. Whilst not designed for the purpose, these organizations appear to be able to provide various forms of assistance for their members,[107] including helping with complaints and discussing ways to resolve such problems. Sometimes, and to some extent, these organizations could pressure management if sufficient workers cooperated with the gang. Moreover, in a few cases, these organizations would become the tool by which the migrant workers resorted to retributive action against their supervisors (Yu 1999), including beatings.[108]

After comparing the costs of undertaking different forms of dispute

---

[107] It should be emphasized that the investigation of local gang activities is extremely difficult, as those are mostly underground and informal groups; some even have linkage to criminal triads. This difficulty is realized by other researchers (see for example Bai 2001).

[108] In a survey by Hu and Luo (2001), 29.4 per cent of migrant workers stated that they would resolve the problems by 'mustering a band of brothers' when their interests were infringed.

resolution, informal means may be the choice for most workers because of the higher cost of formal procedures. Under the current regulations, the maximum time for both procedures of mediation and arbitration will be 90 days, and once a case becomes a lawsuit, it will last much longer. Furthermore, workers are not sure they will win after these legal procedures. Compared with urban workers, the situation of migrant workers may be worse because of their shortage of social support in urban areas (Yin 2001) and lack of money to take formal proceedings. According to the statistics of an arbitration committee in 1997, among the cases won by workers, the average proportion of compensation decided by the arbitrators was different between urban and migrant workers. The former could gain 68.4 per cent of their requirement and the latter, only 39.6 per cent (Yu 1999). Therefore, to save costs migrant workers are especially prone to adopting informal means to resolve their conflict with management, as well as being more likely to simply acquiesce to management.

## COLLECTIVE ACTIONS

Collective actions organized by Chinese workers take place within a political context that often associates non-Party sponsored collective actions with subversion, on the one hand, but also an understandable expression of frustration among urban workers who are politically identified as the rhetorical 'masters'. This mix has meant that collective conflicts in China are rather different and certainly more imaginative than most strikes in liberal industrialized countries. Collective actions are officially called *tufa shijia'* (precipitating events) in China,[109] and include processions, petitions, sit-down demonstrations and strikes, which are invariably spontaneously organized by workers. In the 'Regulations on Handling Collective Event of Public Order by Public Security', issued by the Ministry of Public Security in May 2000, 'precipitating event' is given the title of 'collective event of public order', referring to such actions that 'assemble crowds and jointly commit actions that violate state laws and regulations, disturbing public order, endangering public security, infringing upon citizens' safety of the person and the security of public or private property'. This covers illegal assembly and demonstrations joined by many people (although the exact number is unclear); actions in demonstration and *xinfang* that seriously disturb public order; workers', students' and shopkeepers' strikes that seriously affect social stability; and assemblies organized by illegal and 'evil' religious

---

[109] *'Tufa shijian'* is a word frequently used by the top leaders of the government in their speeches and in MoL documents from 1995 (Zhu 1996b: 113-18; MoL 1995).

organizations. It also covers crowds assembling to besiege the Party, government or judicial departments; and crowds organized to block traffic, to endanger the traffic security and to occupy important public places (Fu 2000). The significance of this long list is that all these forms of collective action take place sporadically, but frequently, in most cities of China. Such a range of activities includes non-work-related conflicts but workers and supporters of workers engage in all types of collective action. This makes conflict in China a part of the fabric of society and one that carries deep political significance, even if conflicts are articulated in forms of economic grievances. However, it is an illogical leap of imagination to connect these growing forms and numbers of mass conflicts with calls for liberal notions of democracy or as challenges to the authority of the CCP. If anything, workers' protests should be considered in quite the opposite context, a demand for socialist democracy and appeals to the CCP to heed the calls of the masses and abide by principles of socialism.

## *Strikes*

Since the beginning of the second round of reform (1992 to date), the PRC has been experiencing a third wave of strike and collective conflict escalation.[110] Compared with the first and the second periods of strike activity, the current period of conflict has been continuing for more than ten years, with no signs of diminishing.

Workers in China have found the strike weapon to be an effective means by which they can exert pressure on management as well as on the government, because the latter always gives priority to maintaining social peace. Therefore, in recent years, workers more frequently resort to strikes to express their complaints. However, for political and legal reasons, as a type of 'emergent event', strikes are usually called 'work stoppages' or 'work slow-down' in China and at present there are no official statistics about strikes nationwide.[111] The number of strikes is often included in the number of collective labour disputes. Therefore, research on strikes can only depend on regional statistics or case studies discovered by researchers or reported in the media.

---

[110] The first climax of strike activity in the PRC occurred in the 1950s due to lockouts and shutdowns of factories in the process of struggles between capitalists (entrepreneurs) and the CCP. The second climax was in the year 1956 when some workers' rights were reduced by the policies of socialist reconstruction of ownership. The government successfully put down these strikes by employing some appeasement policies (Chang 2002b).

[111] In all published statistical compendia, strikes are included in the item of collective labour disputes. See, Department of Policy Studies, ACFTU. *Chinese Trade Unions Yearbooks*, NBS and MoLSS *China Labour Statistics Yearbooks*.

The present phase of increased strike activity may be characterized in the following way. First, the frequency and number of people involved are both increasing. According to an outdated research conducted by the MoL, the number of workers involved in strikes increased by 100 per cent between 1990 and 1994, putting the PRC in the first place among 17 countries and regions studied.[112] Second, the strikes are invariably caused by employer infringements of workers' interests. So the strikes are always related to the individual's labour rights and seldom result from negotiating and implementing collective contracts. Moreover, often at the start of a conflict, management had tried to suppress aggrieved workers using some form of illegal intimidation. Once the aggrieved workers no longer tolerate this, conflict escalates, tensions become explosive and collective actions follow. A strike that occurred in a Japanese-invested enterprise in Fujian Province indicates this point well. After 34 workers jointly complained to their supervisor, all of them were given a disciplinary warning. The workers then responded with a strike joined by 400 people (Lin and Chen 1993). Third, strikes are generally focused on 'obtain[ing] alteration in the work situation or the employment relationship' (Hyman, 1984: 136), and so long as these are dealt with to the workers' satisfaction disputes tend to be resolved quickly; if they are handled insensitively they escalate. Fourth, workers themselves initiate these strikes, without the support or approval of their trade unions. This demonstrates clearly that the unions are not workers' organizations. However, we know that many union cadres are highly sympathetic to strikers and sometimes, more instrumentally, use the potential for strikes as a bargaining tool to encourage FIEs and POE owners to establish official unions in their plants (Fu et al. 2001). However, as strikes are illegal acts and having learned their lessons from supporting students in 1989, the official unions try to, or are asked to, act as conciliators between workers and management during industrial actions.

## Legal Provisions on Strike

Strictly speaking, Chinese law neither allows nor prohibits strikes. In brief, 'basically the existing legal system evades the problem of strikes' (Chang and Zhang 1993: 322–23). This is something of an anomaly in a market economy (Chang 1998; Shi 1999) and perhaps not even legal. Article 8 of the International Covenant on Economic, Social and Cultural Rights (ICESCR) states that 'Parties to this Covenant undertake to ensure the right to strike, provided that it is exercised in conformity with the laws of the particular

---

[112] The five years' data were: 243000 in 1990, 288600 in 1991, 268400 in 1992, 310300 in 1993 and 495600 in 1994 (Research Team of MoLSS 1997).

country'. This covenant, ratified by the Standing Committee of the National People's Congress of China in March 2001, has provided a legal base for legislation to define a right to strike in China. By joining this covenant, the Chinese government has promised to provide workers with the right to strike.

It should be noted that the amended Trade Union Law (2001) has made much progress in this direction. Concerning the actions of stoppage and slowdown, Article 27 of the Trade Union Law provides that:

> in the events of stoppage and slowdown at enterprises or institutes, the trade unions shall, on behalf of workers and staff, consult with the enterprise, institution, or other parties concerned, reflect the views and demands of the workers, and put forward ideas for a solution. The enterprise or institute shall work to meet the reasonable demands of workers and staff. The trade unions shall assist the enterprises or institutes to resume production and restore work order as soon as possible.

Although the concept of 'strike' is not used in this law, the words 'stoppages' and 'slowdowns' undoubtedly act as an equivalent. This article has two important implications. First, it provides a legal basis for workers' actions of stoppage and slowdown. These actions, for a long time, were seen as 'disrupting production' and prohibited by law and work rules. Second, it defines the status of trade unions as the 'representative of workers and staff' in events of stoppages and slowdowns, differing from the provision in the Trade Union Law of 1992, which stated the responsibility of trade unions as 'dealing with the happenings with the management together' (Article 25).[113] Therefore, the amended law recognizes not only the validity of strikes organized by labourers spontaneously, but also the status of trade unions as the representative of workers and staff in a strike.

However, it also falls far short of the strike legislation suitable for a market economy. There is an anomaly in having strikes initiated by labourers but managed by trade unions once they have been started. Moreover, the right to strike implied in the Trade Union Law is only a passive recognition, not an active provision. It does not explicitly stipulate the right to strike and therefore cannot provide a legal basis for framing more detailed rules. Whilst a positive right to strike is also absent in the UK, for example, the legal tradition is very different. In China there is a tendency to see things as illegal or ambiguous unless legally permitted, whereas Anglo-Saxon law tends

---

[113] Article 25 of the Trade Union Law (1992) stated that when slowdowns and stoppages take place, trade unions shall recover the normal state of production as soon as possible by consulting and settling workers' requirements through cooperation with the management or authorities concerned.

towards freedom unless proscribed. Nevertheless, the new law does pave the way for further legislation and this is significant (Qiao 2002: 243–51).

The legalization of the right to strike requires proper legal and social circumstances, especially a trade union that can really represent the workers' interests. Once the Chinese workers are legally entitled to the right to strike, what they need is a legal trade union, not an 'official union' or 'yellow union' controlled by the employer. The status and function of Chinese trade unions, especially those in non-publicly owned enterprises, lead people to doubt their capability to shoulder the responsibility for organizing collective labour disputes and strikes. In the case where the trade union is unable to organize the strike, while the worker's spontaneous strike is prohibited, the effect of strike legislation is to restrict strikes. Therefore, only by combining this law with legislation on freedom of association and the right to collective bargaining can Chinese legislation give a substantive right to strike to workers.

## Demonstration and Petition by Workers

A survey by the ACFTU reports that in recent years collective events keep increasing in some areas and industries (ACFTU 2002: 438). Although detailed information about these events is rarely reported in Mainland China, some common points of these events can still be found from overseas media and some papers published in the journals issued by domestic colleges that belong to the Ministry of Public Security. First, more people have been involved in these events. To give just a few examples, around 20 000 workers joined a demonstration caused by wage arrears in February 2000 in Liaoning Province (*Financial Times* 4 April 2000: 1). A demonstration occurred in March 2002 in Daqing City, Heilongjiang Province that involved 50 000 workers (BBC 13 March 2002; Liu 2002). These workers usually received widespread sympathy from citizens because others (or their relatives) have much the same experiences. According to a survey in Changchun City, Jilin Province, 73.8 per cent of respondents showed their sympathy toward others' collective action, such as collective *xinfang* (Song and Wang 1999: 271–83). The government's biggest fear in these mass demonstrations is the chance a 'chain reaction' maybe set up around the country. Once other workers in the same region understand these collective actions will bring about the results they want, more events would follow (Fan 2001) and encourage workers to think that collective actions are the best alternatives to achieve redress (Lei 2001). Second, actions such as demonstrations, petitions and blocking the road or railway lines often accompany these mass collective actions. Strictly speaking, these events are not industrial actions, but political actions targeting government rather than employers. The dominant status of the government in the labour market has transformed some conflicts between workers and management to ones between workers and government. For SOE workers, they well understand that they may be laid off and become unemployed because of the privatization and corporatization policies actively being pursued by the government. Moreover, many workers and citizens are angry that, whilst their wages are delayed and benefits cut, they see managerial corruption and increased pay disparities tolerated by the government. Some POE and FIE workers have realized that their marginal status is caused by the close relationship between their employers and local government officials. Many believe that, as the trade unions become hopeless, only by collective actions can such workers exert pressure on the government and force them to adopt administrative measures and policies to compel the management to make decisions favourable to the workers. Third, these events mainly occurred in North-east and South-west regions of China where older SOEs are located. In addition, the action is usually concentrated in old industries such as coal mining, steel, textile and military production, which either lack raw materials or face declining product markets (Fang 1998; Zheng 1998). These collective actions were aimed not at overturning the power of government but at asking for assistance from the government. Generally, workers asked the government to pay some attention to their 'right to subsistence' (F. Chen 2000). The slogans found in many collective events also revealed the orientation of these actions (Lee 2000).[114] In some events, workers voice their demands to punish corrupt officials. According to F. Chen (2000) and Jiang (2000), suspected managerial or cadre corruption is a crucial reason that can stir up collective actions.[115] Fourth, a problem closely correlated with 'emergent events' is the forming of spontaneous organizations of workers (unofficial trade unions). According to China's laws, except for the ACFTU, other trade unions are illegal (see Chapter 5). However, since there is no trade union in some enterprises and industries or the existing trade unions fail to represent the workers' interests, sometimes workers set up organizations of their own, which usually form in the process of initiating labour conflicts. Such spontaneous organizations are illegal since they have not gone through formal recognition procedures. [116] Although some of these organizations have the characteristics of a trade union, they are not known as 'trade unions', but as 'associations of workers' or 'workers' welfare unions'. Most of them are loosely set up in order to address a conflict

---

[114] The most common slogans used in these actions were 'We Want to Work' and 'We Want Food'.

[115] In F. Chen's (2000: 51) opinion, workers tend to acquiesce to corruption in their factories so long as they do not see it as affecting their own lives in a significant way.

[116] In recent years, these workers' organizations developed rapidly. In the first half of 1999, more than 30 such informal organizations were found in Beijing, an increase of 23 per cent from the same period in 1998 (Bai 2001).

and so have no formal structure or title. They are considered by some scholars to 'quasi-organizations'. However, these 'spontaneous' collective actions and organizations have certain leaders and core members of their own who organize and lead these actions. For a long time, these organizations, existing publicly under the title of 'trade union' or some other similar titles, have been banned, but increasing collective actions bear witness to the failure of this policy. Therefore, the CCP and government appear still not to know how to deal with these organizations.

The spread of collective actions in recent years has attracted increased attention from the central government. These actions have been defined by the Ministry of Public Security as ones that 'violate state laws and regulations, disturbing public order, endangering public security, infringing upon citizens' safety of the person and the security of public of private property'. However, the central government formulates a series of cautious principles to deal with these events, such as 'cautiously using police force, weapons, police equipment and adopting coercive measures' (Fan 2001). When suppressing collective events, the department of public security should first be accompanied by cadres of some other departments, propagating the policies and laws concerned and persuading participants to cease their unlawful actions. If this does not work, local leaders should show themselves at the scene and give a response to people's demands and answer their questions, or promise a deadline to study and reply to people's requirements. Third, the officials who are in charge of quelling these events should take some strategies, such as 'breaking up the whole into parts' to relax the tension (Peng 2002). However, the department of public security will take coercive measures after the events finish, and arrest the organizers. Generally, except for some short-term financial alms and some casual policy of conciliation, the government will not use more effective means to deal with the underlying causes of these events (X. Liu 2002).


## CONCLUSION

Whilst industrial relations conflict is primarily a conflict over the terms and conditions of labour, this is an inherently political as well as economic conflict. Strikes and demonstrations, grievances and lawsuits are about using power to leverage concessions from the other side, to empower workers to get their demands met by their employers. In China, there is an added political edge to these conflicts, both because the government is intimately entwined with the economy and employers, but also because of the sensitivities of the pretence of market socialism. After the privatization of so many SOEs and the establishment of modern governance system in these enterprises, the workers in the former public sector are increasingly being confronted with the same employment conditions and labour market as their counterpart workers in the private sector. On the one hand, both kinds of workers tend to identify their interests, rights and status with each other so as to show a united possibility of new class; on the other hand, the different causes and issues of labour conflicts in nature make workers adopt different ways to deal with these labour conflicts. Therefore, an organizational basis for a long-term labour movement is still hard to see in China (W. Chen 2001).

The central government, besides its administrative procedures, has established a legal procedure to handle labour disputes in the 1980s. However, the new surge in labour conflict shows the failure of this procedure because it has done little to quell the rising tide of labour protests in recent years. Government policies towards these collective actions adopt a conciliatory tone, and so long as these disputes remain localized and workplace based, mass suppression is avoided. These policies, over the short term, have their effect of maintaining social stability, but in the long term, the potential for a chain reaction still exists, and for those found to be ringleaders of collective actions, there is little justice.

# 8. Collective contract

As a mechanism for adjusting labour relations, the collective contract system can be traced back to the 1950s when private firms existed in China. After the nationalization of industries and commerce and handicraft reforms in 1958, along with the nationalization and collectivization of private firms, the collective contract system was abandoned. This system was resurrected by the ACFTU at the beginning of the 1990s with the aim of safeguarding the interests of workers. However, at that time the system was only experimental, being tested in selected enterprises in several areas and organized by the ACFTU alone. After the beginning of the second round of economic reform in 1992, the Trade Union Law (1992) granted enterprise-level unions the right to conclude collective contracts with the management of their enterprises. The Labour Law (1994) strengthened this right and provides the ACFTU with the responsibility (and opportunity) to spread this system throughout the country. At the closing ceremony of the Second Meeting of the Executive Committee of the ACFTU in December 1994, Wei Jianxing, the chairperson of the ACFTU, stated that the crucial task facing the unions was to conclude collective contracts with enterprises, which he saw as the crux to implementing the Labour Law (*Gongren ribao* 13 December 1994: [1]). After this meeting, the ACFTU took three years to implement the collective contract system on a national scale. By October 2001, according to ACFTU statistics, 510 000 enterprises had concluded such agreements, covering 75.7 million workers and staff members. Of these, FIEs, POEs and TVEs accounted for 318 800 agreements, covering 17.64 million workers and staff members (*Renmin ribao* 20 November 2001 [1]).

This chapter will firstly describe and evaluate these and other relevant legal regulations with respect to the collective contract system, and then examine the way the system was implemented in practice, paying particular attention to the role of the government. Next, we will focus our discussion on the operation of the collective contract procedures, in terms of negotiation structures and processes, and the clauses of collective contracts. Through these discussions, we will provide an illustration of the features of labour relations discussed in the previous chapter.

# THE LEGAL FRAMEWORK OF THE COLLECTIVE CONTRACT SYSTEM

The 1994 Labour Law only states that the staff and workers of an enterprise as one party may conclude a collective contract with the enterprise on matters relating to labour remuneration, working hours, rest and vacations, occupational health and safety, and insurance and welfare (Article 33). This principal regulation does not seem to provide a legal basis for the setting up of a collective contract system (Wang 2001). On 5 May 1994, the MoL (1994b) issued the 'Provisions on Collective Contracts', which provided more detailed regulations on the proposed collective contract system, including such matters as the required contents of contracts, the election of negotiating representatives, the terms of contracts, the conditions for modifying and revoking contracts and the procedures for contract examination and disputes settlement. On 8 December 2000, the MoLSS (2000) issued the 'Measures (for Trial Implementation) of Collective Wage Consultation'. This required the employers and workers (represented by management and unions) in enterprises to collectively consult on matters of the wage system, form of wage payments and the level of wages, and to conclude a special contract specifying the terms and conditions agreed to. This regulation is made in the context of the government's seeking to remove itself from micro-level management of wages, and the regulation shows its attempts to replace government decree with market-based settlements, albeit within a nationally imposed regulatory framework. These three laws establish the Chinese system of collective contracts and their main characteristics will be discussed next.

## *The Role of the ACFTU in Collective Consultation*

The monopolistic status of the ACFTU in China means that its enterprise-based unions invariably become the assigned representative for consultation with management. There is no need to prohibit employers from entering into collective contracts with other unofficial workers' organizations because such organizations are themselves illegal. There is one exception to this, Article 33 of the Labour Law states that 'in an enterprise where the trade union has not yet been set up, [a collective contract] shall be also concluded by the representative elected by the staff and workers with the enterprise.' This provision provides an interesting loophole, which in theory provides workers with the possibility to establish employee representatives in cases where there is no official union present, which means most of the private sector. However, according to the law, workers can only select representatives for the purposes of collective negotiation but not for the organization of an alternate trade union. In practice, this provision has apparently never been exercised, simply because it is very difficult for workers to organize a bargaining party without the protection and assistance of a trade union. Nor is it likely that private employers would be willing to bargain in good faith with such representatives. Without union backing these representatives would be easily intimidated, and given buoyant labour markets there is no guarantee the representatives would stick around long enough to see the negotiations through. Finally, it is unclear whether the government or ACFTU would like such ad hoc elected representatives to establish official trade union status (and therefore ACFTU affiliation), or seek to challenge them by establishing an official union in their place. All this is hypothetical, though, because the bottom line is that ACFTU union organizing precedes the process of establishing collective contracts, and this in turn, at least in the initial wave of signing collective consultation agreements, means it was largely confined to the public sector.

## *Bargaining Unit*

To define coverage of an agreement it is necessary to identify the bargaining unit. In China, on the one hand, the laws discussing collective consultation ambiguously define a bargaining unit to consist of all the people in an organization (either a small firm or a large corporation), except the members of the board of directors (if such a board or committee exists) and senior managers (such as the general manager and his or her deputies).[117] On the other hand, the laws provide a rather vague concept of membership of a bargaining unit, which covers the staff and workers in an enterprise, which may include all rank-and-file workers as well as the managerial personnel at medium levels (for example the manager of a sales department) and lower levels (e.g. supervisor on production lines), without considering his or her job duties and work assignments. Once the contracts were concluded, theoretically, the staff and workers, including the people appointed by the legal representative of the enterprise as his/her representative during collective consultation, would be covered by the contracts.

---

[117] This exception is not explicitly defined by the laws. The 'Provisions of Collective Contract' states that the representative of an enterprise shall be the legal representative of the enterprise or the representative appointed by the legal representatives of the enterprise (Article 9). The 'Measures (for Trial Implementation) for Wages Collective Bargaining' also requires that the representatives of enterprise shall be the legal representative and other people appointed by the legal representative, or other managerial people by the written authority of the legal representative (Article 10).

## *Contents of Collective Contracts*

Differing from the laws in some Western countries (Leap 1991), the laws relating to collective contracts in China are primarily substantive, rather than procedural, leaving little room for the parties to negotiate the terms of an agreement. The laws dictate the main provisions that a collective contract should include and provide little procedural rules or guidelines on how the parties should deal with each other. The main provisions of a collective contract should include the following (Wan 1998: 6050):

1. remuneration, including wage levels, and distribution and payment methods;
2. working hours, including daily working hours and weekly working days;
3. rest and holidays, including regular rest days, holidays, family leave and annual leave;
4. social security insurance and welfare, including details such as pension, medical care, life insurance and other matters, in particular, supplementary insurance as well as employee benefits, health, cultural and sport facilities;
5. occupational health and safety, including the working environment, safety facilities, protective equipment and physical examinations for employees;
6. terms of the collective contract;
7. procedures for modification to, as well as termination and expiry of, the collective contract;
8. rights and obligations of the parties in performing the collective contract;
9. provisions for the handling through consultation of disputes arising from the performance of the collective contract;
10. liabilities for breach of the collective contract; and
11. other items which both parties believe should stipulated (Article 6).

Whilst within each provision there may appear to be much scope for negotiation, other rules and regulations set minimum wage standards, holiday entitlements and so on, and these become 'norms' against which minor adjustments are made. Moreover, once an agreement has been signed it is registered with the ACFTU but also must be approved by the appropriate local labour bureaux. These bureaux pay particular attention to the substantive provisions and reject a good number of agreements for containing clauses which agree to less than the legal minimum provisions (Article 24[3]) of 'Provisions on Collective Contracts').

## *'Negotiation in Good Faith'*

Some common concepts about collective bargaining in industrialized countries have been introduced in Chinese laws, such as the prohibition of 'unfair labour practices'. Perhaps the most significant obligation is that the employer should 'bargain in good faith'. This provision in effect amounts to a government decree that employers must consult with their trade union counterparts over issues directly affecting workers' employment conditions. These are mandatory requirements for all employers, with the exception of those SOEs that are stopping production or in the process of bankruptcy. The obligation to 'bargain in good faith' also requires that the enterprise should 'supply their counterpart [that is, the trade union] with the conditions and data relating to collective consultation under the precondition that divulgence neither violates the provisions of law and regulations on secrets nor involves exposing the commercial secrets of the enterprise' (Article 13 of 'Provisions on Collective Contracts'). In addition, the laws forbid an employer or legal representative from restraining or coercing an employee representative in the exercise of their rights. For example, managers are not allowed to revoke the labour contracts of employee representatives within five years from the date at which they took up the position, so long as the normal period of their employment contracts cover this period, and except where the individual is grossly negligent (Article 11 of 'Provisions on Collective Contracts'). Nor can managers engage in any discriminatory policies towards employee representatives (Article 14 of 'Measures for Wages Collective Consultation'), such as demotion, or unfavourable job assignments.

## *The Role of the Labour Bureaux*

Central government commissions, departments and bureaux, as well as Party organs, the ACFTU and so on, are organized structurally down through the provinces to the local level. The MoLSS has its own organization of labour administration departments we may call 'labour bureaux'. These are responsible for examining collective contracts and handling disputes which may arise during collective consultation processes. The 'Provisions on Collective Contract' entitle the bureaux to register the collective contracts after they have been concluded (Articles 21, 22). [118] The collective contract shall go into effect automatically if no objections are raised by the labour bureaux within 15 days from the date of receiving the copy of the collective contract (Article 27).

The labour bureaux are also given the responsibility of handling any

---

[118] The labour administrative departments would stress the following contents in examining a collective contract: (1) whether the qualifications of two parties of a contract are in conformity with the stipulations of laws and regulations; (2) whether the collective consultation is conducted in accordance with the principles and procedures as provided in laws and regulations; and (3) whether the specific labour standards are as provided in laws and regulations (Article 24 of the 'Provisions on Collective Contract').

labour disputes that may occur during the collective consultation process. According to the 'Provisions of Collective Contract', where the two parties are unable to settle a dispute arising during collective consultation, either party or both parties may file a written application for coordination and settlement with the labour bureau. In turn, the local bureau should normally conclude a settlement within 30 days from the date of deciding whether to accept the case (Article 32, 35). These stipulations include a provision that industrial actions, such as strikes and work stoppages, are illegal during the collective consultation process (see Chapter 7). In the two sets of administrative regulations issued by the MoLSS, 'extremist acts' are prohibited in general. Even though no definition of 'extremist acts' is provided, given the context of China it may be assumed from the reaction of the labour bureaux to such actions that both individual actions, such as personal abuse, or collective actions, such as a strikes or demonstrations, appear to be considered extremist.

Generally, at its initial stage, the legal regulations for the collective contract system have reaffirmed the exclusive status of the ACFTU to represent workers and have established a negotiation structure at the employment unit level. In this system, the labour bureaux at each level of the country are entitled to examine the legality of collective contracts as well as settle 'disputes of interest' between both parties during their negotiation. This appears to place the MoLSS as the third party, coordinating industrial relations, thus replacing the traditional role of the ACFTU. The ACFTU, for its part, is given a clearer worker advocacy role, and perhaps even the resemblance of true trade unionism. Whilst it is clear that the MoLSS is increasing its sphere of influence and replacing many of the traditional roles of the ACFTU, we need to examine further whether the ACFTU is willing, or will be permitted, to take the side of workers.

# IMPLEMENTATION PROCESS OF THE COLLECTIVE CONTRACT

While the previous administrative mechanism to allocate wages, job positions and so on has now largely disappeared even from the public sector, new forms of regulation have yet to take their place effectively. This leaves workers vulnerable to the newly empowered managers but also means the government agencies previously charged with regulating labour relations are reluctant to let go completely and are often able to justify their continued 'interference', albeit on a diminishing number of labour issues. Collective contracts offer one of those rare opportunities to legitimate regulation, whilst appearing to follow government policy of allowing economic transactions (including the cost of labour) to be regulated by the market.

The role of representing workers to conclude collective contracts is viewed by the leadership of the ACFTU as a chance to transform the status and functions of trade unions. At the Second Meeting of the Twelfth Executive Committee of the ACFTU in December 1994, the implementation of collective contracts was first identified as one of the focal points for future union activity. At this meeting, the ACFTU outlined a 'General Train of Thought for Trade Unions' which claimed:

> taking the implementation of the Labour Law as a chance and a starting point, driving trade unions' various jobs, pushing forward trade union reform, building and striving to boost trade unions' work to a new level, and playing a more perfect role in reform, development and social stability. (Wei 1995: 1421; ACFTU 1995: 351–7)

In the ACFTU's working schedules drawn up for 1995, 1996 and 1997, implementing the collective contract system ranked as the highest-priority task that had to be undertaken by the trade unions at all levels. With such a strong commitment to collective contracts, there developed a number of definable stages to the ACFTU efforts to construct and propagate the collective contract system.

## Experimental Phase (1995)

In this phase, the ACFTU saw the implementation of the collective contract system as its exclusive task, and not wishing to involve other government organs. After the Second Meeting of the Twelfth Executive Committee, the top leaders of the ACFTU placed great emphasis on implementing the collective contract system. They repeatedly emphasized that concluding collective contracts with management 'is a right granted by law' and 'the trade unions at all levels should be adept in exercising this right' (D. Zhang 1996: 531–38). On 17 August 1995, the ACFTU issued the 'Methods for Trial Implementation of Equal Consultation and Concluding Collective Contracts' (*Gongren ribao* 9 September 1995). This document lays down a series of points, covering the terms of the consultation and contents of contracts, the procedure for signing an agreement, modification and revocation of a collective contract once signed, and the duties of superior unions in the implementation of the collective consultation system. In this document, which has 42 clauses, there are only two clauses relating to the duties of the labour bureaux, each concerned with settling labour disputes and examining contracts. From this, it can be seen that the ACFTU paid little attention to the government and saw the contracts as falling almost exclusively within its own sphere of influence.

Almost immediately a conflict between the ACFTU and the MoL was created over jurisdictional boundaries. After the Labour Law was published in 1994, the MoL had experimented with the collective contract system in 350 enterprises around the country. However it had not planned to implement this system extensively, at least over the short term. Its work was focused on popularizing the labour contract system in enterprises at that time. In accordance with a speech made by Jiazhen Zhu, the Vice-Minister of Labour:

> The labour contract system defines a legal labour relationship, to establish a labour relationship between two parties, and so it is at the first place. The collective contract system is to adjust labour relations on the basis of the labour contract. Therefore, it is at the second place. (1996c: 96–100)

His opinion obviously conflicted with that of Wei Jianxing, who viewed the implementation of collective contract system as 'the crux of implementing the Labour Law'. It became apparent that because of a lack of government support and resistance to coordination between the union and the ministry, the achievements in implementing collective contracts remained limited. By the end of 1995, nationwide, there were only around 48 000 enterprises (mostly SOEs) that had concluded collective contracts. In the course of experimentation, the local unions had realized that the implementation of collective contracts was not an easy task for the trade unions to accomplish by themselves. Some unions acknowledged that support from various government departments was also needed. Some local trade unions tried to invite the leadership of local governments and the Party organs to participate in the implementation of collective contracts, establishing a steering group consisting of the top leaders from three parties (government, Party and trade unions). The trade unions, in the name of this group, initiated the policies relating to the collective contract system, published the 'model contact' and controlled the progress of implementation. This method gave birth to the model for the future implementation of the collective contract system in 1996.

## Comprehensive Implementation Phase (1996–97)

In this phase, the ACFTU had realized that, by itself, it was impossible to carry out the collective contract system quickly. On 17 May 1996, the MoL, the ACFTU, the SETC and the CEDA issued a joint circular that informed the public that the collective consultation and contract system would be gradually introduced. The circular stated that these four government or quasi-government organs required their own subordinates at all levels to follow the 'united leadership' of local governments and the Party committees, and to coordinate closely with each other to jointly ensure implementation of the system (Department of Policy and Law 1996 (7): 27–9). This document indicated that the contradiction between the ACFTU and the MoL had been eliminated, as well as that 'the implementation of the collective contract system is no longer a task of trade unions only, but a common responsibility of trade unions, management and government' (Yang 1997). The character of the implementation of collective contracts also changed from a quasi government-initiated project whose success (and thus in the main failure) was largely determined by economic forces and the weak political power of the unions. This changed to become a government activity in accordance with the requirements of the leadership of local governments and Party organs, which ensured the primacy of politics over economies was re-established.

The document also provided a model method for implementing the collective agreements, drawing on the experiences of the experimental stage. This model can be summarized into five steps:

1.  three parties – the Party committee, government organ and trade union compose a leading group, with the top leaders of Party organ or government as the head;
2.  the leading group convenes mobilizing meetings and distributes indexes (statistical quotas) to subordinate organs;
3.  the trade unions draft a document concerning the implementation of the collective contract system and issue it in the name of the leading group;
4.  the trade unions design a model contract and still popularize it in the name of the leading group (although this does not necessarily happen); and
5.  the trade unions, through their organization structure, oversee the progress of implementation.

This model was duplicated at all levels so that the collective contract system was instituted in different regions and industries as the same model. Research by Q. Li (2000, 2002) in two cities and a number of fieldwork sites in 1998 to 1999 found that cadres reported very similar experiences of implementation. In the second half of 1996, the process of implementation accelerated with the support of local governments and Party organs. By the end of the third quarter of 1996, 76 647 enterprises concluded collective contracts nationwide, and by the end of the next quarter, this number reached 135 386, an increase of 76 per cent within three months (ACFTU 1997: 57).

The implementation of collective contracts is similar to the process of carrying out most government policies. This process involves a number of stages, starting with a period of experimentation. The ACFTU began to experiment with collective contracts from 1992, when the Trade Unions Law was passed. Even though the experimental sites were limited to a few regions and enterprises, these sites provided experiences and lessons for the ACFTU in developing its process model. From the beginning of the second phase, the ACFTU headquarters instituted a mechanistic quota system setting out targets for the number of contract signings per year, which are then allocated to provinces and industries and so on down the chain of command.[119] This system is fairly coercive in nature, and is designed to ensure compliance by subordinate unions in the hierarchy. The headquarters at the top constantly increases the quotas it sets, to drive greater implementation.[120] As a result of trying to over-fulfil their tasks, the trade unions at subordinate levels inflate their achievements in relation to the quota they were allocated to fulfil, which results in cumulatively inaccurate data at the national level. Finally, the hierarchical system is backed by a set of rewards and punishments. The fact that in 1996, the implementation of the collective contract system could reach more than 200 per cent increase should be attributed to the way the planned quota system is introduced. However, this method leads to a number of problems related to the accuracy of data, emphasis on quantitative rather than qualitative achievements and so on. These will be discussed in the next section.

The next stage in promulgating collective contracts involved implementing the collective contract system nationally, through organizing relevant staff and coordinating various relationships between levels of the union and other organizations concerned. The lesson learned from the first attempts at implementing collective contracts taught the ACFTU that the support and intervention of the Party organs and governments at all levels was essential for the unions to fulfil their own statistical targets, and this they did systematically in the second attempt at national coverage. The top leaders of the ACFTU required trade unions at all levels:

> should ask for the support and leadership from the Party and government in their initiatives, should carry out their work under the

---

[119] This is a common method for propagating ACFTU policies (for example establishing unions in FIEs follows the same practice).

[120] For instance, in the 'Main Working Points of 1995' issued by the ACFTU on 30 December 1994, the ACFTU only required that 30 per cent of FIEs should sign collective contracts. At the Third Meeting of the Twelfth Executive Committee of ACFTU in December 1995, Wei Jianxing, the Chairman of the ACFTU, besides repeating the quota for FIEs, required that more than 30 per cent of the SOEs and the COEs should sign collective contracts. At the Fourth Meeting of the Twelfth Executive Committee of ACFTU in December of 1996, the ACFTU required that by the end of 1997, the contract signing rate in SOEs and COEs must reach 50 per cent and in FIEs with unions, 40 per cent. At the Fifth Meeting of the Twelfth Executive Committee of ACFTU in December of 1997, the rate for enterprises in which public ownership occupies the leading position was raised to more than 70 per cent.

united plan of the Party organs, should report to the Party organs about
the problems and workers' needs created in the implementation as well
as to notify the government. (D. Zhang 1996: 531)

By the end of 1996, leading groups were established in 30 provinces,
autonomous regions and municipalities all over the country. All these groups,
usually headed by the top leaders of the Party organs or governments,
published their own policies concerning the implementation of the collective
contract system.

The ACFTU also established a supervisory system to manage and regulate
subordinate unions in their fulfilment of assigned quotas. Using the vertical
structure of the ACFTU and following the classic administrative management
system common in bureaucracies, with a top-down control structure, adapting
to information supplied from the bottom up. Trade unions at all levels should
regularly report their progress in implementing the collective contract system
up the hierarchy, and this is called a 'reporting and notification system' in
China. The superior unions, on the basis of these statistics, would
periodically inform juniors as to the progress, experience and problems, as
well as the system of rewards and punishments to press their subordinates to
fulfil the index they were assigned.

In short, the implementation of collective contracts in China has
demonstrated the dominant position of the government, whose attitude is the
crucial factor defining success (Li 2000; Warner and Ng 1999) of the system.
The support from the government and the Party organs was mainly in the
form of administrative instruments. These instruments, characterized by the
power of and obedience to the Party, carry the weight of mandatory
instruments (Mao 1996). By utilizing these forms of measures, the ACFTU
and its subordinate unions at all levels could overcome various obstacles and
resistance to attain quantitative targets for establishing the collective contract
system in all kinds of enterprises. In the second phase, with the increase of
the government and Party's invention, implementation was greatly
accelerated, and as a result the process became an administrative procedure in
which the government plays a primary role. The ACFTU is able to undertake
the administration and control of the system in the name of the Party. This
role is not limited to the regulation of collective consultation (Warner and Ng
1999), but expands to the whole process of implementation.

## AN ANALYSIS ON COLLECTIVE CONTRACT CLAUSES

Li (2000) examined a number of SOE–ACFTU collective contracts, and
drawing on this research and subsequent studies (2002) a brief summary of

some of the key points will be presented here, as a means to illustrate the lack of 'negotiation' involved in formulating collective contracts, in the public sector at least. The contracts are composed of three main categories of clauses, which can be placed in order of priority or importance. The first category of clauses covers principles that set out some terms of reference for the contract, such as the parties, aim of the contract, the status of the union, the process of consultation. The second category are clauses containing stipulations or provisions to be implemented, and make up the main body of

*Table 8.1 Classification of clauses in five collective contracts*

| Enterprises | Total clauses | Principle / % | Implementation / % | Commitment / % |
|---|---|---|---|---|
| A | 53 | 5 / 9.4 | 39 / 73.6 | 9 / 17.0 |
| B | 59 | 8 / 13.6 | 43 / 72.8 | 8 / 13.6 |
| C | 46 | 5 / 10.9 | 34 / 73.9 | 7 / 15.2 |
| D | 49 | 3 / 6.1 | 37 / 75.5 | 9 / 18.4 |
| E | 36 | 5 / 14.0 | 23 / 64.0 | 8 / 22.2 |

Source: Li Q. (2000)

the contract. Both parties' rights and obligations are included, such as recruitment of the labour force, wage and salary, working conditions, training and so on. The third category is related to the commitments of terms and duration of contract. A statistical representation of contents of contracts may be seen (in Table 8.1) by counting the number of clauses and apportioning them between the three categories of clauses for five contracts.

Table 8.1 indicates that, of the three categories of clauses in five collective contracts, the number of implementation rules took up an average of 70 per cent of the total number of clauses. However, as discussed below, this high proportion does not mean the actual implementation provisions in collective contracts have practical effectiveness.

Li (2000) found that the process of agreeing the contents of the contracts carried the status of 'administration' which needed to be completed, rather than a mechanism to change or negotiate the relationship between management and labour. This was possible because the employers in SOEs are not the managers but the state agencies and organs. However, the process of formalizing relations in the written form of contracts presented the potential for conflicts to be highlighted. To solve this, and because the procedure had been given the air of an 'administrative chore to complete', both parties tended to rely heavily on contracts others had already signed and the model agreements distributed by the ACFTU. Table 8.2 provides statistics of implementation clauses in the five collective contracts. The implementation clauses can be divided into three categories: clauses defined by the laws, clauses negotiated with reference to law and clauses determined by the representatives after negotiation.

As shown in Table 8.2, in all contracts, the proportion of implementation clauses defined by the labour law was over 50 per cent. This kind of clause is usually a duplication of legal provisions, merely adding the names of the parties concerned in the appropriate places. Among the five contracts Li (2000) examined, the proportions of clauses negotiated with reference to law are different, from the highest 35.0 per cent in B to the lowest 17.4 per cent in E. Even here the discussions between the parties usually resulted from ambiguity in the legal provision as they covered the particular circumstances in each work unit or enterprise. For example, according to the regulation there is no clear timetable for determining when employers should provide regular gynaecological disease examination to female workers. Table 8.2 also shows that in all collective contracts, the negotiated clauses occupy a smaller proportion, from the highest of 17.4 per cent in E to lowest of 5.4 per cent in D. In fact, this kind of clause has a real effect on improving the benefits of workers and staff members.

*Table 8.2  Classification of implementation clauses in five contracts*

| Enterprise | Implementation clauses | Defined by laws / % | Negotiated with reference to law / % | Negotiated / % |
|---|---|---|---|---|
| A | 39 | 24 / 61.5 | 11 / 28.2 | 4 / 10.3 |
| B | 43 | 22 / 51.1 | 15 / 35.0 | 6 / 13.9 |
| C | 34 | 22 / 64.7 | 10 / 29.4 | 2 / 5.9 |
| D | 37 | 26 / 70.3 | 9 / 24.3 | 2 / 5.4 |
| E | 23 | 15 / 65.2 | 4 / 17.4 | 4 / 17.4 |

Source: Li Q. (2000)

All the collective contracts are highly similar in structure and clauses, because a model contract was circulated by the local trade unions to enterprises for their reference in drafting. Taking case B's collective contract which had the most implementation clauses (43 in total) as a benchmark, in comparison with another two collective contracts in A and C in the same city, 32 (82 per cent) of the 39 implementation clauses in A's contract were identical to those in B's contract, and 28 out of C's 34 terms in the same category resembled those of B as well. At the same time, 38 of B's 43 terms could be found in contracts concluded in both A and C, representing 88 per cent repetition of clauses. This group of figures at least reveals that the representatives of negotiation in three enterprises relied heavily on the model contract and previous contracts drafted by other enterprises.

The examples discussed here illustrate the problem of the context in which the collective contracts are 'negotiated'. On the one hand there is little interest in entering into conflict over such 'administration' anyway, and on the other, the strong legal and normative provisions make it easy for the administrators' negotiating the contracts to fall into line and accept as many provisions already agreed or suggested by others (outside the enterprise) as possible. However, as a result, more substantial clauses that can be used to resolve some practical problems concerning the interests of workers are lacking in most contracts.

# VARIATIONS IN THE SYSTEM OF COLLECTIVE CONSULTATION

The formal bargaining structure is defined as the bargaining unit. As discussed before, there is no concept of 'bargaining unit' in Chinese law of collective contracts. The Labour Law states that the staff and workers of an enterprise, as one party, may conclude a collective contract with the enterprise, as the other party, on matters relating to labour remuneration, working hours, rest and vacations, occupational health and safety, and insurance and welfare. From the provisions of current laws, the scope of the bargaining unit and the scope of the unit in which the collective consultation is carried out completely overlap.

Moreover, the consultation structure in China, where it does exist, is highly decentralized. Given the dominant position of the public enterprises when the Labour Law was originally drafted and the great similarities of pay and conditions between enterprises, it would have been possible to negotiate collective contracts at regional or industrial levels. However, the government opted for decentralized consultation down to the level of work units. The political rationale for such a highly decentralized design structure has been, to some extent, due to the desire to reduce the possibility for large-scale labour disputes that might have been 'encouraged' if consultation was set at a more centralized level.

Whilst this highly decentralized structure greatly disadvantages workers, it has the major advantage of being flexible enough to adapt to changing ownership structures for the government. However, in practice the 'new economic organizations', such as FIEs, POEs and TVEs, which exist in ever increasing numbers and employment, present a major challenge to the collective contracts system. Most of these firms are medium-sized and small enterprises and a majority of their workers come from rural or less industrialized areas with lower education levels and less 'street knowledge' than their urban counterparts in being able to protect their interests. Moreover, faced with widespread discrimination, these migrants often have neither a union, nor effective means to establish one, and so they often have inadequate protection from employer abuses. This allows employers to impose low wages, forced overtime working, delays to pay, poor working conditions and occupational injuries, especially in labour-intensive manufacturing enterprises. At the same time, the unionization rate in these enterprises is very low. In some enterprises with trade unions, the implementation of collective contracts is difficult because of the high rate of turnover of unions' cadres, as well as employer resistance. This is a problem to which the ACFTU has paid considerable attention for a number of years now, but with patchy results. In the document jointly issued by the MoL, the ACFTU, the SETC and the CEC in July of 1996, it states that in the areas where small-sized FIEs and POEs are concentrated, a professional or industrial association of primary trade union may be established. They can collectively consult and conclude collective contracts on behalf of workers and staff, with the relevant enterprises. This regulation has allowed the ACFTU and various provincial trade unions to experiment with new forms of unions, as discussed in Chapter 5, and to create a new level of consultation above the level of the enterprise.

The regional system of collective consultation and contract in most areas follows the structure presented in Figure 8.1, which is called 'three types of enterprises', 'three levels' and 'three forms' of collective consultation. 'Three types of enterprises' refers to FIEs, POEs and TVEs. 'Three levels' includes city, county (or district under the city) and township. 'Three forms' refers to three kinds of collective contracts, based on the template contract provided by the united trade unions. These include, first, contracts concluded by the grass-roots unions and the employer under the direction of the united trade unions at the enterprise level. Second, they include contracts concluded by the employer and the united trade unions on behalf of employees in enterprises without a grass-roots union. Third, they include contracts concluded by the united trade unions and the association of employers. These three kinds of collective contracts, in fact, are based on the template contract designed by the association of trade unions in the respective regions.

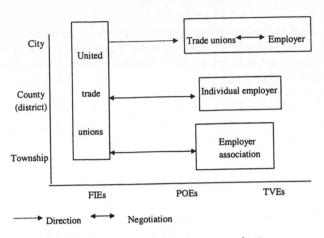

City

County
(district)

Township

FIEs          POEs          TVEs

⤍ Direction   ⟷ Negotiation

*Figure 8.1 Regional structure of collective consultation*

We will examine the implementation and operation of collective contracts in more detail by using a couple of case studies drawn from the public and private sectors. Whilst we have argued that there is a high degree of similarity between both sectors, there are marked differences in operation, and sometimes the same result comes from two quite different internal processes.

## Negotiation Process in an SOE

In 1998, Q. Li (2000) studied the process of collective consultation in one SOE in northern China, employing 2000 workers and staff. Figure 8.2 sets out the major events in the consultation process that occurred in this SOE.

The process shown in Figure 8.2 can be divided into four phases. The first phase may be termed 'preparation and propagation', in which after receiving a directive from the superior trade union, the chairperson of grass-roots union reported to the Party committee about the desire to institute the collective contract system in the enterprise. A 'leading group of collective contract' was then set up in which the Party secretary acted as the head and the chairperson of the union and the enterprise director as the deputy head. The leading group convened a meeting to lay out a detailed schedule for the process. The union, through streamers, blackboards, close-circuit television, internal broadcasts and an internal journal, explained and publicized the significance of collective consultation to workers. The union also held courses for the chairpersons of workshop unions, the representatives of female workers and the workers' congress, studying labour regulations concerning collective contracts and relevant ACFTU documents. After that, a 'collective consultation team' consisting of ten representatives from both parties was set up, in which the management representatives were appointed by the director, and the workers' representatives, except the chairperson of the union, were elected though the workers' congress.

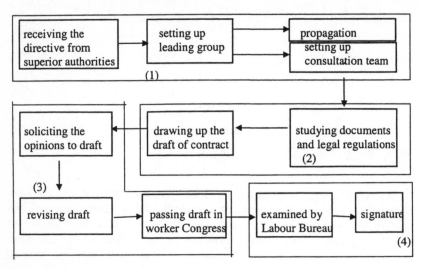

*Figure 8.2 A classic consultation process in 'A'*

The second phase involved drawing up a draft collective contract. Before drawing up the draft, the collective consultation team studied the Labour Law, the legal regulations pertaining to the Labour Law and the relevant ACFTU documents. The first version of the draft was written after several team meetings. This was a result of combining the representatives' opinions, 'model contract' and examining other enterprises' collective contracts.

The third phase was concerned with discussing, revising and passing the draft collective contract. By holding forums, the members of both the leading group and consultation team heard opinions and recommendations from workers and staff members on the draft contract, and then entrusted the job of making revisions to the union. After revision, the draft was forwarded to a WC for discussion and adoption.

The fourth and final phase involved examination and a signing ceremony. The trade union, in the name of the leading group, submitted the adopted draft to the local labour bureau for examination. This draft became an effective collective contract automatically (in the absence of any official queries) within 15 days upon submission and receipt of the draft by the labour bureau. After that, a formal signing ceremony was held in the meeting hall of the enterprise and some top leaders from superior agencies and trade unions were invited.

The evidence in another four SOEs that the authors has visited subsequent to the case given above all indicated that these enterprises experienced a similar process of collective consultation. The process of consultation lasted one to two months, depending on the time available and the requirement of the superior agency and trade unions.

The process appears open and valuable to all parties interested in liberal democratic and pluralist versions of industrial relations. Workers and staff are made aware of their rights, of laws and of the contents of their labour contracts. Moreover, through their involvement in the implementation of the collective contract system, the intention of the ACFTU is to institute a new mechanism to adjust labour relations and, at the same time, to stress its image as 'representative of workers'. Although the government and the ACFTU are able to design this system as a form of public policy and implement it through their own administrative channels, the system itself seems incongruous with the feature of labour relations in enterprises, namely 'weak labourer versus strong employer' and non-performing trade unions. Consequently, implementation at enterprise level relies more on form than content and there are two fundamental problems with the system, relating to the aims and the process of negotiation.

After the collective contract system was implemented in the enterprises, the first problem created was that the original aim for implementing collective contracts had become altered. In SOEs, the unions are not in a position to represent workers' interests. Although they have been officially given this position after reform, the official unions' multiple roles often mean in practice that they continue to be little more than welfare agencies. No doubt, having been given the responsibility to negotiate with enterprise management in law and on behalf of workers and staff members, the unions have been placed in an awkward position that is not one the union cadres are accustomed to. One way to deal with this problem is to set up a tripartite leading group with the secretary of the Party committee as the head and the chairperson of the union and the director as deputies, as we saw in the case presented above. This shifts responsibility away from the union cadre and ensures that the cadre is seen to follow the Party line, rather than perhaps stirring up trouble among workers. The whole course of collective consultation is actually dominated by this leading group. It has authority in determining the representatives of both parties, sets out the period and process of consultation, and examines the last draft of the contract before submission to the labour bureau. Sometimes, the secretary of the Party committee should preside over the consultation meetings in the capacity as the head of the leading group. In the course of consultation, the management and union are combined together by this leading group without even a formal division of interests between them. In this way, there is a total absence of 'parties' in the negotiation process. This is not just an absence of the appearance of conflict, which may exist within the private meetings of the leading group, but a systemic removal of formal interests between the individuals involved in the leading group. Therefore, the aim of negotiation is twisted. The organizers (Party committee, management and union in SOEs) do not strive to institute a mechanism to adjust labour relations, but to fulfil the quota assigned them by their higher authorities. The quickest and easiest way to meet the quota for all parties involved is through cooperation.

Usually, after the contract passed the examination of the labour bureau, in all the enterprises studied, a ceremony to officially sign the contract was held, even if the collective contract had already come into effect. Compared with the other activities involved in the collective consultation process, the three parties involved within the SOEs appear to place most importance on this ceremony. A few top leaders of their superior authorities would be invited, and the higher the level the enterprises rank in the administration, the higher the level of 'top leaders' could be invited. Through this ceremony, the three parties wanted to convey nothing more than to publicize to their superior authorities that they had fulfilled the duty assigned to them. In this way the collective contract agreement became a vehicle for cadres in the enterprises to ingratiate themselves with their bosses for the future.

The absence of unions as representative organs for workers and unions' subordinate status within enterprises led to few points of contention in the process of negotiations and effectively made confrontation between the two parties impractical. At the negotiation table, the two parties strived to decrease their differences to the minimum point, if debates were not avoided altogether. This was common to all five enterprises visited (Q. Li 2002) and was seen in other studies. Two issues that were debated in the five enterprises studied, revolved around annual paid vacation and the system for regulating annual salary rises. The former, in fact, was caused by ambiguity the government had given rise to in various labour regulations. According to Article 45 of the Labour Law, all workers and staff are entitled to 'paid annual vacation'. However, the State Council had yet to settle on a minimum requirement for the number of vacation days. [121] This ambiguity led to confusion and debate between representatives of both sides in collective consultation in respect to the duration and calculation of the paid vacation. The difference was usually ironed out when both sides would compromise and adjust their expectations accordingly. The management would agree to annual vacation while the union would make a concession on the duration of vacation, for example decreasing it from seven days to five days or less.

---

[121] The Labour Law reads: 'The State shall practice a system of annual vacation with pay. Labourers who have kept working for one year and more shall be entitled to annual vacation with pay. The concrete measures shall be formulated by the Sate Council.' (Article 45).

Another point of debate concentrated on 'annual wage increments'. Almost all managers were reluctant to commit to an automatic annual wage rise for workers. In SOEs, although some managers were willing to increase wages for workers, they would not promise in print the exact incremental amount that they would pay. They felt insecure about future business growth and worried about a possible labour dispute resulting from any breach of promises. In this particular case, the trade union has to concede to management's terms. In the contracts with an 'annual salary increment' clause, they usually read: 'the wage level of workers and staff members will follow the principle of keeping the growth of total amount of wages below the growth of labour productivity'. In these contracts, there were no other clauses relating to the margin by which wages should increase.

In reality, the negotiation process has been distorted, losing its role as 'a formal channel through which the differing interests of management and employees may be resolved on a collective basis' (Salamon 1992: 311) or 'an institution designed to achieve a balance among a number of these conflicting goals between management and unions' (Kochan and Kata 1988: 9). Instead, within China, without a constituency within the enterprises, the trade unions are unable to negotiate and the employers hold power within the constraints of Party leadership. Moreover, there is no evidence the Party is unhappy with this outcome.

## Collective Consultation in Private Enterprises

The last decades saw a great development of non-public enterprises in China. In these enterprises invested by the multinational companies, overseas and domestic Chinese, the implementation of collective contracts shows different tendencies from those described in the public sector.

In some of the private sector enterprises, discussed in Chapter 3 as having a high public profile and an image to protect or promote in China, the collective contract system tends to be more formally and seriously undertaken. This tendency is due to a number of reasons, for example, most employers come from industrialized countries where they are used to collective bargaining. Moreover, such employers are eager to appear law-abiding in China, as well as to stifle opposition to their investment in China from unions at home. These make the employers eager and open to engage in collective consultation. In contrast to public enterprises, the identities of labour and capital and the hierarchical structure that binds them are explicit and irrefutable. Whilst this leaves workers helpless in the face of despotic employers, it allows for clearer lines of demarcation for negotiating issues and representatives in pluralist employer settings. Following this, the separation between the two parties is associated with clear understandings of each party's interests over which to bargain.

With the exception of some joint ventures, the position of trade unions in these enterprises is simply defined as the representative of workers and the cadres of unions have a strong sense of the need to protect the interests of workers in the cases where the union leader is not a management stooge. When such enterprises were established, a grass-roots union was usually organized as part of the employer's high-profile acceptance of Chinese laws and based on pluralist principles. In some well-established joint ventures, the cadres of unions have developed a set of working practices which are different from the ones in public enterprises. Given these favourable conditions, the collective contract system has been established quickly in some large-sized FIEs, which have also satisfied the interests of both the employers concerned and the government, by establishing 'harmonious' labour relations. This occurs not so much because workers are directly involved in negotiating with their employers to further their interests but more indirectly. Workers are presented with an agreement which reflects their interests as mediated by the union, and a formal contract system provides workers with a clear choice on whether to continue (or take up) employment in such an enterprise. In other words, the clarity of the contracts may not represent the interests of the workers, but overt conflict is avoided because of the voluntarist nature of the labour market, a worker unsatisfied with the contract will look for a job elsewhere rather than, say, strike for better terms.

In fact, the collective contract system was introduced in some large-sized joint venture enterprises, such as Beijing Jeep Ltd, Beijing Babcock & Wilcox Company and Shanghai Volkswagen Automotive Company Ltd, in the early 1980s. Summarized below are the key activities of collective consultation in these enterprises, which show clearly the differences from public enterprises. First, the trade unions paid more attention to the preparation stage. Rather than propagating and mobilizing workers, the trade unions concentrated on collecting the demands and opinions of workers. In preparing the negotiation proposal, they would try to find out as much as possible about the legal situation and their employers' financial performance to support their proposals. They would also design their own strategies and principles for dealing with the other party (Trade Union Committee, Beijing Nankou SKF Railway Bearing Ltd 2001). Second, the issues covered were more directly related to aspects of labour relations than in the public sector, and covered many aspects of employment. Besides the usual topics of increasing wage payments, the union pressed for more issues to be negotiated. These included issues relating to methods of wage payment, benefits (for example housing), overtime and overtime wage payment, and calculating standards for seniority. Standards of laying-off were also subject to negotiation (Investigation Team of China Federation of Trade Unions of

Machinery and Metallurgical Industry 1996; Trade Union Committee, Beijing Babcock & Wilcox Company 2001; Trade Union Committee, Beijing United Food Ltd 2001). Third, some grass-roots trade unions have gradually learned how to handle negotiation tactics and techniques. Some union cadres are able to design sophisticated negotiation strategies involving high, medium and bottom lines for their wage negotiation (Investigation team of China Federation of Trade Unions of Machinery and Metallurgical Industry 1996). They are also able to communicate with senior managers through informal conversations, or exert pressures through Chinese senior managerial personnel (Trade Union Committee, Beijing Nankou SKF Railway Bearing Ltd 2001; Trade Union Committee, Hangzhou Toshiba Mechanical and Electrical Product Ltd 1995). Fourth, the process of negotiation has in practice become a negotiation between foreign investors (in the case of FIEs) and Chinese trade unions, even in cases where the foreigner holds a minority share. It is not uncommon that some issues are very difficult to negotiate and lead to disputes and tension between the two parties. Therefore, compared with the process in public enterprises, the consultation in these kinds of enterprises would last several months or even more than half a year.

In most POEs and less conspicuous FIEs, especially those enterprises invested by overseas Chinese, the collective contract system is completely different again. These enterprises are largely beyond the official trade unions' reach. Even in those enterprises that have been organized by grass-roots unions, the unions are often dominated by the employers, or headed by the relatives of employers or the managerial personnel sent by the employers. In a few cases where the union cadres are elected by workers, the cadres themselves are still in a difficult position to call for collective consultation because of their vulnerability as employees' and worry of threat to their own 'rice bowls' (Office of Collective Contract 2000; Zhongshan Federation of Trade Unions 1999). The employers in these enterprises share some common opinions to oppose or resist collective contracts because they worry about the restraints brought about by the contract, in terms of working hours, rest and vacation, wage payment, overtime and working conditions (Liu 1999). The local authorities are also reluctant to implement this system on such employers, often because their personal interests lie with such private owners. Therefore, most collective consultations in these enterprises are mere formality under the 'persuasion and arrangement' of local trade unions. [122] Sometimes, this nominal process was also simplified or omitted when the employers promised to agree to the template contract provided by the local

---

[122] For example, some local unions sent work teams, usually led by their vice-chairperson, to POEs and TVEs set up to promote the collective contract system. In these enterprises the teams' direction would go through the whole process of consultation, from mobilizing workers to determining representatives, designing a draft of the contract, to arranging the negotiation procedure (Federation of Trade Unions, Xiantao City 1996).

trade unions.[123]

## CONCLUSION

During the course of reform, a great change has taken place in labour relations. First, while the government gradually withdraw from labour relations, management have gained more autonomy and control over these relations in a modern enterprise system. Second, with the development of privatization, while the number of private enterprises is increasing, most medium-sized and small enterprises have changed to become private enterprises. This makes it more difficult for the government to control labour relations than before, both with less direct control over such enterprises and also with the sheer growth in their number over the past 20 years. The ACFTU, as a branch of the government, faces similar difficulties, and finds it especially hard to enter into the new forms of enterprises to establish grass-roots unions. The 1994 Labour Law provides the ACFTU with an opportunity to change its image and function, as well as a chance to enter into these new types of enterprises by implementing the collective contract system. At the start, the central government and the ACFTU intended to establish a collaborative system of labour relations and then, recover their control over these relations (Warner and Ng 1999: 303)

However, in the course of implementing collective contracts, similar opposition confronted the ACFTU, which faced resistance from employers and management, as is common in industrialized and, especially, industrializing countries. In contrast to capitalist countries, where bargaining grew out of struggle and a process of institutionalization, the ACFTU, as the official trade union with support from the government and Party, was able to enforce a system from the top down. In SOEs, the trade unions, through the assistance of the government, forced management to accept this system. The statistics from the ACFTU indicate that by the end of the 1990s, the rate of concluding collective contracts in SOEs was much higher than that in the

---

[123] Template contracts designed and provided by local trade unions at different levels offered convenience for both parties to simplify the negotiation process. For example, based on template contracts issued by the Guangdong Federation of Trade unions, the Federation of Trade Unions in Zhongshan City, Guangdong Province designed similar contracts for its subordinate unions (Zhongshan Federation of Trade Unions 1999). Such contracts are duplicated by trade union journals to become regional collective contracts used by local association of trade unions (Jiaojiang Federation of Trade Unions 2000).

private sector,[124] because the trade unions' work in private enterprises is much more difficult and less rewarding. They have to set up grass-roots unions first and then put forward their requirement of collective consultation in the face of considerable resistance from most private enterprises. In recent years, the ACFTU has focused attention on these enterprises, but it is difficult to create much enthusiasm for the work among union cadres. The likely rewards, in terms of funds from union dues, and kudos from fulfilling union organizing quotas, compared to the chances of union survival and the potential to annoy local Party leaders and government cadres, result in patchy efforts to unionize the private sector.

Under such circumstances, rather than an internally bargained compromise between the grass-roots unions and management, collective contracts in both publicly and privately owned enterprises are the result of 'external' compromises. For SOEs, this is a compromise between the managers and their superior agencies (including the superior trade unions subordinated to these agencies). When the managers in these enterprises promise to conclude a contract with the trade union, except for providing some template collective contracts and introducing a model process of collective consultation, the superior agencies and trade unions would not encourage or require more from employers. Therefore, in these kinds of enterprises, collective consultation usually involved few topics of negotiation and the contracts lacked clauses or content that might reflect such agreements as were based on compromises reached after hard bargaining. In private sector enterprises, the compromise is one between three parties: the owners, the local government and local trade unions. After the owners of these enterprises agreed to set up grass-roots unions, both government and trade union would no longer pay attention to who controls these grass-roots unions and the process of collective consultation. Therefore, within the enterprise, the process of collective consultation is not one based on rule making, involving a power relationship between organizations (Flanders 1969: 19).

Through the implementation of the collective contract system, the intention of the ACFTU is to institute a new mechanism to adjust labour relations, and at the same time to stress its own image as 'representative of workers'. Although the government and the ACFTU are able to design this system as a form of public policy and implement it through their own administrative channels, the system itself seems incongruous with the feature of labour relations in enterprises, based on 'weak labourer versus strong employer', and the 'trade unions as mere welfare agencies'. Consequently,

---

[124] For example, in some provinces and municipalities directly under the central government, the signing rate of collective contract in public enterprises had been more than 90 per cent while the collective contact in private enterprises was still in the experimental phase (Wang H. M. 2000: 11923; Xie 2000: 18182).

implementation at the enterprise level has made little difference to workplace-based industrial relations. Given the situation in which the identities of both parties have not been clearly defined in the public sector and the bargaining power of employer outweighs that of the employees in private enterprises, there will in practice be no 'competitors' at the negotiation table. Moreover, due to the dominant role of government in labour relations in the public sector and its strategies of 'limited intervention' in labour relations in private enterprises, employers will permit few topics for negotiation. Some issues concerned with the interests of workers, such as job security, and wage increases and so on, are sometimes not the sort of topics that the trade union can or is willing to bargain over effectively. Finally, in the many cases where the trade unions are absent, controlled by employers or very weak, in both public and non public enterprises, the trade union itself is unable to lead the process of negotiation. However, the model designed by the local Party and government organs and the superior trade unions for collective consultation does not provide adequate assistance on how to negotiate in these circumstances.

The system of collective contracts, theoretically designed by the superior authorities as an effective mechanism to help adjust labour relations, has undergone major revision when it comes to be applied in practice. Even though the collective contract could be concluded between the management and the union in many enterprises, the whole process of collective consultation is little more than administrative compliance with quotas assigned from above.

# 9. Conclusion

This chapter will provide a short overview of the main arguments presented in this book. This will be done first by exploring the common themes in Part 1 and Part 11 of the book respectively, and then bringing these together to present more thematic arguments. These arguments are centred on the role of the state, the declining position of workers and an analysis of the nature of conflict in Chinese industrial relations. The chapter will then address the future direction of the development of industrial relations in China by presenting a brief critique of convergence theories, and then present an overview of the tensions that will influence the development path.

## SUMMARY OF CHAPTERS

This book has examined various aspects of the development and current situation of industrial relations in China. The institutional actors were first examined in individual chapters (state, employers, workers and trade unions) and for each a number of issues were covered of particular relevance to the nature of the actor and the most important points highlighted within the context of China. The titles of the various actors, reflected in the chapter headings, are the same as those in industrial relations counterparts in liberal capitalist countries, and the nature and interests of these actors increasingly resemble their capitalist counterparts. However, there are characteristics that set Chinese actors apart from their western namesakes because of the post-planned economic context and the historical roots of these actors in this system. The most obvious is that the ACFTU is not a union but a quasi-government organ, but there are other illustrations. Differences between public and private, between orientations to managerial authority and the application of government legislation are all different from liberal-capitalist institutional arrangements. Moreover, government legislative regulation continues to emphasize the content of industrial relations outcomes as much, if not more than, the procedures and processes by which outcomes are made. There are also other explanations for the difference between the nature of actors between capitalist and Chinese contexts, most notably in the nature of the worker. Urban workers, especially those older than 40, maintain strong socialist expectations over a limited number of 'basic interests'. However, this urban socialist worker is rapidly becoming the minority, as rural people leave the peasantry and become wage labourers in cities or on farms, and as younger workers need to find jobs in the private sector.

Neither the political, economic and social context of post-planning or late industrial development are unique to China but, taken together with ideological and real cultural traditions, the nature of actors is complex and their trajectory of future identities uncertain. Two actors, the state and the quasi-state institution of the trade unions, are fairly clear about what they seek to gain from industrial relations, although within each, and especially within the ACFTU, there are differences of how to achieve the aim of maintaining social peace. The differences centre on the degree of independence the unions should have from state and the CCP. The other two actors most closely involved in the daily activities of industrial relations, workers and managers and employers, hold more diffuse interests, that depend on their position within the political economy. However, the argument of the chapters has been that there is a clear tendency towards homogenization of interests within the category of worker and of employer, which is leading to a much clearer set of issues over which industrial relations conflicts can be expected to take place in the future.

The second part of the book dealt with a few selected areas in which the actors come together to interact in industrial relationships. Whilst analysis covered all aspects of the industrial economy, particular attention in each chapter was given to the public sector for framing analysis. This is because it is still the dominant sector, but also because change is greatest in this sector as the market economy is used as a political wedge to force greater responsibility for enterprise performance on their managers. Whilst in the 1980s it is fair to say the state maintained a strong influence over industrial relations in the public sector, altering the basis of relations but also ensuring the privileged position of the urban state worker, it sacrificed other workers to the full ravages of capitalist exploitation in the private sector. This policy was possible mainly because the vast majority of the workers in the new despotic economy were peasants who had always been the underclass of China, and this formed the 'mock dual economy' (quoting the title of the article by Christiansen 1993, who details this in terms of transfer pricing from rural to urban areas). However, in the 1990s the government moved emphasis both to more general macro-level management and to institute controls over the private sector. Thus, union organizing, collective bargaining and labour law provisions increasingly focused on enabling the state to regulate private sector labour relations (BBC 1 January 2001). It may be argued that, in turn, the government has tried to establish a level playing field for all types of enterprises and to standardize labour conditions across the economy during the 1990s, through institutionally regulated bargaining, conflict management and other policies. However, whilst this may be the intention of the CCP and the wish of the ACFTU, there is no evidence that provincial and local-level government cadres think the same way and nor in practice have the same policies been applied in the same way across all sectors of the economy and for all workers. In consequence, huge variations in the way local governments treat different enterprises remain. Variation is more pronounced within the private sector because the public sector continues to have more formal relations with different government agencies, which standardize relations and practices.

## MAIN ARGUMENTS

In this book we have sought to draw out three main arguments. The government continues to play a dominant role in industrial relations in China, the position of workers is steadily declining and overt conflicts of interest are becoming more pronounced.

### *The Dominance of the State*

In examining China, we have painted a picture in which the Party-state remains in control of industrial relations at all important levels and in a number of important ways. These include the methods used in capitalist countries, such as legal control, direct employment and control over the ideological agenda, if not its substance. Whilst not unique, the state in China also uses less common methods of control, such as through the operation and control of quasi-state organs, especially the trade unions, and through more pervasive legal regulation.

The ACFTU is a state organ, which in the early stages of the foundation of Communist China hotly debated whether the unions should be independent from the state bureaucracy or an appendage to it. This debate reopened in the early stages of Deng's agenda of reform. In both cases, the prospect of the unions representing workers' interests against the Party-state was alarming to the CCP (McElroy 2000). In both cases, the ACFTU cadres who propagated pro independence were purged or 're-educated' (Sheehan 1998). Compared with the restriction of organizing trade unions, the policy for organizing employer associations seems quite easy. Based on several national employer associations, various local, regional and industrial employer associations have been set up in recent years. They are tacitly approved or supported by government organs, although there are also increasing moves to regulate these, such as in restricting the employer representation in tripartite industrial relations to the CEC.

The regulation of collective bargaining, conflict resolution and so-called 'democratic management' all point not only to state regulation of the public sector (McNally 2002), but with the new century, to an increasing concern with introducing and adapting these regulations to suit the private sector environment. Consequently, these new institutional arrangements often appear to be copies of advanced capitalist economies, such as in the institution of tripartism and the legislative framework. However, on closer examination, invariably the resemblances mask very different practices. The outward appearance seems often to be contrived to promote China's international image as a modern pluralist political economy and to stem Western criticism of its authoritarianism. Close examination, as provided in the preceding chapters, shows these practises extend Party and government control in two ways: by reinforcing and extending reporting mechanisms which ensure a top-down line of authority, and by stipulating the content of procedures more than the process of relations. In these ways, cadres in the employer and union institutions, the labour department and so on identify their own interests with those above them in the hierarchy, rather than those below. Moreover, by stipulating content, the state both reduces the terrain of potential conflicts between parties and (re)introduces a uniform set of labour standards that to some degree makes it appear that the state is promoting equity, even if belatedly. At the same time, ambiguity in the application of laws provides the state at various levels with the flexibility of not being constrained by such laws.

Whilst Mainland scholars rarely criticize anyone these days, the primary focus of much overseas research is polemic, to seek to change or at least to identify someone to blame. Invariably it is the Party-state that is seen as the root of all evil (sometimes literally) for either being conservative (meaning socialist, in the eyes of many liberal critics) or authoritarian (meaning pro-capital in the eyes of many radical critics). Indeed the state should carry much blame for what is wrong with the industrial relations system in China because, as we have argued consistently throughout the book, the state is the main player, the dominant power in shaping the institutions and processes of industrial relations in the country. However, there are a number of problems with 'CCP-bashing'.

First, there is confusion over the interests of the CCP. Whilst some argue the Party-state is holding back progress by slowing down the pace of economic reform of SOEs, providing opportunities for rent-seeking, and so on, others argue the CCP is at the vanguard of authoritarian-capitalist development. These equate to liberalist or radical perspectives of political economy and, consequently see the treatment of labour very differently. The liberalists contend that the legacy of socialism restrains efficient allocation of labour resources and dilutes rational (economic) decision-making, with incomplete laws, excess labour, an inefficient public sector and so on. For the radicals, the problem is the suppression of labour (the polar opposite of the liberals). Local Party cadre corruption and the like are taken as evidence of the state sponsoring capitalist development, using Party control of the state apparatus to ensure benefits flow to a small group of Party elite. The point is, whilst there may be both elements within the Party pushing development towards liberalism and pulling back towards conservatism, the general theoretical tendency must be one way or the other. The evidence does not support the liberal argument, simply because China has a phenomenally successful economy so far. Claims that if the state had reduced or removed its role, performance would have been even better, amount to mere flights of fantasy, given the history of economic development to date in China and the world. The radicals appear closer to the mark, but the state is a more complex actor than simple authoritarianism allows for. Whilst some institutions of the state wish to suppress workers, other elements wish to promote some view of justice or simply recognize that Party survival depends on meeting the interests and cultivating loyalty among the army, the peasants and the workers. Moreover, the state could feasibly develop a differential policy, both promoting less exploitative forms of industrialization, whilst suppressing those still working in those industries. It is very difficult, for example, to see an alternative for the government but to maintain some form of regulation over labour migration from rural to urban areas (although the methods might be very different than at present). In this way, the state could feasibly promote social progress, whilst simultaneously suppressing elements of the working class.

Second, it is not clear that there is any alternative to strong state involvement in development. As discussed elsewhere (Nolan and Wang 1999; Taylor 2002), 'big bang' economic reform has proven to be an abject failure, so a sudden withdrawal of the state would plunge China into Russian-style mafia-capitalism at best and, given the predominantly agrarian economy of China, African or south Asian levels of poverty at worst. Strong developmental state policy, such as that followed by Japan, then South Korea, Singapore and Taiwan provides a more stable growth model. However, all these economies were far more urbanized at the start and the foundations for developmentalism were set within a framework that included strong worker activism followed by severe repression of labour unions. However, a developmentalist role for the state necessarily continues to place the state as the central actor, and there is little the Chinese state has been doing that the Japanese, Taiwanese or South Korean governments have not been doing (So and Chiu 1995). Yet, as argued previously, China is extremely different from these Asian capitalist development models, with its vast geography, period of non-capitalist economic relations and continued ambivalence towards socialism.

## Workers and Unions

Within a capitalist economy, the employer holds the greatest power in deciding the terrain as well as the outcomes of industrial relations. In a totalitarian system it is the state that controls labour standards. Whilst developing states often have a strong element of state leadership, the state has nevertheless taken on stewardship of the economy for the express purpose of promoting the rapid capitalist development. As Deyo (1989: especially 89) argues, this is often achieved by representing the interests of an expressly narrow group of elite capitalists within the country or particular foreign multinationals with considerable economic ties to the authoritarian elite, and thus development occurs specifically within a context where capitalist and state elite interests coincide. Globalization appears to be strengthening a tendency towards state capitalist alliances, which in turn makes the situation for workers in different countries progressively worse (Berger and Borer 1997; Chang 2002b; Mok and Cai 1999; Solinger 2002).[125] Despite all the rhetoric of the 'socialist market economy', or 'market socialism with Chinese characteristics' the developmentalist model the Chinese leadership is following strongly resembles state-sponsored capitalist development. This inevitably means labours' interests are subsidiary to economic development (that is, employer interests). This can easily be seen in terms of the organizational strength of both employers and workers. Although there is a unified organizational system of trade unions, these trade unions have been neither organized around the interests of workers nor allowed to act wholly as workers' representatives at any meaningful level. In contrast, employers and managers not only have authority in organizing and allocating personnel in their enterprises, but also enjoy more influence in their social and political organizations (management and employer associations) than do workers. What merits particular attention is that along with the continuous ascending social status of employers, there has been a new tendency in Chinese trade unions to establish closer relationships with employers, even admitting them

---

[125] The process of internationalization based primarily on colonialist expansion led to the systematic exploitation of workers in satellite and dependent countries, but the post-Second World War development of globalization has led to significant retrenchment and loss of privileges for the core powerful countries. The implications of the break-up of the soviet system was to accelerate the globalization processes to some degree and although China had developed its market economy prior to this collapse, the liberalist path was vindicated and the Chinese leadership embraced the World Trade Organization as it sought to capitalize on its favourable position within the capitalist globalization agenda.

to the membership of trade unions over the last two years.[126] This is perhaps the clearest illustration to date that the workers do not have legal recourse to trade unions in the sense the term is understood within industrial relations.

Within the public sector, to some degree at least, workers may continue to use the union as any other government agency, alongside the more common complaint route of going through management, to air grievances. In the private sector the process of industrial relations is dominated and controlled by employers. Since the trade unions have no clear function in the private sector, industrial relations mainly takes the form of individual labour relations, namely the labour relations between individual labourers and their employer. Not only the decision and practice of labour standards, work rules and employment conditions, but also the management and settlement of labour disputes, are undertaken through individual labour relations. This not only severely disadvantages workers but also creates an extremely volatile climate for industrial relations. Moreover, as more public enterprises privatize or corporatize, their management appears more eager to adopt private sector methods to manage all matters, including labour, and hence this volatility is spreading throughout urban China.

The ACFTU has thus been presented with shifting sands of relevance. The absence of the *danwei* in the private sector and the recent rise in redundancies in SOEs mean the organizational base and relevance of the trade unions have gone. Without this base, the unions appear powerless to resist managerial economistic agendas, and workers are well aware of this weakness. As in other countries, when the unions appear powerless in the face of employer onslaught, the ACFTU appears to be increasingly turning to legislative means to further its own and its member's interests. However, this has two problems. First, in promoting laws, the ACFTU enters into 'turf-wars' with the MoLSS, which is supposed to take that role within government systems. In order to activate any legislative programme which stands a chance of being enacted, the ACFTU has to subordinate itself to the MoLSS both in the enactment process and in the monitoring of laws once applied. Up to the present, the strength of the ACTFU lies in its direct link and (since June 1989) subordination to the party, which gives the ACFTU a political and ideological foundation for its work. Far from being a weakness (Chan 2000:

---

[126] A prevalent view inside Chinese trade unions is that if entrepreneurs can join the Party, why can they not join trade unions (Wang 2002: 7)? Many people, including high-level cadres in the trade union, promote the admission of 'new classes' (including private entrepreneurs) into the trade union (Zhou 2001). Previously whilst managers could join the union, plant directors in public enterprises and the owners in privatly owned firms could not. However, many unionists and especially Mainland labour researchers have strongly opposed extending membership in such a way. They argue that joining and forming a trade union are basic rights of workers and that to admit employers into the trade union not only acts against the principles of international labour conventions, but also against Chinese labour laws (Chang 2001).

35–6; Pan 2002: 2), this party backing at the national level has allowed the unions to maintain calls for balanced development, campaign against excessive economism and promulgate highly advanced legal codes to protect workers. MoLSS has a more complex set of stakeholders, which appears to firmly place it within a capitalist development camp, and thus ACFTU subordination to this has often meant laws have been made unworkable through ambiguous provisions and uneven application.

## *Nature of Conflict*

The development of the form and system of industrial relations is new for China, but in arguing this, we have in mind a specific definition of what is meant by industrial relations. This definition assumes that there is an industrial relationship only in a situation in which there is a clear conflict of interest between the owners of the means of production and the producers of commodities, workers, and that this conflict takes on a primarily economic manifestation. China is only now beginning to develop such clearly defined interests. Of course, China has had numerous periods of conflict throughout its history and even clear illustrations of industrial relations at certain times and in a few locations in the first part of the twentieth century.

There are some who argue that China has a cultural tradition that is strongly familial, affecting the social relations of the *danwei* (Sil 1997; F. Wang 1998: 105–12) and Chinese business practices (Selmer 1998; Wright et al. 2002; Wong and Slater 2002: 344–5). Although it is important to recognize cultural influences on the manifestation and articulation of interests, conflict is and has always been systemic to Chinese society (Perry and Sheldon 2000; Sheehan 1998). China moved from feudal to totalitarian regimes of different colours, with only a brief and partial exposure to the cowboy capitalism of early capitalism (Lu and Perry 1997b) and the dependent colonial capitalism of Japanese-occupied areas (Warner 1995). Within the Mao period of the CCP, conflicts were primarily cultural and political, between different factions and ideological positions as regards the role of China as a communist state and in regard to the way power would be distributed within the totalitarian regime (Ladany 1988). Whilst there were conflicts of interests, all economic conflicts were subsumed within the political culture of revolutionary politics (Sheehan 1998), or immolated at the local level, often by party leaders, which displaced overt industrial relations conflict. Instead, there was a political-ideological implicit negotiation over the distribution of rewards for effort within enterprises. The state tried to contain conflicts over rising unemployment and periods of falling standards of living were with the ideological tool of accusing dissenters of syndicalism

(Sargeson 1999). Given this politicized context, and the fact that the state was the ultimate employer, conflicts tended to be articulated as conflicts between the workers and the authorities, (rather than managers and workers).

It is in this context that the urban worker was given the much discussed 'iron rice-bowl' (Leung 1988). This is quite unlike the Japanese system of lifetime employment guarantees. In Japan, for the minority of male employees working in large firms, an average at its height of around 20 per cent of the workforce, the employment bargain was the result of bitter and protracted conflict between employers and employees. The iron rice-bowl existed in feudal China under the bureaucratic imperial factories and processing plants, and some scholars make the same linkage between these early stages of industrialization in China and the development of paternal-capitalist development (Ling 1996) in Japan over the last century (Chan 1995a, 1997; Unger and Chan 1995). However, this link is tenuous in both cases as the early experience of capitalism in both countries was to tear down many of these social connections between land-owning feudal elites and urban entrepreneurial racketeering. Similarly, the peasants were ripped from their servile rural communities and often sold by their parents into mass dormitories and factory lives where their every moment was monitored and controlled. Food and shelter was not part of a bargain, but a means to extend control over workers and stop them escaping. As more modern factories formed with higher technological requirements and as men began to replace women in the workplace, these 'facilities' were invariably withdrawn (Taylor 1999a). The difference between China and Japan lies in the way these extra job guarantees got (re) introduced. In China, the best similarity is with public sector workers, both the mandarins of the old court system of imperial China and the civil servants of German and to a lesser extent other European countries. Workers are employed to serve some notion of the public good, rather than private interests. For sure, people enter these jobs for personal career advancement, but in the full knowledge that the employment system will neither make them rich nor redundant.

As such, the basis of the labour process is quite unlike the capitalist system, in which the job of the agents of capital, the managers, is to extract knowledge from workers of the skills of the labour process and embody them in machines and routinized and segmented work processes (Braverman 1974) so as to cheapen the value of labours' input and weaken their bargaining position over the price of their labour. Instead, the labour process in public sectors everywhere consists of a tension between generalizing the knowledge and skills of employees to all relevant parts of the bureaucratic system and ensuring equity of service delivery and treatment though standardization.

Whilst it may be unfashionable to think of the public sector in the liberal West in such terms these days, the drives to consumerism and privatization are attacks on the ideological value of 'the public'. In this last sentence lies the ideological foundation of the Chinese employment system of the communist era. Whilst it was not socialist, it was publicly orientated. Despite political infighting, personal aggrandisement and all the other accusations the liberalists can throw at the Mao period of China, the orientation of publicly owned enterprises, of government bureaucracies and even the Party hierarchy was that despite the petty realities of daily politics and personality conflicts, the function of their organizations was to promote some sense of the public good. This is in contrast to capitalistic enterprises whose specific function is to serve the private interests of the owners, who, with increased use of US-style share ownership schemes for directors, and Japanese style corporate cross-ownership cartels, are also the senior managers.

Thus far, we have skirted around the central element that helps us understand what shapes industrial relations, which is power. Once we understand the institutions, history and experiences of industrial relations at a descriptive level, the processes that bind together and or tear actors apart are essentially facets or manifestations of power. Take, for example, the dilemma facing the ACFTU. At present its relevance to industrial relations is on the wane, its welfare functions stripped away and its representative role unsure. The official unions are seen as either useless or as instruments of state suppression. Both opinions derive from alternative interpretations of the power of unions. In fact the unions have almost no latent power; their power depends on serving the interests of the CCP. Without the CCP credentials, why should anyone listen to the ACFTU? If the union was to change to derive its power base from representing employers or workers it could remodel itself, as many within the union organization would wish in China. However, this again confronts problems of power – why should the CCP let the unions break free and be independent of its control? If the ACFTU could ensure social stability it might be attractive to the government in this time of deepening conflict to allow independence. This certainly corresponds to liberal-pluralist notions of trade unions acting as conflict managers. However, these notions have a naive and narrow view of power. Workers would only join a union that would fight for their interests, and so the power base of mass unions like the ACFTU depends on delivering improvements in class-based interests, which clearly flies in the face of the CCP's interests in continued political hegemony. Why should the parent let go of the child, knowing the child will soon sue them for every penny they can? This, of course, is a one-dimensional view of power (Lukes 1974), and power acts in more sophisticated ways, such that seeming compromises can appear to be reached. Workers can accept a weak union that at least represents some of their material interests, and the CCP can accept a union that more effectively immolates worker unrest in this way. The workers can accept enterprise unions controlled by the CCP, over independent unions that tend to collapse or be suppressed by the state. This is because workers are conscious of their power position within the Chinese communist state, just as workers recognise their weak position within capitalist regimes (Lukes's 1974 second view of power). Moreover, the CCP leadership knows that its control over the country is not total, and so needs to accept dissent and conflict at levels that do not threaten, but in some ways help maintain its monopolistic status. In this way unions, where they exist, have a role as conflict managers.

However, many workers are not covered by unions. Most new enterprises formed since reform began have avoided unionization or usurped the system of union recognition to establish management-controlled organs. In these cases, overt conflict is rife, through not only rising strikes, high levels of labour turnover and public demonstrations, but also through brutal managerial suppression, often tacitly supported by local governments (Chan 2001). Migrant workers are especially vulnerable, resulting from a history of discrimination towards the rural population (Sargeson 1999), and this discrimination extends to migrants working in the public sector as well, who are often denied union representation. Rising gaps between rural and urban populations are driving ever greater numbers of rural migrants to look for work in urban enterprises; this division and the discrimination they face in securing and maintaining such jobs presents a potentially explosive tension within Chinese society.

## CHANGING WORKPLACE INDUSTRIAL RELATIONS

In deciding the extent of change, the literature has focused on the role of the government, on workplace employment relations, and particularly on the status of workers. The key underlying impediment to change at the workplace and for workers individually (micro level) is seen as the characteristics of the Party-state (macro level). Radical writers on China seem more perturbed by this than the liberals, perhaps because the latter see this as a short-term problem to be eroded as China modernizes. For many radical writers, such as Sheehan (1998) and Chan (2001), the problem lies in the communist elite being able to remain in power, changing their Maoist green jackets for pinstriped suits because of the lack of democracy in China. Whilst there is some debate as to whether the Party cadres are becoming the new entrepreneurial elite (for example Oi and Walder 1999, Yep 1999), the general argument is that Party hegemony leads to incipient totalitarianism. Whilst this has an undoubted truthful edge, there is an inherent revisionism to this particular form of leftist argument. The basis of socialist political economy is democratic centralism, in which decisions are arrived at democratically (with full and free debate and access to decision-making processes for all) with centralist implementation. Whilst China is not a democracy, it has a shorter journey to travel to obtain real democracy than most industrialized countries. Although this is not to argue that there are any leaders in the current CCP who are willing to take the first step. It is thus quite possible, though unlikely, that China will become a socialist society if the rupture happens in a certain way, whereas it is extremely unlikely this will happen in the liberalist west and the UK and US in particular.

With the reform of labour relations, managers have gradually become an independent 'employment actor' (*yonggong zhuti*) according to the regulations (Chang 1995a; Qi and Xu 1995; Wang 1993). They gain greater autonomy in recruiting and dismissing workers. They now have the power to determine the number and conditions under which workers are recruited, and base these according to their production requirements and demand for labour (Qi and Xu, 1995; Wang 1993). Moreover, they gain autonomy to discharge and lay off workers in light of workers' performance and production requirements (Wang 1993; Zhu 1995). These regulations, even if still limiting the scope of managerial actions, at any rate provide them with a legal basis for their actions and constitute a set of 'managerial rights'. Further, managers gain determination of affairs with respect to internal personnel management, such as deciding the wage system, promotion and punishment mechanism, and work quotas in their enterprises (Han and Morishima 1992; Warner 1995). These changes mean that workers start to face their managers, rather than the state, directly as the primary actor in determining their work and compensation, even in the public sector.

Lu (2002: 51) argues that 'besides managerial staff of state and society, the private entrepreneurs and managers have been included in the class of those controlling or managing economic resources'. Whilst at a political level the CCP still publicizes the guideline of 'relying on the working class wholeheartedly', owners of capital and managers are the social classes to which the officials at all levels attach importance and on whom they rely in the reform process. Lu goes on to argue that:

> The social foundation of the Party in power is more and more being replaced by the classes in possession of economic and culture resources, such as the managerial class, professional and technical classes and private entrepreneurs. (Lu 2002: 38)

Whilst Lu appears to support this change and used this argument to encourage the CCP to allow entrepreneurs to join the Party, there also appears to be some evidence that this may be the attitude of many in the upper echelons of the CCP. After all, as Dai (2001a) argues, industrial workers have become the smallest membership category (that is, with the lowest membership rates) of the CCP now. Several years before, entrepreneurs could just enter into the local people's congress as deputies or political consultative conference as members. In recent years, by entering into the government directly, their role transformed from mere participation to gaining a real grip on power at the local level to some degree.[127]

In studying these changes, Chinese scholars are reluctant to go so far as to explicitly state that these actors are engaging in an 'employer-employee' relationship, owing to the political connotation this implies. Chang (1995a) and Feng and Xu (1993) each employ the term 'stratum' (*jieceng*) in explaining the status of workers and managers after reform started. This term implies that there is a substantial gap between managers and workers, even if their official interpretations mean both still belong to the same 'class'. Chang (1995a) argues that a new social group a 'labourer stratum', has been created. Chang demonstrates that the 'labourer stratum' has become an independent social group by illustrating such changes as a relationship based on directors as managers and workers as those managed, on income disparities, workers' rights defined by labour regulations, workers' attitude and values, and modes of social interaction after reform started. Based on a survey during the period of 1991 to 1992, Feng and Xu (1993) take the view that the former difference between workers and managers was based on an 'administrative wage system'. At the beginning of reform, management gained more autonomy and, in the meantime, workers had experienced a decrease in their social status. Along with the implementation of the contract responsibility system, further reforms have expanded the gap between managers and workers in terms of interests and income, leading to a change within the structure to form a sub-stratum of labour. Therefore, between workers and managers, there are widening gaps beyond the former 'administrative differences', such as gaps in economic status (for example income, housing conditions), social and political status (for example political prestige, social rights and popularity).

White (1996) is perhaps the first scholar who unequivocally indicates that the Chinese workers, in the process of reform, have become 'wage labourers and commodities'. In a paper examining the social status of Chinese trade unions in transition, he suggests that:

> An increasingly wide gap has opened up between the official ideological description of workers as 'masters of the enterprise' and the reality that they are turning into wage labourers in increasingly profit-oriented enterprises and into commodities in increasingly competitive labour markets. (1996: 440)

---

[127] An anecdote from one of the authors (Chang) when conducting research in a southern province in 2001 illustrates this problem. In a case where the official term of a 'leading team' (a party-led political management committee) had expired, a basic requirement imposed from higher authorities in the government for selecting members for a new leading group was the inclusion of representatives from entrepreneurs. However, no such requirement was given concerning representatives of the workers or the unions.

Many authors both local and overseas agree that a division of interests surfaces between workers and their employers (R. Jiang 1996; Qi and Xu 1995; Walder 1991; Zhang 1997; Zhu 1995).[128] After enterprise managers obtain power and flexibility as well as responsibility, the costs, prices and profits become increasingly important concerns for them and press them to take every means available to enhance productivity (Ip 1995; Lin 1992; Peng 1998; Tang et al. 1996; Walder 1991; Warner 1995; Zhang 1997). Managers have a strong incentive to extract the maximum amount of labour effort at minimum labour costs in order to increase (if not actually maximize) profits (Groves et al. 1995; Tang et al. 1996; Zhang 1997). Obtrusive control is used to achieve these goals (Lin 1992). This situation is most keenly seen in non-public firms (Chan and Senser 1997; Goodall and Warner 1997; Qiao 1995), but also in some SOEs (Zhao and Nichols 1996). Chan argues that:

> Managers have shown a great inclination towards [the] use of Taylorist management techniques. Their measures include tightening labour discipline, imposing heavy penalties, raising production norms, and restructuring the award system ... The latter half of the 1980s witnessed degenerating management labour relations, and poor working conditions became one of the main causes of an increasing number of strikes.[129] (1997: 356)

Urban state workers in particular have lost many of their privileges relative to other social groups; they have reduced tenure rights, increased wage disparities, increased workforce segmentation and stratification, and reduced wages for those in unprofitable enterprises (Karmel 1996; O'Leary 1998; Tang et al. 1996; Walder 1991). Compared with workers, managers have become increasingly aware of their personal interests and income disparities (Qi and Xu 1995; Walder 1991; Zhang 1997). These aspirations for personal interests are due to their emerging relatively independent employment status and their rights to earn surplus income under the law (Chang 1995b). This is set to worsen as enterprises become more independent (Qi and Xu, 1995), and the friction and conflict between workers

---

[128] 'Interests' is used in its Marxist meaning of objective interests pertaining to a class in a given stage of economic development.

[129] In fact, Taylorist management techniques had been introduced into the Chinese SOE by the Soviet Union from the 1950s when the first 156 SOEs were established under Russian assistance. Chan probably means that Taylorist principles were more rigorously applied than before, and this would certainly be the common view among managers. However, we must be careful not to assume that whilst the Taylorist management technique of work evaluation is used, the results of any productivity increase are utilized according to the Taylorist-Fordist mode of accumulation purported by the regulationists.

and managers is likely to worsen (Tang et al. 1996; Wang 1993; Walder 1989; Yu 1986).

Generally, all people share the view that the Chinese economic reform has brought about great changes in labour relations, which affect all forms of enterprises, but especially SOEs. They usually base their arguments on four aspects of reform policies: the withdrawal of government, the implementation of labour contracts, the enhancement of managers' authority and the establishment of new management mechanisms. The withdrawal of government from direct involvement in employment leads workers and managers to become two opposing actors in labour relations, instead of the managers and workers as employees and the state as the employer and its agencies as the ultimate managers. This relationship is further defined by the labour contracts. Associated with the gain of authority, managers in SOEs take profits as their primary objective. This leads to a division of interests between themselves and the workers they employ. All these indicate an evolving system of labour relations towards the orientation of market.

## DEVELOPMENT OF A WORKING CLASS

In the transition to a market economy, the working class is in the process of changing and restructuring. However, government agencies and quasi-government organizations, including the ACFTU (993, 1997), continue to refer to the working class as comprising workers, managers and intellectuals. A few scholars have started to examine the internal changes of this class, through either large-scale surveys (Lu 2002) or case studies (Liu and Zhou 2002). In their case study in four SOEs in Beijing, Shenyang and Shanghai, Liu and Zhou distributed 857 questionnaires, strictly categorizing the respondents into workers (415), technicians (166) and managers (276). They followed this by interviews with 80 people drawn from the three groups. Their methodology was constructed to control for as many variables as possible and concentrate on differences within the official working class. They found that all worker respondents believed they belonged to the working class, while 57.9 per cent and 54.4 per cent of technicians and managers respectively, thought that they form a part of the working class. However, only 22.6 per cent of worker respondents thought that senior managers belonged to the working class. At the same time, 72.6 per cent and 68.8 per cent of them respectively accepted workers in TVEs and FIEs as members of the working class. This indicates that whilst horizontal differentiation is increasing, traditional vertical divides are melting away. It is clear that workers are beginning to change their orientation towards class inclusion and exclusion; in other words, they are developing a new class identity.

The working class, formerly composed of urban workers, has transformed from a rhetorical leading class into 'wage labourers' or 'hired labourers', which consists of urban workers and workers who make their living by selling their capacity to labour. Scholars have noted that the labour contract system and related legislation implemented since 1986 have clarified the relationship between those working in enterprises, who can be addressed as 'workers', and those referred to as 'employers' (Ng and Warner 1998). When workers lose many of their privileges relative to other social groups, they increasingly become aware of their personal interests and income (Qi and Xu 1995; Walder 1991; Zhang 1997). These aspirations for personal material interests occur because the dependence of workers on their enterprises is broken after reform and their rights to earn income under conditions of the labour market become enshrined in law (Chang 1995a).

Managers and staff now form an independent social stratum. From the micro point of view, this change is reflected in their differences from workers in aspects of social status and rights defined by law, ideological consciousness and values based on their social experience (Chang 1995b). From the macro point of view, privatization and the modern corporate system both encourage and force managers to gain power and flexibility, as well as responsibility. Costs, prices and profits have become increasingly important concerns for them and pressed them to take every means available to enhance productivity whilst seeking to minimize labour costs (Ip 1995; Lin 1992; Peng 1998; Tang et al. 1996; Walder 1991; Warner 1995; Zhang 1997). Their relationship with the workers is one between managers and managed, with different material interests. It is likely that the reason why workers saw less difference between themselves and middle managers (and technicians) in Liu and Zhou's (2002) survey than with senior managers, is that the middle managers, as is sometimes the case in public sector enterprises in capitalist countries, can appear to have ambiguous class identities. However, this is likely to be short-lived, as the market economy sorts out the structure of divisions of interests within enterprises more clearly.

The Chinese reform also leads to homogenization of a new working class in which the differences between the workers labouring in different types of enterprises and those from urban and rural areas are gradually narrowing. In urban areas, the workers in the public sector have lost most of their material privileges formerly enjoyed under the planning system, such as job security, enterprise-orientated insurance and welfare benefits. Like their counterparts in the private sector, they are under the increasingly strict supervision and tight control of management. However, the most significant tendency towards homogenization is that the distinction between the urban workers and rural workers is undergoing a gradual transition, although it is not exactly certain what the end result will be. Despite attempts to stratify workers by breaking up the working class into Weberian-style social groups, as discussed earlier in the chapter, we should consider class in a narrower Marxian sense. The major contrast in China has traditionally been between the urban worker and rural peasants, who comprised 80 per cent of the population and received lower incomes and much fewer welfare and social benefits than the urban minority. This distinction will be of declining relevance in the future, which will have important political, social and economic repercussions. The distinction arose because of three main factors.

First, the revolution in China was predominantly a peasant based. Whilst this tends to marginalize the significant contribution strikes in Guangdong, Shanghai and elsewhere had on the formation of revolutionary consciousness among urban labour, Mao's tendency to rely on the peasantry was underscored in both the Cultural Revolution and the recruitment grounds of the Peoples Liberation Army. The vast peasant population and the rapid development of urban coastal areas, together with the reliance on the peasants by the CCP, all reinforced a clear division between urban and rural workers.

Second, in economic terms, there was transfer pricing from rural to urban areas (Christiansen 1993), so that income inequalities were not simply the result of superior productivity in cities but also of wealth redistribution to urban areas. This kind of economic growth model is very similar to Meiji and Taisho Japan, which also used rural surpluses to promote urban industrialization. However, unlike Japan, at least thus far, the transfers continue, exacerbating inequality, which further fuels rural migration to cities.

Third, whilst money flowed from the country to the urban areas, strong limits on labour movement, through household registration (*hukou*), were and are maintained. This results in large differences in income and material living standards between workers in coastal urban areas and the vast hinterland of peasants. The urban workers were, thus, a politically less significant force than the peasants,[130] but they were economically more privileged, which acted more or less successfully as a system of balance and counterbalance. The urban workers undoubtedly existed both as a political faction and as a socio-economic class, but the basis of their class relations was somewhat awkward and ambiguous, as discussed earlier in the chapter.

However, there do appear to be signs of class development across the rural urban worker divide. If so, this is significant for the development of Chinese industrial relations, because the state can no longer rely on urban–rural divisions to maintain control, and the development of an objective working class begs the question as to whether an employer class will also emerge.[131]

---

[130] The trade union movement that was active in the early 1950s was neglected and withered, a tangible sign of the lack of significance the CCP assigned to urban workers.

[131] Whilst we have not argued this, there are many writers already claiming the development of an identifiable bourgeois class in China (Clara 2002).

There are five main factors influencing the development of an objective working class, which breaks down this rural–urban segregation.

First, whilst the effects of China's joining the World Trade Organization may have been exaggerated and reify a particular event, the resultant market openings will very likely affect the agricultural sector in some dramatic ways. With strong farming lobbies in the US and the EU, trade liberalization in the area of foodstuffs, and particularly in market segments where these countries are competitive, is likely to force open agricultural policies in China, which have already been fairly market driven for decades. In order to compete, it will be essential for the Chinese farms to adopt farming practices that rely on machinery, which in return requires economies of scale. This will encourage larger farms, and whilst these may be based on village co-operatives, the division of labour and separation between workers and technocrats will become necessary. It is not enough for the Party secretary to learn about the latest husbandry techniques and fertilizers from training courses by local state bureaucracies or overseas aid organizations. They will need farmers, with a stake in making a profit, and probably even business managers. This will transfer control (even if legal property rights remain fudged) to the managerial/farmer class. The majority of peasants will become farm hands. As such, the countryside will start to resemble the cities in class divisions, and it will only be a question of time before full property rights will be given to the farmer elite through the quasi-privatization that is already taking place.

Second, whilst it is possible that the commercial success of some areas of the countryside able to produce cash crops may make them attractive enough to stem migration to urban areas, it is likely that the vast majority of peasants will be pushed off the land through mechanization and be forced to search for jobs in the cities. With rising unemployment in the cities and fewer jobs to be had, as an increasing number of enterprises switch from socio-political concerns to economically 'rational' behaviour, domestic consumption will become the key determinant of aggregate employment levels. Thus, a potential exists for the even more severe competition for jobs and heightened resentment among the urban population towards peasant migrants undercutting urban wages. However, unless there are dramatic policy changes, the profile of a large mass lumpen proletariat and a smaller pool of urban skilled workers will probably emerge. The distinction between being a labourer on the land and a labourer in a factory will matter little as urban unemployed and the migrant peasant compete for jobs, with migrants taking up jobs urban workers refuse to do to some extent. Whilst there are differences in aptitude to industrial work, physical endurance, and even in discriminatory prejudices among recruiters, there is likely, over time, to be a merging of the two groups of workers. The exception to this will be the continual steam of new migrant peasants, filling in the most disadvantaged group.

Third, TVEs have been the private concerns of village and township elites or, in some prosperous or advantaged locations, the whole community has become the collective employer of enterprises which rely on imported labour from other poorer communities. As such, TVEs have been divisive organizations, advantaging some whilst benefiting little or even disadvantaging others. Whilst the significance of TVEs is on the wane, the process of simple industrialization and non-agricultural commercialization has brought about two potential changes in peasant consciousness. One of these is that many of the rural areas have been introduced to industrial work and new kinds of commodity markets, other than those for farm produce, and this has eroded the urban rural distinction. The other potential change is that the division between village heads and the elite, on the one hand, and the peasant labourers, on the other, has highlighted not just inequality of access to political influence, but real economic separation. As a variant on this theme, the rise of landlord or prosperous villages also highlights the divisions between the 'haves' and the 'have-nots'.

Fourth, whilst industrialization mainly occurred in the coastal regions, the communist government quickly sought to weaken the coastal provinces' hold over industry by locating many large industrial complexes in inland regions in the 1950s and 1960s. As the economy was reintegrated with world capitalism in the 1980s, the coastal provinces have again become advantaged, with their proximity to ports and global trade routes. Consequently, the large industrial complexes became uncompetitive, and as the Chinese market opened up to foreign investors and products in the 1990s, many enterprises could not cope. This heightened a division between the coastal and inland regions, and one of the responses has been for inland provinces to relax *hukou* (urban residency permit) requirements, probably in order to provide a more (legally) accessible pool of cheap labour in an attempt to regenerate their failing economies. Moreover, the glaring inequalities maintained through the *hukou* have been a potential flashpoint for labour unrest, and the removal of such a contentious policy removes a potential threat to social stability, in cities already experiencing daily protests by workers laid off or with unpaid wages. Nevertheless, within the context of the Chinese government's preference for reform strategies based on incremental change and generalizing policies only after experimental phases in one or two locations, it will be a matter of time before *hukou* restrictions will be relaxed or abolished in all major industrial cities (with the possible exception of Beijing). Without the political division based on *hukou*, the distinction between peasant and urban worker will be further undermined.

Fifth, as a result of these changes, the objective foundation of a working or labouring class is forming, which contains not only the urban industrial worker but a growing percentage of the vast number of peasants as well. Whilst this argument may be highly contestable, it is supported by the experience of other economies that industrialized. More importantly, economies that do not integrate the peasant class into the industrialized market economy, face degrees of uneven development that create social instability. The Chinese peasant has been revolting against exploitation roughly once every 100 years for over 2000 years. They will inevitably revolt again, if they are denied access to urban labour markets, and if capitalism leads to greater economic benefits for urban workers. If, however, they are given free access to urban labour markets, but without the development of capitalism within the agricultural sector, China will face the economic malaise of many stalled industrializing economies, such as India. Thus, economic rationalization of farming is a necessary requirement for economic growth, whilst containing the dialectic of forging a more homogenous working class in opposition to the employing elite. Moreover, maintaining the division between peasants and urban workers, each with its own constituency, can potentially spit the CCP.

## Class-consciousness

Whilst there may be an objective movement to class formation, the development of class identity is more complex. The working class of China has a number of impediments to gaining this identity, and transforming itself, in Marxist terms, from a class in itself to a class for itself.

First, in general the mass of workers have not understood what the market economy means to them. The promises held out by the CCP based on the early reforms, when wages rose and unemployment fell, were high, but subsequent reality has neither kept pace with rising expectations, especially among the younger generation, nor with those early gains, as benefits have been distributed increasingly unequally. However, there is still a degree of dependence on the state to solve problems and a degree of nostalgia for the past or hope for the future, which displaces the need to face the grim realities of the present predicament many workers are in. Those workers directly confronting market realities, such as those facing job loss, are beginning to understand the meaning of marketization. An example of this division within the working class can be seen in a survey of workers who were kept on or made redundant from SOEs (Department of Policy Studies, ACFTU 1999: 1045–99). Workers who were made redundant, as opposed to those who were not, were much more apt to consider management as corrupt, industrial relations to be bad and their interests to have always been different from those of their employer. In contrast, those continuing to work were positive about the level of participation, competence of managers and the state of industrial relations in their enterprise. This can be seen in SOE workers clinging on to their posts even if they are not paid. This is a practical response, given the lack of opportunities to solve the present situation for many, but the vain hope for the future, especially in the twin carrots of CCP leadership towards a better tomorrow and the economic Santa-Claus of China's entry to the World Trade Organization, mask the reality that most, especially older and women, workers are unlikely to see any improvement. Without facing the stark realities of the impersonal market, many workers lack the inclination to seek to adapt to the labour market though retraining or facing their demeaned status in the market economy.

Second, whilst Sheehan (1998) has documented a history of labour conflicts which show it is a myth to think Chinese workers were ever passive, there are problems in developing broad-based fronts which are independent of orchestration from above. As such, Chinese workers do not have a clear conception of the need to act collectively (and nor has this been permissible). As Engels wrote, trade unions are the organization that workers form and through which they develop class identity (Marx and Engels 1956: 67). Workers' collective consciousness should lead to an intuitive desire to join or organize trade unions to protect their interests. There are many examples of such organizing, often spontaneously in the course of sporadic collective struggles, but there are two impediments to broader-based collectivistic attitudes. First, there has been a general lack of pressure from workers to urge trade union reform in China, to set up unions in the private sector (where there is more scope and space for representative activities) and to press union representatives in existing plant-based unions to be more active in protecting worker demands. Second, the official union structure and police actions both discourage independent organized collective action (as discussed in Chapter 5).

The whole drift of post-Second World War labour consciousness in advanced industrialized countries has been towards fragmentation, and a decline in trade union consciousness has gathered pace towards the end of the century. Thus, a lack of strong workerist identity in China should be expected. However, given the rhetoric of socialism, workers as 'masters of their enterprise' and 'leaders' of Chinese communism, a critical edge exists in China for cultivating collectivist attitudes. Ironically, to a large extent the continual need for the government and Party to retain direct management of the development of industrial relations in China is to forestall such collective consciousness, to maintain social stability.

As a major actor in the industrial relations system, workers in China are undergoing a historical transition into a new working class. From rhetorical masters of society and enterprises, and a real elitist position, the urban worker is being returned to the status of 'employed workers' at the mercy of the labour market, which is itself increasingly becoming a buyers market. Under the prevailing circumstances of privatization and market-oriented reform, the social and political status of Chinese workers has declined from a relatively privileged class into that of 'hired hands' selling their labour on the open market. In these circumstances, given problematic reform policies, the nature of the market itself and the underdevelopment of class consciousness, workers' economic and social rights cannot be adequately protected by law or workers' own collective efforts. Therefore, the Chinese working class cannot strive for or protect their rights and interests, nor does the state wish to see this happen.

## FUTURE DIRECTIONS

History almost always proves academics to be poor judges of the future course of history and so we will not embarrass ourselves by presenting our own readings of the stars. It is clear that the state is playing and will continue to play the leading role in the development of capitalism in China. However, what this implies for the development of industrial relations, and for society more generally, is by no means clear. In place of a detailed analysis of the character and development of the Chinese state, most western commentators fall back on convergence theory, suggesting that China is destined to follow some preordained path of development, or try to guess what will happen in China by finding comparators elsewhere, most usually with the developmental state in East Asian late industrialization. However, such comparisons are unconvincing because they ignore the fundamental differences between China and the rest of East Asia. In particular, the Chinese state is under the control of a Communist Party that led a nominally socialist revolutionary transformation of a peasant country and has turned towards the market after 40 years of building a monolithic state socialism. Moreover, China is an enormous and very diverse country marked by regional inequalities, which have been intensified by China's incorporation into the world economy.

China is following its own course. We cannot predict in which direction China will go, but we can identify the pressures and so the possibilities. These range from China becoming unambiguously a capitalist state to actual revolutionary socialism. Clemens (1999) provides three main future directions: Singaporean style authoritarian capitalism, Russian collapse or some kind of hybrid socialist market economy envisaged by Deng (1994b: 1415). His argument is that change is inevitable, and that China cannot develop in the same way it has been doing over the past 30 years. To restate this in a slightly different way, one can envisage a number of future directions. Authoritarian capitalism with labour subordination and suppression (Unger and Chan 1995), liberal capitalism (Prybyla 1996) with a Dunlop's (1958) industrial relations system (Chan 1995b; Ng and Warner

1998), a Hong Kong variant of this (Ip 1999, White et al. 1999),[132] Russian-style crony capitalism or complete collapse (G. Chang 2001). Looking at these as a set of paired choices, we have Western versus Eastern capitalism, unitary versus a pluralist political framework, and strong state versus weak state development. It is likely that the CC-CCP will not change its desire for hegemonic control in China and so the authoritarian politics remains the primary goal of state management. However, there is also a clear desire for liberal economic planning, which tends to indicate a likely path is towards the Singaporean model. However, Singapore is a tiny ex-colony established, albeit with some reluctance, under British supervision. There is no precedent in reality for China to follow in seeking this path. The implosion model of Russia is the only and least desirable model with strong reference points for China.

The eventual outcome will ultimately depend on two industrial relations actors, the state and the workers. Managers and entrepreneurs are predictable, their profit and careerist interests can easily be understood, and their 'commitment' to Chinese development will invariably depend on how much of these they calculate they can appropriate depending on the political economic system. The state and the workers, as they always have in China, create the dynamics of tension between change and stability. To the CCP, economic development is a political tool to maintain hegemony and nothing more. For their part, workers face a number of problems in trying to articulate their interests. The degree to which they act as a class in and of itself is the main shaping force in this, but within this complex formation of (or failure to form) class identity there are a number of important tensions: sectional interests, background experience, degree to which the state unions partly mollify concerns and so on. The state in turn depends on the compliance of the workers to accept segmentation, and for many, great uncertainty and worsening labour conditions, which thus far, has largely been successful. The future, however, is impossible to predict, because it is based on political and class-based struggles. However, the idea of a smooth transition to some form of capitalism is exceedingly unlikely. The reform process in China started because of conflicts within the existing system; the process of change is itself a conflict negotiation process and the outcomes, should they not lead to socialism (as they are unlikely to do at present) will be predicated on institutionalized conflict arrangements.

---

[132] Though in practice the evidence for such claims is restricted to a narrow set of industrial relations issues and almost always using the empirical example of Guangdong, the neighbouring province to the Hong Kong SAR.

# References

ACFTU. 1987. *Zhongguo zhigong duiwu zhuangkuang diaocha* (A survey of Chinese staff and workers). Beijing: Gongren chubanshe.

ACFTU. 1991. *Zhongguo gonghui nianjian: 1991* (Chinese Trade Unions Yearbook: 1991). Beijing: Zhongguo tongji chubanshe.

ACFTU. 1993. Guanyu zhigong de zhengzhi diwei he zhengzhi guanxi de diaocha (A survey on workers' political status and political relationship). In *Zouxiang shehuizhuyi shichang jingji de zhongguo gongren jieji: 1992 nian quanguo gongren jieji duiwu zhuangkuang diaocha wenxian ziliaoji* (The Chinese Working Class in the Transition to Socialist Market Economy: A Collection of Documents and Materials of Enterprise Employee Survey in the Whole Country in 1992). ACFTU. Beijing: Zhoguo gongren chubanshe.

ACFTU. 1995. *Zhonghua quanguo zonggonghui qishinian* (Seventy years of the ACFTU). Beijing: Zhongguo gongren chubanshe.

ACFTU. 1997. *Zhongguo gonghui nianjian: 1997* (Chinese trade unions yearbook: 1997). Beijing: Zhongguo tongji chubanshe.

ACFTU. 1999. Guanyu jiaqiang xin jingji zuzhi gonghui gongzuo de yijian (Opinions about strengthening the work of trade unions in new economic organizations) (29 January).

ACFTU. 2000. *Zhongguo gonghui tongji nianjian: 1999* (Chinese Trade Unions Statistics Yearbook: 2000). Beijing: Zhongguo tongji chubanshe.

ACFTU. 2001. *Zhongguo gonghui tongji nianjian: 2000* (Chinese Trade Unions Statistics Yearbook: 2000). Beijing: Zhongguo tongji chubanshe.

ACFTU. 2002. *Zhongguo gonghui nianjian: 2001* (Chinese Trade Unions Yearbook: 2001). Beijing: Zhongguo gonghui nianjian bianjibu.

Ahlstrom, David, Garry Burton and Eunice S. Chan. 2001. HRM of foreign firms in China: the challenge of managing host country personnel. *Business Horizons.* 59–68.

Anonymous. 1983. *Qiye zhigong daibiao dahui zanxing tiaoli* (Interim Provisions on Workers' Congress). Beijing: Falu chubanshe.

Anonymous. 2001. Taishan gangtie gongsi zhigong dongshi jianshi renzhen lvxing zhize (The employee directors and supervisors can seriously fulfil their duties in Taishan Iron and Steel Corporation). http://www.grrb.com.cn. 30 July.

Anonymous. 2002. Why employee directors feel difficulty to play their roles, *Zhuzhi renshi ba* (Daily of Organization and Personnel). 79. http://www.chinesemanagers.com/skyd/skyd3.htm.

Ashwin, Sarah and Simon Clarke. 2002. *Russian Trade Unions and Industrial Relations in Transition*. Basingstoke: Palgrave.

Asia Monitor Resource Centre. 1995. *Conditions of Workers in the Shoe Industry of China*. Hong Kong.

Bai, Ningxiang. 2001. Feizhengshi gongren zuzhi: yige jidai zhengshi de shehui wenti (Informal organizations of workers: a social fact needs to be faced). In *Liangan sandi de laodong zhengce yu laodong guanxi* (Labour Policy and Labour Relations in Mainland China, Taiwan and Hong Kong), edited by Centre for Studying Relationship between the Two Sides of the Taiwan Straits. Hong Kong: Xianggang haixia liangan guanxi yanjiu zhongxin. 211–26.

Bao, Guimin. 2001. Lun xiangzhen qiye yu zhengfu de guanxi (On the relationship between TVEs and township government). *Shehui kexue zhanxian* (Battlefront of Social Science). 1: 8–14.

BBC. [various dates]. *BBC Monitoring Asia Pacific – Political*.

Beijing Federation of Trade Unions. 2001. *Gonghui tongxun* (Trade Unions' Information). 11. http://www.bjzgh.gov.cn.

Berger, T. Mark and Douglas Borer. 1997. *The Rise of East Asia: Critical Visions of the Pacific Century*. London: Routledge.

Bian, Yangjie. 1992. *Work-unit structure and status attainment: a study of work-unit status in urban China*. PhD Dissertation, State University of New York at Albany.

Bian, Yangjie, John R. Logan, Hanglong Lu, Yunkang Pan and Ying Guan. 1997. Work units and housing reform in two Chinese cities. In Xiaobo Lu and Elizabeth J. Perry (eds). *Danwei: the Changing Chinese Workplace in Historical and Comparative Perspective*. Armonk: M.E. Sharpe.

Biddulph, Sarah and Sean Cooney. 1993. Regulation of trade unions in the People's Republic of China. *Melbourne University Law Review*. 19: 253–92.

Blackman, Carolyn. 1997. *Negotiating China*. Australia: Allen & Unwin.

Blecher, Mark J. 2002. Hegemony and Workers' Politics in China. *China Quarterly*, 170 (June): 283–303.

Boisot, Max and John Child. 1990. Efficiency, Ideology and Tradition in the choice of transactions governance structures: the case of China as a modernizing society. In Stewart Clegg and Gordon Redding (eds). *Capitalism in Contrasting Cultures*. Berlin: Walter de Gruyter.

Bowles, Paul and Xiaoyuan Dong. 1999. Enterprise ownership, enterprise organisation, and worker attitudes in China's rural industry: some new evidence. *Cambridge Journal of Economics*. 23: 1–20.

Braverman, Harry. 1974. *Labour and Monopoly Capital: the degradation of work in the Twentieth Century*. New York: Monthly Review Press.

Brown, David H. and Mohamed Branine. 1996. Adaptive personnel management: evidence of an emerging heterogeneity in China's foreign trade corporations. In David H. Brown and Robin Porter (eds). *Management Issues in China: Volume I Domestic Enterprises*. London: Routledge.

Brown, David H. and Robin Porter (eds). 1996. *Management Issues in China: Volume I Domestic Enterprises*. London: Routledge.

Bu, Nailin and Jiliang Xu. 2000. Work-Related attitudes among Chinese employees vis-à-vis 'American' and 'Japanese' management models. In Malcolm Warner (ed).

*Changing Workplace Relations in the Chinese Economy.* Basingstoke: Macmillan Press.

Cai, Yongshun. 2002. The Resistance of Chinese laid-off workers in the reform period. *China Quarterly.* 170 (June): 327–44.

Carroll, Thomas and Anthony Bebbington. 2001. Peasant federations and rural development policies. In Andes. In John D. Montgomery and Alex Inkeles (Eds). *Social Capital as a Policy Resource.* Boston: Kluwer Academic Publishers.

Central Committee of the Chinese Communist Party. 1987. Zhonggong zhongyang di shiyijie sanzhong quanhui jueyi (The Resolution of the Third Plenary Session of the Eleventh Central Committee of the CCP). In *shiyijie sanzhong quanhui yilai zhongyao wenjian xuandu: shangce* (A Selection of Important Documents since the Third Plenary Session of the Eleventh Central Committee of the CCP: 1st volume), Department of Document Studies, CPC. Beijing: Renmin chubanshe. 1–14.

Chan, Anita. 1993. Revolution or corporatism? Workers and trade unions in post-Mao China. *The Australian Journal of Chinese Affairs*, no. 29: 31–61.

Chan, Anita. 1995a. The Emerging Patterns of Industrial Relations in China and the Rise of Two New Labour Movements. *China Information.* 9(5): 36–59.

Chan, Anita. 1995b. Chinese enterprise reforms: convergence with the Japanese model?. *Industrial and Corporate Change.* 4(2): 449–70.

Chan, Anita. 1997. Chinese danwei reforms: convergence with the Japanese model?. In Xiaobo Lu: and Elizabeth J. Perry (eds). *Danwei: The Changing Chinese Workplace in Historical and Comparative Perspective.* Armonk: M.E. Sharpe.

Chan, Anita. 2000. Chinese trade unions and workplace relations in state-owned and Joint-venture enterprises. In Malcolm Warner (Ed). *Changing Workplace Relations in the Chinese Economy.* Basingstoke: Macmillan Press.

Chan, Anita. 2001. *China's Workers Under Assault.* New York: An East Gate Book.

Chan, Anita and Robert Senser. 1997. China's troubled workers. *Foreign Affairs* 76(2): 104–17.

Chang, Gordon G. 2001. *The Coming Collapse of China.* New York: Random House.

Chang, Kai. 1988a. Gongchao wenti de diaocha yu yanjiu (A survey of workers' protest movements). *Dangdai gonghui wencong* (Collected Papers on Contemporary Trade Unions). Beijing: Gongren chubanshe. 1: 51–8.

Chang, Kai. 1988b. *Lilun gonghuixue gailun* (Compendium of Trade Union Science), Beijing: Jingji guanli chubanshe.

Chang, Kai. 1993a. Shichang jingji tiaojian xia de laodong guanxi yu gonghui (Labour Relations and trade unions in a Market economy). *Gonghui lilun yu shijian* (Theories and Practices of Trade Unions). 1: 2–5.

Chang, Kai. 1993b. Laodong guanxi yu gonghui lungang (An outline theory of labour relations and trade unions). *Gonghui lilun yu shijian* (Theories and Practices of Trade Unions), no. 3: 13–16.

Chang, Kai. 1995a. Daolun: zhongguo laodong wenti yanjiu de yiban lilun he fangfa (Introduction: general theories and methodology of studies of China's labour issues). In *Laodong guanxi, laodongzhe, laoquan: dangdai zhongguo laodong wenti* (Labour Relations, Labourers and Labour Rights: Labour Issues in Contemporary China). Beijing: Zhongguo laodong chubanshe.

Chang, Kai. 1995b. Laoquan baozhang (Safeguarding labour rights). In *Laodong guanxi, laodongzhe, laoquan: dangdai zhongguo laodong wenti* (Labour Relations, Labourers and Labour Rights: Labour Issues in Contemporary China). Beijing: Zhongguo laodong chubanshe.

Chang, Kai. 1998. Globalization and China's Labour Legislation. *Asian Labour.* September/ December: 33–45.

Chang, Kai. 2001. Organize trade union according to law is basic right of Labourer. *Workers' Daily.* 19 March.

Chang, Kai. 2002a. WTO, laodong biaozhun yu laoquan baozhang (WTO, labour standards and protection of labour rights). *Zhongguo shehui kexue* (Chinese Social Science). 1: 127–36.

Chang, Kai. 2002b. Lun zhongguo bagong quanli de lifa (On China's legislation on right to strike). *International Conference of Industrial Relations and Labour Policies in a Globalising World* (January). Peking University, Beijing.

Chang, Kai, Qi Li and Bama Athreya. 2001. A Comparison between International Labour Standards and Chinese Labour Standards. Research report, Washington: International Labour Rights Fund. *Unpublished.*

Chang, Kai, Qi Li and Yuanwen Liu. 1999. Zhigong Jiceng minzhu canyu yanjiu (A study on the employees' participation in enterprises). In *1997 zhongguo zhigong zhuangkuang diaocha* (Survey of Chinese staff and workers in 1997). Department of Policy, ACFTU. Beijing: Xiyuan chubanshe.

Chang, Kai and Derong Zhang. 1993. *Gonghui fa tonglun* (General Theory of Trade Union Law). Beijing: Zhonggong zhongyang dangxiao chubanshe.

Chen, Feng. 2000. Subsistence crises, managerial corruption and labour protests in China. *The China Journal.* July: 41–63.

Chen, Hong-Yi and Scott Rozelle. 1999. Leaders, managers, and the organization of township and village enterprises in China. *Journal of Development Economics.* 60: 529–57.

Chen, Ji. 1999. *Gaige zhong de gonghui he gonghui de gaige* (Trade Unions in Reform and Reform of Trade Unions). Beijing: Zhongguo gongren chubanshe.

Chen, Jiagui and Qunhui Huang. 2001. Woguo butong suoyouzhi qiye zhili jiegou de bijiao yu gaishan (A comparison of corporate governance between different types of enterprises). *Jingji Redian* (Economic Hot-points). 7: 23–30.

Chen, Wentong. 2001. Dui woguo xian jieduan shehui xingtai jiqi laodong he laodongzhe jieji he boxiao de sikao (A thinking to social formation, labour, labourers, classes and exploitation in current China). *Dangdai shijie yu shehui zhuyyi* (Modern world and socialism). 4: 10–17.

Chen, Yiqi. 2000. Yujian xinxinag minzu: nan zhongguo taizi qiye de laodong guanxi (Meeting a burgeoning nationality: labour relations in Taiwanese-invested enterprises in South China). In *Haixia liangan de laozi guanxi he laoodong zhengce* (Labour Policy and Labour Relations in Mainland China, Taiwan and Hong Kong). Hong Kong: Xianggang haixia liangan guanxi yanjiu zhongxin.

Chen, Yizi. 1990. *Zhongguo: shinian gaige yu bajiu minyun* (China: A Decade's Reform and Democratic Movement in 1989). Taipei: Lianjing chuban shiye gongsi.

Chen, Xiangming. 2001. Both glue and lubricant: transnational ethnic social capital as a source of Asia-Pacific subregionalism. In John D. Montgomery and Alex Inkeles (eds). *Social Capital as a Policy Resource.* Boston: Kluwer Academic Publishers.

Cheng, Xiaonong. 2001. Who can coordinate the labour relations in SOEs (*Shui lai xietiao guoyou qiye de laodong guanxi*). http://newssearch.bbc.co.uk/hi/chinese/china_news. 1 May.

Child, John. 1994. *Management in China during the Age of Reform*. Cambridge: Cambridge University Press.

Child, John and Yanni Yan. 1999. Investment and control in international joint ventures: the case of China. *Journal of World Business*. 34(1): 3–15.

Child, John and Yuan Lu (eds). 1996. *Management Issues in China: Volume II International Enterprises*. London: Routledge.

China Enterprise Association and China Investigation System of Entrepreneur. 2001. 2000nian qian hu guoyou qiye jingyingzhe wenjuan diaocha baogao (A survey report on 1000 SOEs managers in 2000). *Gongchang guanli* (Factory Management). 7: 6–7.

China Enterprise Confederation and China Enterprise Directors Association http://www.cec-ceda.org.cn.

China Investigation System of Entrepreneur. 1997. Dangqian woguo qiye jingyingzhe dui jili yu yueshu wenti kanfa de diaocha (An investigation into Chinese entrepreneurs' views on the encouragement received and restrain placed under the existing conditions). *Guanli shijie* (Management Worlds). 4.

China Investigation System of Entrepreneur. 1999. Yingjie zhishi jingji tiaozhan: shiyi zhi jiao de zhongguo qiye jingyingzhe (Facing the challenges from knowledge economy: the Chinese entrepreneurs before millennia). *Guanli shijie* (Management Worlds). 4.

China Investigation System of Entrepreneur. 2000. Zhongguo qiye jingyingzhe duiiwu zhiduhua jianshe de xianzhuang yu fazhan (The situation and development of Chinese entrepreneurs [2000]), *Guanli shijie* (Management Worlds). 4.

China Labour College (ed.) 1993. *Xiang shichang jingji guodu shiqi de zhongguo gonghui gongzuo* (The Trade Unions' Work during the Transition towards Market Economy). Beijing: Zhongguo dabaike quanshu chubanshe.

Chiu, Catherine and Bill Taylor. 2001a. Labour regulation in foreign funded firms in socialist China: the relation between the origin of capital and the control of labour. In Glenn Drover, Graham Johnson and Julia Tao (eds.). *Regionalism and sub-regionalism in East Asia: the dynamics of China,* Huntington: Nova Science.

Chiu, Catherine and Bill Taylor. 2001b. Shuchangdi jilyu: zhongguo hexin giyeneide hezuo' (The discipline of the market: consent in core firms in China) in Y.S. Cheng, S. Yu, K. Chang and B.L. Leung (eds). *Haixia liangan sandide* lauzu guanxi yu laugong zhongtse: yanjiu zhuanshu diliuhao (Labour relations and labour policy in China, Hong Kong and Taiwan: research monograph No. 6) Hong Kong: Xiang gang Haixia liangan guanxi yanjiu zhongxin [Hong Kong Two-coasts Relations Research Centre].

Choi, Eunkyong and Kate Xiao Zhou. 2001. Entrepreneurs and politics in the Chinese transitional economy: political connections and rent-seeking. *The China Review*. 1(1): 111–35.

Christiansen, Flemming. 1993. The legacy of the mock dual economy: Chinese labour in transition 1978–1992. *Economy and Society*. 22(4): 411–36.

Clarke, Simon. (ed.). 1995. *Management and Industry in Russia: Formal and Informal Relations in the Period of Transition*. Aldershot: Edward Elgar.

Clements, C. Walter. 1999. China: alternative futures. *Communist and Post-Communist Studies.* 32: 1–21.

Coll, Joan H. 1993. The People's Republic of China. In Miriam Rothman (ed). *Industrial Relations around the World: Labour Relations for Multinational Companies,* New York: Walter deGruyter.

Dai, Jianzhong. 2001a. Xian jieduan zhongguo siying qiyezhu yanjiu (A study on private entrepreneurship in contemporary China. *Shehuixue yanjiu* (Sociology Studies). 3: 65–76.

Dai, Jianzhong. 2001b. Zhongguo siying qiyezhu yanjiu (A study of POEs' owner), *Zhongguo renmin daxue xuebao* (Journal of People's University). 2: 12–16.

Deery, Stephen and Richard Mitchell (eds). 1993. *Labour and Industrial Relations in Asia: Eight Countries Studies.* Melbourne: Longman Cheshire.

Deng, Xiaoping. 1983. Gongren jieji yao wei shixian sige xiandaihua zuochu youyi gongxian: zai quanguo zonggonghui di jiu ci quanguo daibiao dahui shang de zhice (The working class should make outstanding contributions to the four modernizations: speech at the 9th National Congress of the ACFTU). In *Selected Works of Deng Xiao-ping (1975–1982).* Editorial Committee for Party Literature, Central Committee of the CPC. Beijing: Renmin chubanshe. 124–29.

Deng, Xiaoping. 1994a. Speech at receiving the members of the Drafting Committee of Basic Law of Hong Kong Administrative Region (16 April 1987). In *Selected Works of Deng Xiaoping: 1982–1992.* Translated by the Bureau for the Compilation and Translation of Works of Marx, Engels, Lenin and Stalin under the Central Committee of CCP. Beijing: Foreign Languages Press.

Deng, Xiaoping. 1994b. Establishing socialism with Chinese characteristics (30 June 1984). In *Selected works of Deng Xiaoping: 1982–1992.* Translated by the Bureau for the Compilation and Translation of Works of Marx, Engels, Lenin and Stalin under the Central Committee of CCP. Beijing: Foreign Languages Press.

Denigan, Mary. 2001. Defining public administration in The People's Republic of China: a platform for future discourse. *Public Performance and Management Review.* 24(3): 215–32.

Department of Information. 2001. *Gongshang xingzheng guanli tongji huibian* (Statistical Compilation of Industrial and Commercial Administration [1990–2000]). Beijing: National Bureau of Industrial and Commercial Administration.

Department of Overall Planning, Ministry of Labour. 1989. *Guide to Labour Management of Enterprises with Foreign Investment in China.* Beijing: Laodong renshi chubanshe.

Department of Policy and Law, Ministry of Labour. 1983. *Laodong zhengce fagui zhuankan* (Special Volume of Labour Policies and Regulations).

Department of Policy and Law, Ministry of Labour. 1985. *Laodong zhengce fagui zhuankan* (Special Volume of Labour Policies and Regulations).

Department of Policy and Law, Ministry of Labour. 1994. *Laodong zhengce fagui zhuankan* (Special Volume of Labour Policies and Regulations).

Department of Policy and Law, Ministry of Labour. 1996. *Laodong zhengce fagui zhuankan* (Special Volume of Labour Policies and Regulations).

Department of Policy Studies, ACFTU. 1999. *1997 zhongguo zhigong zhuangkuang diaocha* (Survey of the Status of Chinese Workers and Staff in 1997). Beijing: Xiyuan chubanshe.

Department of Policy Studies, ACFTU. 2000. *Zhongguo gonghui tongji nianjian: 2000* (Chinese Trade Unions Statistics Yearbook: 2000). Beijing: Zhongguo tongji chubanshe.

Department of Policy Studies, State Bureau of Labour. 1981. *Laodong zhengce fagui huibian* (Collection of labour policies and regulations). *Unpublished.*

Department of Trade Unions Science, China Institute of Labour Movement. 1993. *Xin shiqi gonghui gongzuo zhongyao wenjian xuanbian* (Selection of Important Documents about the Trade Unions' Work in New Period). *Unpublished.*

Department of Trade Unions Science, China Institute of Labour Movement. 1999. *Xin shiqi gonghui gongzuo zhongyao wenjian xuanbian (1993–1998)* (Selection of Important Documents about the Trade Unions' Work in the New Period [1993–1998]). *Unpublished.*

Deyo, C. Frederic. 1989. *Beneath the Miracle: Labour Subordination in the New Asian Industrialism.* Berkeley: University of California Press.

Dickson, Bruce J. 2001. Cooperation and corporatism in China: the logic of party adaptation. *Political Science Quarterly.* 115(4): 517–40.

Ding, X.L. 2000. The illicit asset stripping of Chinese state firms. *China Journal.* 43(1): 1–28.

Ding, Xuezhi and Dong Zhao. 2002. Guanyu woguo minying qiye zhili jiegou de yanjiu (A study on governance structure of private enterprise). *Shaanxi jingmao xueyuan xuebao* (Journal of Shaani Economic and Trade Institute). 15(1): 40–3.

Du, Jian and Weizhen Zheng. (Ed.). 1995. *Shehui baozhang zhidu gaige* (Reform of the Social Security System). Shanghai: Lixin kuaiji chubanshe.

Dunlop, John. 1958. *Industrial Relations Systems.* New York: Henry Holt.

Economic and Business News. 2000. Zhigong dingshi he jianshi zai hebei sheng qiye zhong fahui zhongyao zuoyong (The employee directors and supervisors played an important role in corporation in Hebei province). *Xinghua News Agency*: http://news.old.fjii.com/allnews. 15 June.

Fan, Fuming. 2001. Quntixing lanche duanlu shijian de tedian he chuzhi duice (The characteristics and policies on collective events of blocking traffic). *Tiedaobu zhengzhou gongan guanli ganbu xueyuan xuebao* (Journal of Railway Ministry Zhengzhou Police College). 2: 3–6.

Fan, Gang (ed). 1994. *Zouxiang shichang (1978–1993): zhongguo jingji fenxi* (Toward Market [1978–1993]: An Analysis of the Economy of China), Shanghai: Shanghai renmin chubanshe.

Fan, Qimiao. 1994. 'SOEs' reform in China: incentives and environment. In Qimiao Fan and Peter Nolan (eds). *China's Economic Reforms: The Cost and Benefits of Incrementalism.* New York: St. Martin's Press.

Fan, Zhanjiang. 1998. *Laodong zhengyi chuli* (Settlement of Labour Disputes). Beijing: Falv chubanshe.

Fang, Dan and Yungao Lin. 1990. *Gonghui diwei yu zhineng yanjiu* (Study of the Status and Functions of Trade Unions). Shenyang: Liaoning renming chubanshe.

Fang, Shan. 1998. Dalu guoqi gaige xia de shiye zhuangkuang (Unemployment in mainland China SOEs under reform). *Zhongguo dalu yanjiu* (Study of Mainland China). 44(8): 17–29.

Federation of Trade Unions, Xiantao City. 1996. Jiji zhidao he bangzhu xiangzhen qiye qianding jiti hetong (Playing a full role in directing and assisting the TVEs to sign their collective contracts). *Zhongguo gongyun* (China Labour Movement). 3: 19.

Feng, Tongqing. 2001. Laozi guanxi de bianhua yu zhongguo gonghui de jiben tezheng (Changes of industrial relations and characteristics of trade unions in China). *Xianggang shehui kexue xuebao* (Hong Kong Journal of Social Sciences). 21: 67–98.

Feng Tongqing and Xiaojun Xu. 1993. *Zhongguo zhigong zhuangkuang: neibu guanxi ji xianghu guanxi* (The Situation of Chinese Workers and Staff: Internal Structure and Relationship). Beijing: Zhongguo shehui kexue chubanshe.

Feng, Xiashuang. 1995. Zhujian sanjiaozhou wailai nongmingong de zhuangkuan (The situation of migrant peasant-workers in the Zhu River Delta area). *Zhongguo shehui kexue* (China Social Science). 1: 92–104.

Fewsmith, J. 1994. *Dilemmas of Reform in China: Political Conflict and Economic Debate.* Armonk: M.E. Sharpe.

*Financial Times.* 2000 4 April.

Flanders, Allan. 1969. The nature of collective bargaining. In Allan Flanders (ed). *Collective Bargaining.* Harmondsworth: Penguin.

Fox, Alan. 1966. Industrial sociology and industrial relations. *Royal Commission on Trade Unions and Employers' Associations Research Paper no. 3.* London: HMSO.

Fox, Allen. 1973. Industrial relations: a social critique of pluralist ideology. In John Child (ed). *Man and Organization.* Allen & Unwin.

Frazier, Mark. 2002. *The Making of the Chinese Industrial Workplace: State, Revolution, and Labour Management.* Kentucky: University of Louisville.

Frost, Stephen. 2002. Toys, wages and retail prices. *Asian Labour Update.* 42. January to March 2002.

Fu, Lin, Bill Taylor and Qi Li. 2001. City trade unions and the regulation of industrial relations in FIEs in China: a last chance for the ACFTU to be relevant? *Labour in a Globalising World: The Challenge for Asia.* Hong Kong: City University of Hong Kong, January.

Fu, Youzhi. 2000. Quntixing zhian shjian de shehuixue hanyi (The social meaning of collective public events). *Shandong gongan zhuanke xuexiao xuebao* (Journal of Shandong Public Security College). 1: 81–3.

Gai, Yaomin. 2002. Guoyou qiye shuangchong jingying mubiao de maodun ji gaige chulu (The contradiction of SOEs' dual objectives of management and the way of reform). *Shandong caizheng xueyuan xuebao* (Journal of Shangdong College of Finance). 1: 54–60.

Gao, Shangquan. 1998. *The Second Revolution Historic Change in China's Economic System.* Hong Kong: Joint Publishing.

Gao, Shangquan. 1999. *Two Decades of Reform in China.* (Translated and edited by Yuling Wang.) Singapore: World Scientific.

General Office. 1982. Centre for Economic Law, State Council. 440–72.

General Office. 1997. *Guoyou qiye lingdao banzi kaohe jianshe gongzuo zhidao* (The Direction of Assessing and Building the Leading Body of SOEs). Coordination Group of Strengthening the Building of Leading Body of SOEs. Beijing: Dangjian duwu chubanshe.

*Gongren ribao* (Workers' Daily). various issues.

Goodall, Keith and Malcolm Warner. 1997. Human resources in Sino-foreign joint ventures: selected case studies in Shanghai, compared with Beijing. *International Journal of Human Resources Management.* 8(5): 569–94.

Granick, David. 1990. *Chinese State Enterprises: A Regional Property Rights Analysis.* Chicago: University of Chicago Press.

Gregory, Neil and Stoyan Teney. 2001. China's home-grown entrepreneurs. *The China Business Review.* 28(1): 14–18.

Groves, Theodore. 1995. China's evolving managerial labour market. *Journal of Political Economy.* 103(4): 873–91.

Gu, Shutang, Weian Li and Minghua Gao. 1999. Zhongguo shangshi gongsi neibu zhili de shizheng fenxi (A case study of the governance within China's listed corporations). *Guanli shijie* (Management Worlds). 6: 145–51.

Guan, Huai and Yanchun Cao. 2000. Luelun woguo laodong zhengyi de qiye tiaojie (On labour mediation within enterprise). *Faxue zazhi* (Magazine of Law). 4: 11–12.

Guan Shafeng. 2001. Lun laodongfa yu laodongzhe de renquan baozhang (On labour law and the protection of human rights of labour). *Gonghui luntan* (Trade Union Tribune). 8(1): 51–4.

Guo, Qiang and Guang Li. 2001. Zhongguo qiye zhili jiegou fazhan zhong de wenti: 'xinsanhui' he 'laosanhui' de maodun" (The problems in developing governance structure in corporations: the contradiction between the *xinsanhui* and *laosanhui*). *Laoning ribao* (Liaoning Daily). http://www.injj.com.cn 13 August.

Han, Jiangwei and Motohiro Morishima. 1992. Labour system reform in China and its unexpected consequences. *Economic and Industrial Democracy.* 13(2): 233–61.

Hannan, Kate. 1991. Building socialism with Chinese characteristics. In Hans Hendrischke (ed). *Market reform in the changing socialist world.* Centre for Chinese Political Economy. Macquarie University.

Harwit, Eric. 2001. Chinese Millionaires. *China Business Review.* 28(1): 20–1.

He, Jianzhang. 1990. *Dangdai shehui jieji jiegou he shehui fenceng wenti* (The structure of social class and social stratification). Beijing: Zhongguo shehui kexue chubanshe.

He, Jie. 2001. Zhigong dongshi yineng fei zhigong (The employee director must be employee). http://www.grrb.com.cn/news/news. 27 March.

He, Qinglian. 2000. "Dangqian zhongguo shehui jiegou yanbian de zongtixing fenxi" (A general analysis on the evolution of social structure in contemporary China). *Shuwu.* 3.

Hein, Mallee. 2000. Migration, hukou and resistance in reform China. In Elizabeth J. Perry and Mark Selden (eds). *Chinese Society: Change, Conflict and Resistance.* London: Routledge.

*Henan Ribao.* 2001. (Henan Daily). 27 February.

Heytens, M. Annella, Charles Kuan and John Liang. 2001. Human resources and the transition to sole foreign ownership. *China Business Review.* 28(6): 36–40.

Ho, Peter. 2001. Who owns China's land? Policies, property rights and deliberate institutional ambiguity. *China Quarterly.* 394–421.

Hou, Shan. 2001. Zhengfu zhineng quexian jiqi jiaozheng (The drawbacks of government's functions and correction). *Jiangxi xingzheng xueyuan xuebao*

(Journal of Jiangxi College of Administration). 2: 14–6.

Howell, Jude. 1993. *China Opens Its Doors: The Politics of Economic Transition*. Hemel Hempstead: Harvester Wheatsheaf.

Hsu, C.Y. Immanuel. 1982. *The Rise of Modern China*. Hong Kong: Oxford.

Hu, Jintao. 1993. Speech at the fifth meeting of the Eleventh Executive Committee of the ACFTU (8 December 1992). In *Xin shiqi gonghui gongzuo zhongyao wenjian xuanbian* (Selection of Important Documents about the Trade Unions' Work in the New Period). edited by the Department of Trade Unions Science, China Institute of Labour Movement.

Hu, Jun. 2000. Dui dangqian liyi tiaozheng zhong gongren jieji diwei pingjia de shehuixue sikao (A sociological thinking to the evaluation of status of working class during the adjustment of interests). *Zhonggong ningbo shiwei dangxiao xuebao* (Journal of the Party School of CPC Ningbo Municipal Committee). 22(6): 40–2.

Hu, Liansheng and Ling Yang. 1999. *Dangdai ziben zhuyi de xin bianhua yu shehui zhuyi de xin keti* (New Changes in Modern Capitalism and New Topics in Socialism). Beijing: Renmin chubanshe.

Hu, Shuzhi and Yiyuan Luo. 2001. Shehui shifan: chengshi nongmingong de youminhua qingxiang (Social anomie: the vagrant tendency of migrant workers in urban areas). *Chengshi wenti* (Urban Problems). 2: 43–7.

Huan, Ling and Sun Zhen. 1992. *Zhongguo gaige quanshu: laodong gongzi tizhi gaige juan* (A Complete Works of the Chinese Reform: Volume of Labour and Wage system reform). Dalian: Dalian renmin chuchanshe. 37.

Huang, Yasheng. 2001. Internal and External Reforms: Experiences and Lessons From China. *Cato Journal*. 21(1): 43–64.

Huang, Yueqin. 1994. *Laodongfa lun* (On Labour Law). Taipei: Taiwanzhengzhi daxue laogong yanjiusuo.

Huo, Haiyan. 2000. Nongmingong qunti maodun diaocha fenxi (A study on contradictions among groups of migrant workers). *Zhongzhou daxue xuebao* (Journal of Zhongzhou University). 2: 1–3.

Hyman, Richard. 1984. *Strikes*. 3th edn. Douglas: Fontana.

Hyman, Jeff and Bob Mason. 1995. *Managing Employee Involvement and Participation*. London: Sage.

Information Office of the State Council. 2002. Labour and social security in China (April). http://www.china.org.cn.

Institute of Labour Science, Ministry of Labour and Social Security. 2001. Guoyou qiye xiagang gongren laodong guanxi yanjiu baogao (Study report on dealing with the labour relations of laid-off workers in SOEs). http://www.labournet.com.cn/advertise/labourinstitute..

International Labour Organization. 1993. Case No. 1652, Report No. 286. *ILO Committee on Freedom of Association*, 76 (B–1).

International Labour Organisation. 1977. *Grievance Arbitration: A Practical Guide*. Geneva: ILO.

Investigation Team of China Federation of Trade Unions of Machinery and Metallurgical Industry. 1996. Dui hezi qiye tuixing pingdeng xieshang qianding jiti hetong zhidu de qingkuang de diaocha (A survey on implementing equal consultation and signing collective contract in joint-venture enterprises). *Zhongguo gongyun* (China Labour Movement). 4: 18–21.

Ip, Olivia. 1995. Changing employment system in China: some evidence from the Shenzhen special economic zone. *Work, Employment and Society.* 9(2): 269–85.

Ip, Olivia. 1999. A Case Study of Human Resource Management Practices in the People's Republic of China: Convergence or Non-Convergence?. *International Journal of Employment Studies.* 7(2): 61–79.

Ji, You. 1998. *China's Enterprise Reform: Changing State/Society Relations after Mao*, London and New York: Routledge.

Jiang, Kaiven. 1996. *Gonghui yu dang-guojia de chongtu: bashi niandai yilai de zhongguo gonghui gaige* (The conflicts between trade unions and the Party-state: the reform of Chinese trade unions in the 1980s). *Xiang Gang shehui kexue xuebao* (Hong Kong Journal of Social Sciences). 8: 121–58.

Jiang, Ruxiang. 1996. Fenhua yu zhenghe: guanyu zhongguo shehui wendingxing guocheng de fenxi. (Division and integration: an analysis of stable process of China society), *Guomin jingji yu shehui fazhan* (National Economy and Social Development). 2: 10–13.

Jiang, Zemin. 1992. *Zai zhongguo gongchandang di shisi ci quanguo daibiao dahui shang de baogao* (Report delivered at the 14th National Congress of the Communist Party of China). Beijing: Renmin ribao chubanshe.

Jiang, Zemin. 1997. Zai zhongguo gongchandang di shiwu ci quanguo daibiao dahui shang de baogao (Report delivered at the 15th National Congress of the Communist Party of China) (12 September 1997). *Renmin ribao* (People's Daily). 22 September.

Jiang, Zemin. 2001. Zai qingzhu jiandang bashi zhounian dahui shang de jianghua (Speech at a grand gathering in Beijing marking the 80th founding anniversary of the CPC on 1 July 2001). *Renmin ribao* (People's Daily). 2 July 2001: (1).

Jiang, Zhenchang. 2000. Qianxin yu jinqi dalu gongchao: jiti xingdong duandian (Wage arrears and labour chaos in mainland China: opinions of collective action). *Zhongguo dalu yanjiu* (Mainland China Studies). 43(9): 81–101.

Jiaojiang Federation of Trade Unions, Taizhou city, Zhejiang province. 2000. Dali tuixing cunzhen liangji quyuxing jiti hetong zhidu (Implementing regional collective contract system at township and village levels). *Zhongguo gongyun* (China Labour Movement). 3: 25–6.

Jin, Pei. 1997. *Hequ hecong: dangdai zhongguo de guoyou qiye wenti* (What Course to Follow: The Problems of SOEs in Modern China). Beijing: Jinri zhongguo chubanshe.

Kagawa, Noriko. 2000. The modern enterprise system and corporate governance in China's state-owned enterprise reform. http://www.gwu.edu/~econ270/Noriko.htm.

Karmel, Solomon. 1996. The neo-authoritarian dilemma and the labour force: control and bankruptcy vs. freedom and instability. *Journal of Contemporary China.* 5(12): 111–33.

Knight, John and Song, Lina. 1999. Employment constraints and sub-optimality in Chinese enterprises. *Oxford Economic Papers.* 51: 284–99.

Kochan, Thomas and Harry Kata. 1988. *Collective Bargaining and Industrial Relations :From Theory to Policy and Practice.* 2nd edn. Homewood: Irwin.

Korzec, Michael. 1992. *Labour and the Failure of Reform in China*. Basingstoke: Macmillan.

Kuang, Kuang. 1984. *Zhongguo gongren jieji* (Working class in China). Changchun: Jilin renmin chubanshe.

Ladany, Laszlo. 1988. *The Communist Party of China and Marxism 1912–1985: A Self-Portrait*. Hong Kong: Hong Kong University Press.

Lau, Chung-Ming and Lowell W. Busenitz. 2001. Growth intentions of entrepreneurs in a transitional economy: The People's Republic of China. *Entrepreneurship Theory and Practice*. 26(1): 5–20.

Lau, Raymond. 1997. China: labour reform and the challenge facing the working class. *Capital and Class* 61: 45–81.

Leap, Terry. 1991. *Collective Bargaining and Labour Relations*. New York: Macmillan.

Lee, Ching Kwan. 1999. From organized dependence to disorganized despotism: changing labour regimes in Chinese factories. *The China Quarterly*. 157: 44–71.

Lee, Ching Kwan. 2000. Pathway of labour insurgency. In Perry, Elizabeth and Mark Selden (Eds). *Chinese Society: Change, Conflict and Resistance*. London: Routledge.

Lei, Han. 1997. Woguo gongsi faren jiguan quanli zhiheng jizhi de gongsifa wanshan (On perfecting the regulations in Corporation Law about power control mechanism in governance structure of corporation). *Xibei zhengfa xueyuan xuebao* (Journal of North-east College of Politics and Law). 6: 5–8.

Lei, Ming. 2001. Zenyang duidai quntixing shijian (How to deal with collective events). *Shandong gongan zhuanke xuexiao xuebao* (Journal of Shandong Public Security College). 8: 48–9.

Leung, Wing Yue. 1988. *Smashing the Iron Rice Pot: Workers and Unions in China's Market Socialism*. Hong Kong: Asia Monitor Resource Centre.

Leung, Wai Yue. 1993. Stalinist unions under market socialism, (Working Paper). Department of Political Science, University of Hong Kong.

Li, Clara. 2002. Premier views tax avoidance by business as a bit rich. *The South China Morning Post*. 16 July.

Li, Keming. 2001. Xinfang gongzuo mianlin de xinqingkuang and xin wenti (The new situation and new problems faced by *Xinfang* institution). *Zhongguo jiancha* (China's Supervision). 11: 42–3.

Li, Lulu. 1999. Lun shehui fenceng yanjiu (On studies of social stratification). *Shehuixue yanjiu* (Sociology Studies). no. 1: 101–9.

Li, Lulu and Fenyu Wang. 1992. *Dangdai zhongguo xiandaihua jincheng zhong de shehui jiegou jiqi biange* (The social structure and its changes in the process of modernisation in China). Hangzhou: Zhejiang renmin chubanshe.

Li, Peilin (ed). 1995. *Zhongguo xin shiqi jieji jiecheng baogao* (A report of class and stratum in a new period in China). Shenyang: Liaoning renmin chubanshe.

Li, Peilin, Yi Zhang and Yandong Zhao. 2000. *Jiuye yu zhidu bianqian: liangge teshu quanti de qiuzhi guocheng* (Job Searching, Employment and Institutional Change), Hangzhou: Zhejing renmin chubanshe.

Li, Qi. 2000. *Transition of Labour Relations in Chinese State-owned Enterprises: Case Studies of a Process Dominated by Government*, PhD Dissertation, City

University of Hong Kong.

Li, Qi. 2002. *Gaige yu xiufu: dangdai zhongguo guoyou qiye laodong guanxi yanjiu* (Reform and Repairing: A Study of Labour Relations in Contemporary Chinese SOEs). Beijing: Zhongguo laodong he shehui baozhang chubanshe.

Li, Qiang. 1993. *Dangdai zhongguo shehui fenceng yu liudong* (The Social Stratification and Migration in Contemporary China). Beijing: Zhongguo jingji chubanshe.

Li, Xiaoping and Xian Chen. 2000. *21 shiji shui zhu chenfu: zhongguo qiyejia rencai shichang yanjiu* (Study of the Entrepreneur Market in China). Shanghai: Shanghai jiaoyue chubanshe.

Lim, Min Le and Michael Forsythe. 2002. China's state firms slowing job cuts: reversal is linked to key party meeting. *International Herald Tribune*.

Lin, Yifu, Cai Fang and Li Zhou. 1997. *Choufen xinxi yu guoyou qiye gaige* (Sufficient Information and State-owned Enterprise Reform). Shanghai: Shanghai sanlian shudian and Shanghai renmin chubanshe.

Lin, Yimin. 1992. Between Government and Labour: Managerial Decision-making in Chinese Industry. *Studies in Comparative Communism*. 25(4): 381–403.

Lin, Yi-min and Tian Zhu. 2001. Ownership restructuring in Chinese state industry: an analysis of evidence on initial organizational changes. *China Quarterly*. 305–41.

Lin, Zhengong and Yulin Chen. 1993. Sanzi qiye daigong bagong de tedian he duice (Slow-down and strike in FIEs). *Zhongguo laodong kexue* (China Labour Science). 5: 33–5.

Ling, Huan and Zhen Sun. 1992. *Zhongguo gaige quanshu: laodong gongzi tizhi gaige juan* (A Complete Works of the Chinese Reform: Volume of Labour and Wage System Reform). Dalian: Dalian renmin chuchanshe.

Ling, H.M. 1996. Hegemony and the internationalizing state: a post-colonial analysis of China's integration into Asian corporatism. *Review of International Political Economy*. 3(1): 1–26.

Liu, Aiyu and Hui Zhou. 2002. Zhidu biange guocheng zhong gongren jieji de beibu fenhua yu rentong chayi (The internal differentiation and identical differences of working class in the process of system transition). http://www.ccrs.org.cn.

Liu, Guoguang and Guiying Zhou. 1992. *Zhongguo jingji gaige quanshu (1978–1991): gongye qiye juan* (A Complete Works of the Chinese Reform [1978–1991]: Volume of Industrial Enterprises). Dalian: Dalian renmin chuchanshe.

Liu, Hainian and Lin Li. (eds). 2001. *Yifa zhiguo yu falu tixi de jiangou* (Governing the Country According to Laws and Establishing the System of Laws). Beijing: Zhongguo fazhi chubanshe.

Liu, Kang. 1999. Tuixing jiti hetong zhidu de ruogan qingkuang he yijian (Some problems and suggestions on implementing collective contract system). *Gonghui lilun yu shijian*. 13(6): 45–6.

Liu, Xiaobo. 2002. Jianping daqing liaoyang dengdi de gongchao (A brief comment on the labour chaos in Daqing and Liaoyang).
http://news.bbc.co.uk/hi/chinese/china_news.

Liu, Yufang. 2001. Qiantan gongrenjijie duiwu nribu jiegou bianhua (On the changes occurred within the structure of working class). *Gongren ribao* (Workers' Daily). 26 December 2001: (3).

Liu, Yufang. 2002. Guoyou qiye butong zhigong qunti de xingwei quexiang chayi yanjiu (A study of the difference of behavioural orientation of various groups of workers and staff in SOEs). *Gonghui lilun yu shijian* (Theory and Practice of Trade Union) 16(1): 57–60.

Lu, Feng. 1989. Danwei: yizhong teshu de shehui zuzhi xingshi (Unit: A Special Form of Social Organisation). *Zhongguo shehui kexue* (China Social Science). 1: 71–88.

Lu, Hong. 1999. Cong wuxu dao youxu: xianjieduan laodong zhengyi tezheng fenxi (From disorder to order: an analysis of features of the present industrial conflicts),.*Guangzhou shiyuan xuebao[shehui kexue ban]* (Journal of Guangzhou Normal University [social science edition]). 20(6): 39–47.

Lu, Jianguo. 2001. Guanyu changwu gongkai gongzuo de diaocha yu yanjiu (A survey and study on the work of OCA). In *Gonghui tongxun* (Trade Unions' Information), edited by Beijing Federation of Trade Unions. 6. http://www.bjzgh.gov.cn.

Lu, Xiaobo. 1997. Minor Public Economy: The Revolutionary Origins of the Danwei. In Xiaobo Lu and Elizabeth J. Perry (Eds). *Danwei: The Changing Chinese Workplace in Historical and Comparative Perspective*. Armonk: M.E. Sharpe.

Lu, Xiaobo and Elizabeth J. Perry (eds). 1997a. *Danwei: The Changing Chinese Workplace in Historical and Comparative Perspective*. Armonk: M.E. Sharpe.

Lu, Xiaobo and Elizabeth J. Perry. 1997b. Introduction: The Changing Chinese Workplace in Historical and Comparative Perspective. In Xiaobo Lu and Elizabeth J. Perry (eds). *Danwei: The Changing Chinese Workplace in Historical and Comparative Perspective*. Armonk: M E. Sharpe.

Lu, Xueyi (ed). 2002. *Dangdai zhongguo shehui jieceng yanjiu baogao* (Studying Report on the Stratum in Contemporary China). Beijing: Shehui kexue chubanshe (Social Science Press).

Lu, Yuan. 1996. *Management Decision-making in Chinese Enterprises*. New York: St. Martin's Press.

Lukes, Steven. 1974. *Power: A Radical View*. London: Macmillan.

Luo, Jun. 2000. Assessing management and performance of Sino-foreign construction joint ventures. *Construction Management and Economics*. 19: 109–117.

Luo, Peixin. 2000. Woguo zhigong canyu guanli zhi lifa quelou jiqi wanshan (Employee Participation in China: the flaws of legislation and remedy). *Shanghai daxue xuebao* (Journal of Shanghai University). 4: 73–8.

Luo, Yan and Kui Chen. 2001. Woguo laodong zhengyi chuli de zhidu chuangxi wenti (Study on a new system of labour dispute handling). *Huanan shifan daxue xuebao[shehui kexue ban]* (Journal of Huanan Normal University [social science edition]). 3: 19–22.

Mao, Shoulong. 1996. *Zhongguo zhengfu gongneng de jingji fenxi* (Economical Analysis of Chinese Government's Function). Beijing: Zhongguo guangbo dianshi chubanshe.

Marx, K. and F. Engels. 1956. *Makesi En'gesi quan ji* (Marx and Engle's Thought) Vol. 19, pp. 6–7. Beijing: Renmin chubanshe.

McElroy, Damien. 2000. China's struggles to keep lid on labour unrest Beijing is terrified of a workers' rights movement emerging from the spread of isolated protests. London: *The Sunday Telegraph*.

McNally, Christopher A. 2002. Strange bedfellow: Communist Party institutions and new governance mechanisms in Chinese state holding corporations. *Business and Politics.* 4(1): 91–115.

Mi, Na. 2001. Woguo guoyou qiye qiyejia xianzhuang jiqi chengzhang jizhi fenxi (An analysis on the situation and developing mechanism of entrepreneur in SOEs),.*Yanhai qiye yu keji* (Coastal Enterprises, Science and technology). 6: 10–12.

Ministry of Labour. 1994a. 'Provisions on Collective Contracts' www.molss.gov.cn . May.

Ministry of Labour. 1994b. Guangyu jianli shehui zhuyi shichang jingji tizhi shiqi laodong tizhi gaige zongti shexiang (The general opinions on labour system reform during the period of establishing socialist market economic system). http://www.labournet.com.cn. 21 December.

Ministry of Labour. 1995. 1996nian gongzuo jihua (Working plan for 1996). http://www.labournet.com.cn/fagui.

Ministry of Labour. 1996a. General Outline about Labour System Reform during Establishing Social Market Economy (12 December 1993) In Jianxin Wang (ed). *China Labour Yearbook: 1992–1994.* Beijing: Zhongguo laodong chubanshe. 610–12.

Ministry of Labour. 1996b *'Laodong shiye fazhan di jiu ge wunian jihuan he 2010nian changqi mubiao'* (The ninth Five-Year Plan of labour undertaking development and long-term goals in the 2010s) 21 May. http://labournet.com.cn.

Ministry of Labour. 1999 *Laodong he shehui baozhang shiye fazhan zongti guihua* (General program for the development of labour and social security undertakings) 1 March. http://labournet.com.cn.

Ministry of Labour and Social Security. 2000. Measures (for Trial Implementation) of Collective Wage Consultation.' www.molss.gov.cn. December.

Ministry of Labour and Social Security. 2001. Laodong he shehui baozhang tongji gongbao: 2001nian shangbannian (Statistics bulletin of labour and social security: first half of 2001). http://www.molss.gov.cn/index_tongji.htm.

Mo, Rong. 2002. Jiuye xingshi yiran yanjun (Employment still troubling). In *2002 nian: zhongguo shehui xingshi fenxi yu yuce* (2002: Analysis and Forecast of China's Society), edited by Ru, Xin et al. Beijing: Zhongguo shehui kexue wenxian chubanshe.

Mok, Ka Ho and He Cai. 1999. Beyond Organized Dependence: A Study of Workers' actual and perceived living standards in Guangzhou. *Work, Employment amd Society.* 13(1): 67–82.

National Bureau of Statistics and Ministry of Labour and Social Security. [years 1990–2002] *Zhongguo laodong tongji nianjian* (China Labour Statistical Yearbook), Beijing: Zhongguo tongji chubanshe. various years.

Naughton, Barry. 1997. Danwei: the economic foundations of a unique institution. In Xiaobo Lu and Elizabeth J. Perry (eds). *Danwei: The Changing Chinese Workplace in Historical and Comparative Perspective.* Armonk: M.E. Sharpe.

Ng, Sek Hong and Malcolm Warner. 1998. *China's Trade Unions and Management.* New York: St Martin's Press.

Ng, Sek Hong and Malcolm Warner. 2000. Industrial relations versus human resource management in the PRC: collective bargaining 'with Chinese characteristics'. In

Malcolm Warner (ed.). *Changing Workplace Relations in the Chinese Economy.* Basingstoke: Macmillan Press.

Nishitani, Hashiko. 1992. *Roudouhouchuu kojinyo shuudan* (The individual and the collective in labour law). Tokyo: Yuuhikakubunhan (In Japanese).

Niu, Xiongying. 1999. Guoqi caiyuan fanglue: qiye caiyuan de guocheng fenxi (The strategies of lay-off: an analysis on the process of lay-off in SOEs). *Zhongguo renli ziyuan kaifa* (Human Resources Development in China). 5: 14–15.

Nolon, Peter and Wang Xiaoqiang. 1999. Beyond privatization: institutional innovation and growth in China's large state-owned enterprise. *World Development.* 27(1): 169–200.

Office of Collective Contract, ACFTU. 2000. Guanyu guizhou shanxii liang sheng jiti hetong gongzuo de diaocha (A survey on the work of collective contract in Guizhou and Shanxii province). *Zhongguo gongyun* (China Labour Movement). 6: 7–9.

Ogden, Suzanne. 2000. China's developing civil society: interest groups, trade unions and associational pluralism. In Malcolm Warner (ed.). *Changing Workplace Relations in the Chinese Economy.* Basingstoke: Macmillan Press.

Oi, Jean. 1999. *Rural China Takes off: Institutional Foundations of Economic Reform,* Berkeley: University of California Press.

Oi, Jean C. and Andrew G. Walder (eds). 1999. *Property Rights and Economic Reform in China.* Stanford, California: Stanford University Press.

O'Leary, Greg. 1998. The making of the Chinese working class. In Greg O'Leary (ed.). *Adjusting to capitalism: Chinese workers and the state.* Armonk: M.E. Sharpe.

Ouyang, Jun. 2000. Waizi, siying, xianzhen qiye laodong guanxi zhuangkuang ji zujian gonghui de jinpoxing (The situation of labour dispute and recognition in FIEs, POEs and TVEs. *Gonghui lilun yu shijian* (Theory and Practice of Trade Unions). 14(3): 14–16.

Pan, Philip P. 2002. In China, labour unions offer little protection. *International Herald Tribune.* 16 October: 2

Pan, Yiqing. 2001. Mo rang zhigong dongshi he jianshi zhi cheng tinghui jueshou jiqi (Don't change the employee directors and supervisors to be ornament). *The Xinhua News Agency Report,* 12 March.

Peng, Lingyong (ed.). 1998. Zhongguo qiye laozi guanxi (Industrial Relations in Chinese Enterprises). *Xiandai qiye* (Modern Enterprise). 8: 4–11.

Peng, W. Mike. 2000. Controlling the foreign agent: how governments deal with multinationals in a transition economy. *Management International Review.* 40(2):141–65.

Peng, Qigui. 2002. Chuzhi qunti zhian shijian de jiben duice (Basic policies on dealing with collective public security events). *Renmin gongan* (Public Security of People). 2: 36–37.

Perry, Elizabeth J. 2000. From native place to workforce: labour origins and outcomes of China's danwei system. In Xiaobo Lu and Elizabeth J. Perry (eds). *Danwei: The Changing Chinese Workplace in Historical and Comparative Perspective.* Armonk: M.E. Sharpe.

Perry, Elizabeth J. and Mark Selden. 2000. Introduction: reform and resistance in contemporary China. In Elizabeth J. Perry and Mark Selden (eds). *Chinese Society: Change, Conflict and Resistance*. London and New York: Routledge.

Pistrui, David, Wilfred Huang, Dolun Oksoy, Jing Zhao and Harold Welsch. 1999. The characteristics and attributes of new Chinese entrepreneurs and their emerging enterprises. *Business Forum*. 24(3 and 4): 31–8.

Pringle, Tim. 2001. Industrial unrest in China – a labour movement in the making? http://iso.china-labour.org.hk

Prybyla, Jan S. 1996. On systemic transition: will China go capitalist?. *Journal of Northeast Asian Studies*. Winter: 3–34.

Qi, Zhirong and Xiaohou Xu. 1995. *Zhongguo laodong guanxi daolun* (The introduction of Chinese labour relationship). Hangzhou: Zhejiang renmin chubanshe.

Qiao, Jian. 1995. Waizi touzi qiye laodong guanxi de zhuangkuang he tedian (The situation and features of labour relations in FIEs). In Kai Chang (ed.). *Labour Relations, Labourers and Labour Rights: Labour Issues in Contemporary China*. Beijing: Zhongguo laodong chubanshe.

Qiao, Jian. 2002. Chuzai gaige qianyan de zhongguo zhigong (Employees confronting the reform). In Xin Ru, Xueyi Lu and Peilin Li (eds). *2002 nian: zhongguo shehui xingshi fenxi yu yuce* (2002: Analysis and Forecast of China's Society). Beijing: Zhongguo shehui kexue wenxian chubanshe.

Qin, Ying and Yanfei Wang. 2001. Guoyou qoiye zhigong shiqi shuiping de diaocha he yanjiu (A studies about the employees' morale in SOEs). *Kexue guanli yanjiu* (Studies of Scientific Management). 19(1): 63–7.

Qu, Zhanqiang. 2000. Weihaishi hanzi qiye yu gongyouzhi qiye rufa shijian zhi bijiao (A comparison of precipitating events between Korean-invested enterprises and SOEs in Weihai City). *Shandong gonghui guanli ganbu xueyuan xuebao* (Journal of Shangdong College of Trade Union). 1: 26–7.

Research Team of the Ministry of Labour and Social Security. 1997. Laodong guanxi zhong tufa shijian de chengyin jiqi duice tantao (Causes and solutions of 'emergent events' in labour relations). November. *Unpublished*.

*Renmin ribao* (People's Daily). Various issues.

Rose, Michael. 1988. *Industrial Behaviour: Research and Control*. 2th edn. London: Penguin.

Ross, Robert. J.S. 2001. Vulnerable labour in global capitalism. *Conference: Labour in a Globalising World: The Challenge for Asia*. Hong Kong: City University of Hong Kong. January.

Ruan, Chongwu. 1996. Zai quanguo laodong tijuzhang huiyi shang de jianghua (Speech at the national meeting of directors of labour bureau) (15 December 1992). In Jianxin Wang (ed.). *China Labour Yearbook: 1992–1994*. Beijing: Zhongguo laodong chubanshe. 50–66.

Salamon, Michael. 1992. *Industrial Relations: Theory and Practice*. 2nd edn. Hertfordshire: Prentice Hall.

Sanyal, N. Rajib and Turgut Guvenli. 2001. American firms in China: issues in managing operations. *Multinational Business Review*. 9(2): 40–6.

Sargeson, Sally. 1999. *Reworking China's Proletariat*. Basingstoke: Macmillan.

Selmer, Jan (ed.). 1998. *International Management in China: Cross-cultural issues*.

London: Routledge.

Seung, Wook Back. 2000. The changing trade unions in China. *Journal of Contemporary Asia*. 30(1): 46–66.

Shanghai Federation of Trade Unions. 1999. Shanghaishi zhigong zhuangkuang diaocha baogao (Report of situation of staff and workers in Shanghai). In *1997 zhongguo zhigong zhuangkuang diaocha* (Survey of the Chinese staff and workers in 1997), edited by Department of Policy, ACFTU. Beijing: Xiyuan chubanshe.

Shao, Jingjun. 2001. Xianjieduan xinfang gongzuo de lishi teshuxing (Historical and special characteristics of *xinfang* in current period). *Zhonggo xingzheng guanli* (Chinese Administrative Management). 2: 8–9.

Sheehan, Jackie. 1998. *Chinese Workers: A New History*. London: Routledge.

*Shenzhen fazhibao* (Shenzhen Legality Daily). 1999. 16 August (3).

Shi, Shaoxia and Fuyou Wang. 1999. Lun gongsi zhigong canyu quan (On right of participation of workers and staff in corporations). *Fazhi yu fazhan* (Legal System and Development). 3: 37–44.

Shi, Tanjing. 1990. *Laodong fa* (Labour Law). Beijing: Jingji chubanshe.

Shi, Tanjing.1999. Zhongguo laodong zhengyi qingkuang fenxi he bagong lifa wenti tantao (Discussion on situation of labour disputes and strike legislation in China). *Faxue yanjiu* (Law Research). 6: 54–6.

Shouda, Toushirou. 1979. 'Roudoushijiten' (Labour Law Encyclopaedia) *Roudoujumpousha* (Labour Tri-monthly Report). 12gastsubunhan (December edn). (In Japanese).

Sil, Rudra. 1997. The Russian 'village in the city' and the Stalinist system of enterprise management: the origins of worker alienation in Soviet state system. In Xiaobo Lu and Elizabeth J. Perry (eds). *Danwei: The Changing Chinese Workplace in Historical and Comparative Perspective*. Armonk: M.E. Sharpe.

So, Alvin Y. and Stephen W.K. Chiu. 1995. *East Asia and the World Economy*. California: Sage Publications.

Solinger, Dorothy J. 1997. The impact of the floating population on the danwei: shifts in the pattern of labour mobility control and entitlement provision. In Xiaobo Lu and Elizabeth J. Perry (eds). *Danwei: The Changing Chinese Workplace in Historical and Comparative Perspective*. Armonk: M.E. Sharpe.

Solinger, Dorothy J. 2001. Why we cannot count the 'unemployed'. 167 (September): 671–88.

Solinger, Dorothy J. 2002. WTO entry: will China's workers benefit from this 'win-win' deal?. *China Rights Forum: The Journal of Human Rights in China*. 1.

Song, Baoan and Yushan Wang. 1999. Changchun shi xiagang wenti de chayang diaocha (Lay-offs in Changchun: a sampling study). In Xin Ru (ed.). *1998nian: zhongguo shehui xingshi fenxi yu yuce* (1998: analysis and forecast of social situation in China). Beijing: Social Science Documentation Publishing House.

Song, Nongcun and Huining Ding. 1993. Lun woguo butong guoyou qiye gongren de liyi zhuangkuang (On the situation of interests by workers in different types of enterprises). 14(1): 5–8.

Song, Xiaowu. 1995a. *Changquan guanxi yu laodong guanxi* (Property rights relationship and labour relations). Beijing: Qiye guanli chubanshe.

Song, Xiaowu. 1995b. Local governments as industrial firms: an organizational analysis of China's transitional economy. *American Journal of Sociology.* 101(2): 263–92.

State Commission of the Economy and Trade. 2001. Zhongguo guoyou qiye gaige he fazhan youguan qingkuang (The situation about reform and development of SOEs in China). http://www.setc.gov.cn. 10 March.

State Council. 2002. Guanyu jinyibu zuohao guoyou qiye xiagang zhigong jiben shenghuo baozhang he qiye lituixie renyuan yanglaojin fafang gongzuo youguan wenti de tongzhi (Notice on Making Effort to Ensure a Timely and Full Payment of the Retirement pensions for Retirees and Guarantee the Basic Living Expenses of Laid-off Workers in SOEs), http://www.molss.gov.cn/index_zcwj.htm (accessed August 2002).

Sun, Jiuxia. 2001. Zhujiang sanjiaozhou wailai qiye zhong de zuquan yu zuquan guanxi (Racial groups and racial group relationship in the enterprises from outside in the Pearl River Delta). *Guangxi minzu daxue xuebao [zhexue shehui kexue ban]* (Journal of Guangxi University for Nationalities [philosophy and social science edition]). 23(3): 10–21 and 23(4): 39–46.

Sun, Nanmeng, 2001. Cong qiye zhili jiegou kan guoqi jingyingzhe de xuanze (On selection of SOEs' managers: a viewpoint from corporate governance), *Lilun qianyan* (Forward Position of Theory). 20: 30–2.

Supreme People's Court of the PRC. 2001. Guangyu shenli laodong zhengyi anjian ruogan wenti de jieshi de qicao shuoming (Drafting explanation of the interpretation of some issues in hearing labour dispute cases) (14 February). *Unpublished.*

Tan, Justin. 1999. The growth of entrepreneurial firms in a transition economy: the case of a Chinese entrepreneur. *Journal of Management Inquiry.* 8(1): 83–9.

Tan, Justin. 2001. Innovation and risk-taking in a transitional economy: a comparative study Chinese managers and entrepreneurs. *Journal of Business Venturing.* 16: 359–76.

Tan, Qiucheng. 1998. Zhongguo weishenmo hui chuxian xiangzhen jiti qiye (Why did the collective TVEs appear in China). *Zhongguo nongcun guancha* (Observation in Chinese countryside). 3: 16–21.

Tang, Hengzhao and Bixiang Zhu. 2000. Lun guoyou gongsi zhigong diwei zhidu sheji went (On the problems of system designed for workers' master status in state-owned corporation). *Nanjing ligong daxue xuebao* (Journal of Nanjing University of Science and Engineering). 6: 63–7.

Tang, Jun. 2001. Jiaru WTO yu jiuye wenti ji duice (WTO, unemployment and employment policies). In Kai Chang and Jian Qiao (Eds). *WTO: laogong quanqi baozhang* (WTO and Labour Rights). Beijing: Zhongguo gongren chubanshe

Tang, Shurong and Ongsheng Xi (eds). 1994. *Laodong fa shiwu quanshu* (A complete works of application of labour law). Beijing: Zhongguo gongren chubanshe.

Tang, Wenfang. 1996. *Shui lai zuozhu: dangdai zhongguo de qiye juece* (Who make the final decision: decision-making in current Chinese enterprises). (translated by Yao) Hong Kong: Niujin daxue chubanshe.

Tang, Wenfang, William L. Parish and Tongqing Feng. 1996. Chinese Labour Relations in a Changing Work Environment. *Journal of Contemporary China.* 5(13): 367–89.

Taylor, Bill. 1999a. Japanese employment system and the development of China: a critique of Anita Chan's claims of convergence. *Ritsumeikan Journal of Asia Pacific Studies.* 2: 108–32.

Taylor, Bill. 1999b. Patterns of Control within Japanese manufacturing plants in China: doubts about Japanisation in Asia', *Journal of Management Studies.* 36(6): 851–71.

Taylor, Bill.1999c. Japanese Management Style in China? Production Practices In Japanese Manufacturing Plants. *New Technology, Work and Employment.* 14(2): 129–42.

Taylor, Bill. 2000. Trade unions and social capital in transitional communist states: the case of China. *Policy Science.* 33(3 and 4): 341–54.

Taylor, Bill. 2001. Labour Management in Japanese manufacturing plants in China, *International Journal of Human Resource Management.* 12(4): 600–20.

Taylor, Bill. 2002. Privatisation, Markets and Industrial Relations in China, *British Journal of Industrial Relations.* 40(2): 249–72.

Taylor, Bill and Glenn Drover (2000) Labour Standards and Subcontracting among Transnational Corporations in China and Vietnam: A Comparative Study. Internal City University of Hong Kong Research Report, *Unpublished.*

Tian, Jianjun. 2002. Weihe chidao cixiang guoqi lingdao (Why they knife the leaders of SOEs?). *Beijing Qingnianbao* (Beijing Youth Daily). 25 February (4).

Trade Union Committee, Beijing Babcock & Wilcox Company. 2001. Jianli xieshang tanpan zhidu shi qianding jiti hetong de guanjian (Establishing consultation system is the key of signing collective contract). *Gonghui lilun yu shijian* (Theory and Practice of Trade Union). 10(3): 38–39.

Trade Union Committee, Beijing Nankou SKF Railway Bearing Ltd. 2001. Jianli gongzi jiti xieshang jizhi shi gonghui weihu zhineng zhenzheng luodao shichu (Establishing consultation system on wages to make the trade union play its function of protection). In *Gonghui tongxun* (Trade Unions' Information). Beijing Federation of Trade Unions. 7–8. http://www.bjzgh.gov.cn.

Trade Union Committee, Beijing United Food Ltd. 2001. Tuchu weihu zhineng cujin qiye fazhan (Stressing the function of protection and promoting the development of enterprise). In *Gonghui tongxun* (Trade Unions' Information). Beijing Federation of Trade Unions. 7–8. http://www.bjzgh.gov.cn.

Trade Union Committee, Hangzhou Toshiba Mechanical and Electrical Product Ltd. 1995. Jianli xieshang zhidu baozhang gongzuo hefa quanyui (Establishing the system of consultation and protecting the legitimate rights of workers). *Zhongguo gongyun* (China Labour Movement). 9: 15–16.

Tung, R. 1996. The depletion of state assets in Mainland China. *Issues and Studies.* 22(1): 3–17.

Unger, Jonathan and Anita Chan. 1995. China, corporatism, and the East Asian model. *Australian Journal of Chinese Affairs.* 10: 29–53.

Walder, Andrew. 1986. Communist neo-traditionalism: work and authority in Chinese industry. California: University of California Press.

Walder, Andrew. 1989. Factory and manager in an era of reform. *The China Quarterly.* 118: 242–64.

Walder, Andrew. 1991. Worker, managers and the state: the reform era and the political crisis of 1989. *China Quarterly.* 127: 467–92.

Walsh, James P., Erping Wang and Katherine R. Xin. 1999. Same bed, different dreams: working relationships in Sino-American joint ventures. *Journal of World Business*. 34(1): 69–93.

Wan, Isabelle. 1998. *China Labour and Social Security Law: Essential Facts Explained*. Hong Kong: TransAsia Ltd.

Wang, Aiwen. 1993. *Shehui laodong guanxi: yanbian guocheng de kaocha yu fenxi* (Social Labour Relations: An Examination and Analysis of its Evolution). Beijing: Hongqi chubanshe.

Wang, Chidong (ed.). 1999, *Changwu gongkai minzhu guanli caozuo zhinan* (A Handbook for Opening Corporation Affairs and Democratic Management). Beijing: Dangdai shijie chubanshe.

Wang, Chunguang. 1999. 1997–1998 nian: zhongguo shehui wending zhuangkuang de diaocha (A survey on the situation of social stability during 1997 to 1998). In Xin Ru (ed.). *1998 nian: zhongguo jingji xingshi fenxi yu yuce* (1998: Analysis and Forecast of Social Situation in China). Beijing: Zhongguo shehui kexue wenxian chubanshe.

Wang, Fei-Ling. 1998. *Institutions and Institutional Change in China: Premodernity and Modernization*. Basingstoke: Macmillan.

Wang, Huimin. 2000. Beijingshi zonggonghui (Beijing Federation of Trade Unions). In *Zhongguo gonghui nianjian: 2000* (Chinese Trade Unions Yearbook: 2000). ACFTU. Beijing: Zhongguo tongji chubanshe: 119–23.

Wang, Hongling. 2000. Weituuoren 'zhengfuhua' yu 'fei zhengfuhua' dui qiye zhili jiegou de yingxiang (The effect of entruster's 'governmentalization' and 'non-governmentalization' on corporate governance). *Jingji yanjiu* (Economy Studies). 7: 56–62.

Wang, Peiren. 2000. Qiye gaizhi guocheng zhong de laodong zhengyi wenti yanjiu (A study on the problems in the course of SOEs' reform). *Shandong shehui kexue* (Shangdong Social Science). 6: 91–4.

Wang, Shengsheng (ed.). 1998. *Guoqi gaige ershi nian* (SOE Reform in Twenty Years). Beijing: Zhongguo shenji chubanshe.

Wang, Shitao. 2001. Laodong qinquan ji falv jiuji (Infringement of labour rights and legal compensation). *Dongbei caijing daxue xuebao* (Journal of Dongbei University of Finance and Economics). 4: 89–91.

Wang, Xiangwei. 2002. Workers 'to remain leading class': union chief's comments come as leaders expected to discuss admitting entrepreneurs to Party. *South China Morning Post*. 16 July: 7.

Wang, Yongxi. 1992. *Zhongguo gongyun shi* (History of Chinese Trade Unions). Beijing: Dangshi chubanshe.

Warner, Malcolm. 1995. *The Management of Human Resources in Chinese Industry*. New York: St Martin's Press.

Warner, Malcolm. 1996a. Human resources in the People's Republic of China: the three systems' reforms. *Human Resource Management Journal*. 6(2): 32–43.

Warner, Malcolm. 1996b. Chinese enterprise reform, human resources and the 1994 Labour Law. *International Journal of Human Resource Management*. 7(4): 779–96.

Warner, Malcolm. (ed.). 2000. *Changing Working Relations in the Chinese Economy*.

Basingstoke: Macmillan.

Warner, Malcolm. and Sek Hong Ng. 1999. Collective contracts in Chinese enterprises: a new brand of collective bargaining under market socialism. *British Journal of Industrial Relations* 32: 295–314.

Watson, Tony J. 1980, 1987. *Sociology, Work and Industry*. London and New York: Routledge.

Wei, Jianxing. 1995. Zai quanzong shier jie er ci zhiweihui shang de jianghua (Speech at the Second Meeting of the Twelfth Executive Committee of the ACFTU). In *Zhongguo gonghui nianjian: 1995* (Chinese trade unions yearbook: 1995). ACFTU. Beijing: Zhongguo gongren chubanshe. 14–20.

Wei, Jianxing. 1999. Zai quanguo changwu gongkai jingyan jiaoliu hui shang de jianghua (Speech at the national conference of exchanging experiences of OCA). http://www.bjzgh.gov.cn. 19 April.

Wei, Jianxing. 2000a. Zai quanguo xin qiye gonghui zujian gongzuo huiyi shang de jianghua (Speech at the national working conference of recognition in new enterprises) (12 November 2000). In *Zhongguo gonghui nianjian: 2001* (Chinese Trade Union Yearbook: 2001). Beijing: Zhongguo gongren chubanshe. 8–12.

Wei, Jianxing. 2001. Zai quanguo xinjian qiye gonghui zujian gongzuo huiyi shang de jianghua (Speech at the National Working Conference of Recognition in New Enterprises) (12 November 2000). In *Zhongguo gonghui nianjian: 2001* (Chinese trade unions yearbook: 2001). edited by ACFTU. Beijing: Zhongguo gongren chubanshe, pp. 8–12.

Weldon, Elizabeth and Wilfried Vanhonacker. 1999. Operating a foreign-invested enterprise in China: challenges for managers and management researchers. *Journal of World Business*. 34(1): 94–107.

White, Geoff, Janet Druker, Vivienne Luk and Randy Chiu. 1999. Pay systems and regional convergence: a study of Hong Kong and Guangdong. *International Journal of Employment Studies*. 7(1): 53–78.

White, Gordon. 1996. Chinese trade unions in the transition from socialism: towards corporatism or civil society. *British Journal of Industrial Relations*. 34(3): 433–57.

White, Gordon, Jude Howell and Hsiaoyuan Shang. 1996. *In Search of Civil Society: Market Reform and Social Change in Contemporary China*. Oxford: Clarendon.

Wong, Amy L.W. and Jim R. Slater. 2002. Executive development in China: is there any Western sense? *International Journal of Human Resource Management*. 13(2): 338–60.

Wright, Philip., W.F. Szeto and Louis T.W. Cheng. 2002. Guanxi and professional conduct in China: a management development perspective. *International Journal of Human Resource Management*. 13(1): 156–82.

Wu, Cuiyun. 2001. Tan zhigong dongshi he jianshi zhidu (On the system of employee director and supervisor). http://www.grrb.com.cn/news. 14 July.

Wu, Jinglian. 1994. *Xiandai gongsi yu qiye gaige* (Modern corporation and enterprises reform). Tianjin: Tianjin renmin chubanshe.

Wu, Yaping and Kai Chang. 1995. Laodong guanxi yu gonghui (Labour relations and trade unions). In Kai Chang (ed.). *Labour Relations, Labourers and labour Rights: Labour Issues in Contemporary China*. Beijing: Zhongguo laodong chubanshe.

Wu, Zhongyu. 1997. Woguo danqian guoyou qiye yu siying qiye laodong guanxi bijiao yanjiu (A comparison of labour relations in state-owned enterprises and private enterprises. *Huazhong ligong daxue xuebao* (Journal of Huazhong University of Science and Engineering). 4: 17–21.

Xia, Jizhi (ed.). 1999. *Zhongguo laodongfa ruogan zhongyao lilun wenti he duice wenti yanjiu* (Studies on Some Important Issues of Chinese Labour Law). Beijing: Zhongguo laodong he shehui baozhang chubanshe.

Xian Government. 2002. http://www.xa.gov.cn/rules/zhenbao/200112/right.htm. (accessed July 2002).

Xie, Yanmei. 2000. Guangdongsheng zonggonghui (Guangdong Federation of Trade Unions). In *Zhongguo gonghui nianjian:2000* (Chinese Trade Unions Yearbook: 2000). Beijing: Zhongguo tongji chubanshe. 181–2.

*Xinhua Yuebao* (Xinhua Monthly). Beijing. several issues.

Xu, Chongli and Lin Zhong. 1997. *Zhongguo waizi fa* (Chinese Foreign Capital Law). Hong Kong: sanlian shudian (xianggang) youxian gongsi.

Xu, Xiaohong. 1998. *Zhongguo siyou qiye de laodong guanxi* (Labour Relations in POEs in China). Hangzhou: Hangzhou xinwen chubanshe.

Yang, Xingfu. 1997. Guanyu shishi jiti hetong zhidu de jige wenti (Some problems about the implementation of collective contract system). *zhonguo gongyun* (China Labour Movement). 4: 4–8.

Yeh, Wenshin. 1997. Republican origins of the danwei: the Case of Shanghai's Bank of China. In Xiaobo Lu and Elizabeth J. Perry (eds). *Danwei: The Changing Chinese Workplace in Historical and Comparative Perspective*. Armonk: M.E. Sharpe.

Yep, Kin Man Ray. 1999. *The Rise of Township-Village Enterprise Managers and the Emergence of a New State-Society Relationship in Rural China*. Hong Kong: City University of Hong Kong, Department of Public and Social Administration.

Yi, Ping and Qiwei Li. 2000. Minying jingji he difang zhengfu xingwei (Private economy and the behaviour of local government). *Hunan Economy* (Hunan Economy). 3: 16–18.

Yin, Manxue. 1999. Waishang touzi qiye de laodong zhengyi yu duice (Labour dispute and policy in FIEs). *Zhongguo laodong* (China Labour). 8: 16–18.

Yin, Xiaoqing. 2001. Nongmingong: yizhong jiuye moshi de xingcheng jiqi shehui houguo (Migrant workers: the creation and social result of a new employment model). *Nanjing shifan daxue xuebao [shehui kexue ban]* (Journal of Nanjing Normal University [social science edition]). 9: 50–6.

Yu, Chengpeng. 2001. Woguo siying qiye jiazu guanli dongyin fenxi ji fazhan duice (An analysis on the motivation of development of family management in POEs). *Nanjing jingji xueyuan xuebao* (Journal of Nanjing University of Economics). 3: 33–7.

Yu, Depeng (ed.). 1999. Chengxiang eryuan jiegou yu chengshi wailaigong fanzui (The dual structure and crime of migrant workers). *Zhejiang shehui kexue* (Zhejiang Social Science). 2: 46–50.

Yu, Qinghe (ed.). 1986. *Zhongguo zhigong duiwu zhuangkuang diaocha* (An investigation of the situations of Chinese workers). Beijing: Gongren chubanshe.

Zapalska, Alina M. and Will Edwards. 2001. Chinese Entrepreneurship in a cultural and economic perspective. *Journal of Small Business Management*. 39(3): 286–92.

Zhang, Dinghua. 1996. Zai zhonghua quanzong di shierjie zhiweihui di sanci gongzuo huiyi shang de gongzuo baogao (The working report to the Third Meeting of the Twelfth Executive Committee of ACFTU). In *China Trade Unions Yearbook: 1996*. ACFTU. 531–38.

Zhang, Dinghua. 1999. Zai quanzong shisan jie zhiweihui yantaohui shang de jianghua (Speech at the seminar of the Thirteen Executive Committee of the ACFTU) (23 October). In *Zhongguo gonghui nianjian: 2000* (Chinese Trade Unions Yearbook: 2000). ACFTU. Beijing: Zhongguo gongren chubanshe. 30–5.

Zhang, Rui. 2001. Shehui jingji xingwei zhong de yinxing boyi (The recessive gambling and chess in the social and economic behaviour). *Heilongjian shehui kexue* (Heilongjiang Social Science). 6: 13–17.

Zhang, Yunqiu. 1997. An intermediary: the Chinese perception of trade unions since the 1980s. *Journal of Contemporary China.* 6(14): 139–52.

Zhang, Zaiping. 1996. *Laodong zhengyi* (Labour Dispute). Beijing: Falv chubanshe.

Zhang, Zouji. 1994. Laodong fa chutai shimo (Labour Law: from drafting to promulgating). In Jianxin Wang (ed.). *China Labour Yearbook: 1992–1994*. Beijing: Zhongguo laodong chubanshe.

Zhang, Zouji. 1999. Zai zhongguo laodongli shichang jianshe zuotan shang de jianghua (Speech at the seminar on constructing labour force market in China). http://www.chinafobank.com. 22 June.

Zhao, Hongzhu. 1999. Zai tuixing changwu gongkai jiaqiang qiye mingzhu guanli zuotan hui shang de jianghua (Speech at the Seminar on Implementing OCA and Strengthening Democratic Management in Enterprises). In Jianxin Wang (ed.). *Zhongguo laodong nianjian 1995–1996* (China Labour yearbook: 1995–1996). Beijing: Zhongguo laodong chubanshe. 141–8.

Zhao, Minghua and Theo Nichols. 1996. Management control of labour in state-owned enterprise: case from the textile industry. *China Journal.* 36: 1–21.

Zhao, Rulin (ed.). 1999. *Shichang jingjixue da cedian* (Dictionary of Market Economics). Beijing: Jingji kexue chubanshe.

Zheng, Haihang (ed.). 1998. *Guoyou qiye kuisun yanjiu* (Studies on SOEs' Loss-making). Beijing: Jingji guanli chubanshe.

Zhongshan Federation of Trade Unions. 1999. Waisheng touzi qiye tuixing pingdeng xieshang jiti hetong zhidu de nandian he duice (The hard points and strategies in implementing collective contract system in FIEs). *Gonghui lilun yu shijian* (Theory and Practice of Trade Union). 13(4): 53–4.

Zhou, Yongming. 2000. Social capital and power: entrepreneurial elite and the state in contemporary China. *Policy Sciences.* 33: 323–40.

Zhou, Yuqing. 2001. Issues need to be studied by trade unions at present, *Workers' Daily.* 9 September.

Zhou, Zhenhua. 1994. *Bulu jiannan de zhuanhuan: zhongguo maixiang xiandai qiye zhidu de sisuo* (Difficult Transition: Thoughts on the Movement to Modern Enterprise). Shanghai: Shanghai yiwen chubanshe.

Zhu, Jiazhen. 1996a. Zai quanguo laodong jiancha huiyi shang de jianghua (Speech at the national working conference on labour inspection). In Jianxin Wang (ed.). *Zhongguo laodong nianjian 1995–1996* (China labour yearbook: 1995–1996). Beijing: Zhongguo laodong chubanshe.

Zhu, Jiazhen. 1996b Speech at the Closing Ceremony for the National Working Conference of Settling Labour Disputes (18 November 1995.) In Jianxin Wang (ed.). *Zhongguo laodong nianjian 1995–1996* (China Labour Yearbook: 1995–1996). Beijing: Zhongguo laodong chubanshe.

Zhu, Jiazhen. 1996c. Guanyu geren shouru fenpei he shehui baozhang zhidu wenti (On issues about individual income and the system of social security) (20 December 1993). In Jianxin Wang (ed.). *Zhongguo laodong nianjian 1995–1996* (China Labour Yearbook: 1995–1996). Beijing: Zhongguo laodong chubanshe. 89–101.

Zhu, Ying. 1995. Major changes under way in China's industrial relations. *International Labour Review*. 134(1): 37–49.

Zhu, Ying and Iain Campbell. 1996. Economic reform and the challenge of transforming labour regulation in China. *Labour and Industry* 7(1): 29–49.

Zhuang, Qidong (ed.). 1988. *Laodong gongzi shouce* (Handbook of labour and wages). 2nd edn. Tianjin: Tianjin renmin chubanshe.

Zou, Peng, Wang guoping and Huang Bicheng. 2001. Guoqi li de yangguan xingdong ('Sunshine activity' in SOEs). *Sixiang zhengzhi gongzuo yanjiu* (Study of Ideological and Political Work). 1: 28.

Zweig, David. 2000. The 'externalities of development': Can new political institutions mange rural conflict? In Elizabeth J. Perry and Mark Selden (eds). *Chinese Society: Change, Conflict and Resistance*. London and New York: Routledge.

# Index

accidents, high rate of 98
accounting practices 144
agricultural sector 78, 110, 224
Ahlstrom, David 72, 231
All China Federation of Trade Unions
    (ACFTU) 33, 38–43, 107–15,
    147–50, 167, 182–4, 188, 204, 231
  and Chinese Communist Party 115–19
  structure and organization of 104–5
allowances unpaid 38
appointment and dismissal 139
arbitration 34, 38–9, 155, 158, 163–9,
    174
Ashwin, Sarah 129, 232
Asia Monitor Resource Centre 95, 232
assembly, right of 123
assurance system for living expenses
    91
autonomy 25, 62, 65–7
  in decision-making 53, 56, 111
  in dismissal 218
  lack of 153
  of managers 85, 140, 149
  in recruitment 218
  of trade unions 116

Bai, Ningxiang 173, 232
Bank of China 83
bank loans 53
bankruptcy of firms 36, 38, 93, 127,
    149–51, 160–61, 186
Bao, Guimin 63, 232
bargaining 119, 184, 195, 204
Beijing 43, 56, 95, 128, 148
benefits, reduction of 149
Berger, T. Mark 212, 232
Bian, Yangjie 52, 84, 232
Biddulph, Sarah 115, 117, 120, 232
Blackman, Carolyn 61, 232

Blecher, Mark 92, 93, 99, 232
blue-collar workers 78
Boisot, Max 98, 232
bonus distribution schemes 38, 139, 150
Bowles, Paul 232
Braverman, Harry 78, 215, 232
Brown, David H. 7, 66, 232
Bu, Nailin 99, 232
bureaucracy, Chinese 45

Cadre School of the ACFTU 106
cadres of trade unions 117
Cai, Yongshun 94, 233
capital 54, 89
  and assets 139
  and labour 110
  power of 121
capitalist 23, 44, 55, 68, 75
  development, state-sponsored 212
  economies 7, 47, 57, 212
  entrepreneurs 71
  exploitation 208
  functionaries 89
  organizations 63
Carroll, Thomas 134, 233
Central Committee of the Chinese
    Communist Party (CC-CCP) 20, 21,
    37, 58, 78–9, 129
Chan, Anita 233
Chang, Gordon G. 233
Chang, Kai 233–4
Chen, Feng 179, 234
Chen, Hong-yi 61, 234
Chen, Ji 107, 234
Chen, Jiagui 58, 63, 234
Chen, Wentong 234
Chen, Xiangming, 234
Chen, Yiqi 234
Chen, Yizi 234